Igbo Culture

Second Edition

Reuben K. Eneze

Reuben K. Eneze
10402 Meadowridge Lane
Bowie MD, 20721-2854
Phone 1 (202) 450-0109
reneze@outlook.com

Published by Reuben K. Eneze
ISBN: 978-1-7335505-2-9 (sc)
ISBN: 978-1-7335505-3-6 (e)

Print information available on the last page.

Any people depicted in stock imagery provided by Thinkstock are models, and such images are being used for illustrative purposes only.

Certain stock imagery ©

Thinkstock. This book is printed on acid-free paper.

Because of the dynamic nature of the Internet, any web addresses or links contained in this book may have changed since publication and may no longer be valid.

About the Book

The author presented his book, **Igbo** Culture, in a most convincing way by quoting expert opinions on most of the issues he discussed in the book.

Through his carefully researched work and detailed analysis of facts, he showed in the book that **Igbo** youths working hard like their ancestors can reform Igboland into a new and better civilization by sifting the good aspects of **Igbo** culture into today's way of life.

He started his book by making a brief reference to the possible migration route of **Igbo** ancestors from their earliest settlements in the forest region of central Africa to their present-day settlement in Southern Nigeria of West Africa. He also made a brief reference to the development of the **Igbo** civilization through the period covering the Stone Age and Iron Age civilizations.

He painted a clear picture of the cultural background of the community where the author was born and brought up and lived in for more than sixty years before he traveled to the United States of America. He traced the more than twenty-six generations-deep lineages, beliefs, concepts, customs, and history of **Ihe Shikeaguma** in **Ntuegbe** clan of Enugu State in Southeastern

Nigeria as a sample core **Igbo** culture community. He also delved into the historical links and social formation of this community, with emphasis on genealogy, religion, settlement, language, government, law enforcement, defense, seasons, festivals and residential structures.

He took his readers to **Igbo** thought on: God, self, family, human life, birth, death, spirit, human mind, and reincarnation.

He clearly documented the cultural products of **Igbo** thought which can be seen in the formulation of **Igbo** institutions with special reference to: marriage, the extended family system, the social status structure and title system, festivals, informal education, traditional law, community service, religion, divination, and health care services.

He explained that the symbolism of various articles and some spoken words in **Igbo** culture are products of **Igbo** thought. He referred to ọfọ stick, kola nut, alligator pepper, spears, tribal face marks, body paint, white chalk, and the young palm frond as symbols or instruments of **Igbo** philosophical expressions and concepts.

He showed how **Igbo** culture and philosophy have been affected by the cultures of **Igbo** neighbors in Nigeria and by other foreign cultures with special references to:

(a) **Ugwuele** civilization – (A Stone Age culture) – 1,000,000 B.C. - 500,000 B.C.
(b) **Nri** civilization – (A ritualized Kingship system) – 800 A.D. - 1700. A.D.
(c) **Aro** civilization – (Slave trade and colonial era) – 1700 A.D. - 1850 A.D.
(d) Border civilization – (Slave trade and colonial era) – 800 A.D. - 1900 A.D.
(e) External civilization – (Slave trade and colonial era) – 1700 A.D. - 2000 A.D.

The author concluded his work by making an evaluation of **Igbo** culture. He carefully examined the oriented values of the **Igbo** and highlighted those areas of the **Igbo** culture that should be refurbished and re-infused into **Igbo** life by the **Igbo** themselves in order to transform Igboland into a big theater of modern civilization.

Dr. Mrs. A.V. Iwueke
PAMO University of Medical Sciences
Elelenwa, Port Harcourt
Rivers State, Nigeria.

Table of Contents

Illustrations

Dedication

This book is dedicated to my children;
Adaku, Udegbunam, Chibuike, Enezenta and
Uchechukwu

Foreword

Every society has culture and tradition handed down from generation to generation orally and practically. Culture is a general way of life of a society, which identifies and marks it out from the other societies. The size of a society does not matter; it has a culture discernible in language, custom, religion and values. In consequence, there are various cultures as there are societies in the world and **Igbo** culture is one of them.

Culture is as old as the society itself and its inception is hard to determine, hence the culture of a group can never be exhausted historically and otherwise. For this reason, several books, pamphlets and articles are written both by foreigners and the **Igbo** elites to trace and explain the origin of the **Igbo** community, her culture and tradition. In order to tackle this onerous task, several facets were adopted, such as tracing the coming to be of a village, town, clan, and the **Igbo** as a group. This is exactly what the author did in this book.

Igboland has her genealogy, custom, tradition and certain external influences mainly by the foreigners from Europe. These were the colonial masters and the missionaries. Thus, a lot of her belief system and practices are overhauled by the new faith. The

Igbo culture and history have been transmitted orally and unless there is documentary such as this work the culture may go into extinction. Therefore, kudos to the author who put these facts down for those yet unborn to peruse and understand their culture. He did precisely what Dr. S. **Iwe** rightly observed, that the **Igbo** tradition of verbal documentation has been changed to more effective and reliable methods of record keeping, library, archives and museum.

His method is expository as he brought to limelight the facts of lineage, history, and the custom of the land. This book will educate the youths on the situation prior to the advent of the colonial masters and the missionaries. The author is detailed in his analysis of facts. He contends that culture re-visitation is very imperative now, else the **Igbo** culture goes into extinction. He is of the opinion that certain aspects of **Igbo** customs and tradition should be sifted into Christianity; and that **Igbo** culture should not be thrown to the winds. This work will serve as a handbook to future researchers on **Igbo** culture...

Rev. Fr. Dr. Sylvanus N. Onuigbo.
IECE, Thinkers Corner, Enugu

Acknowledgement

I owe a special appreciation to God Almighty that gave me my caring parents who taught me the oral stories on our roots, and the basic cultural concepts and beliefs in **Ihe Shikeaguma**.

My gratitude goes to my dear wife, **Ngozi** and our children, who by their support have made this work less burdensome.

I am most grateful to my father, **Ekoude Eneze**, and the following elders who through their oral stories supplied me with the basic knowledge with which I started this work.

a. **Chukwu Nevo** (Oracle Agent and founding member of **Ọfia** Oracle).
b. **Anioke Ọnyia** (Yam Farmer and founding member of **Ọfia** Oracle).
c. **Okonkwọ Udeagụ** (Oracle Priest; his father received the first British soldiers in **Ihe Shikeaguma**).
d. **Oje Udeagụ** (Professional hunter and **Magnetopath**).
e. **Chukwu Ọyiwa** (Yam Farmer; **Obunọ** Community leader).
f. **Chukwu Obele** (Yam Farmer; keeper of **Obune** war dance instruments).
g. **Nwike Ogbuu (Obunọ** community leader).

h. **Udeagbala Okafor** (Priest of **Ọgbụlụgbụ** deity).

i. **Ude Ọnụọha** (Priest of **Ani Ihe Shikeaguma** deity).

j. **Nzekwe Chukwuanụọ (Umuhu Owelli)**.

k. Benedict **Okonkwọ (Ụmụanebe Ihe Shikeaguma)**.

l. Cyprian **Ude** (Descendant of **Ogodo Igweonwo Amanakụlụ)**.

m. **Nwaniekwe Ani (Amaọfia Agbogugu)**.

n. Innocent **Ike** (Chairman, **Ihe Shikeaguma** Council of elders).

o. Patrick **Anichukwu** (Secretary, **Ihe Shikeaguma** Council of elders).

p. Pa. Lawrence **Agụ** (Retired teacher, and second son of **Agunevo Ọtusa**, the first Warrant chief of **Ihe Shikeaguma**).

q. H.R.H. Chief **Ejike** Edward **Ọkpa** (Former traditional ruler of **Ihe Shikeaguma**).

r. H.R.H. **Igwe** G.U. **Ochi** (Retired Sch. Headmaster and traditional ruler of **Ogugu**).

I immensely acknowledge the various authors of **Ahiajoku** lecture series whose work sharpened my interest in the study of **Igbo** culture and supplied very valuable expert information on the subject. Their work answered most of the various nagging questions raised by undated oral stories told by my father and his peers.

I give a special acknowledgement to Professor M. A. **Onwuejeogwu** whose lecture on the Evolutionary Trends in the History of the **Igbo**

19

Civilization in the Culture Theatre of Igboland in Southern Nigeria, was the first **Ahiajoku** lecture that I came in contact with, and which inflamed my love for the **Ahiajoku** lectures, and my commitment to this work.

I also acknowledge Rev. Father Dr. S. **Onuigbo,** whose work, The History of **Ntuegbenese,** inspired my commitment to the completion of this book. His work has been a source of pride and fulfillment to me because as a primary school teacher, I taught Rev. Dr. **Onuigbo** in primary one at St. Mary Primary School **Ihe Shikeaguma** when he was only six years old. Rev. Dr. **Onuigbo** gave me valuable advice and wrote the foreword to this book.

My acknowledgement goes also to the various other authors whose books have been of great help to me during the process of writing this book

I acknowledge in a very special way, my good friends, **Chike Ochi** and **Okolie Animba** who gave me valuable suggestions on the book. I sincerely acknowledge Professor Vincent **Onyema Okeke**, of **Imo** State University **Owerri**, **Imo** State, for editing this book.

I also acknowledge my very good missionary friend, Luis Paul S. Baron, SSP, for his assistance to me during the second edition of this book.

Introduction

a: Igbo Culture

The **Igbo** culture is the sum-total of all the socially transmitted behavior patterns, beliefs, institutions, and other products of human work and thought typical of the **Igbo** as a people. The **Igbo** culture can be found in the memories of their old men and women. It can also be found in material objects created by the **Igbo**, such as architectural, historical, archaeological artifacts and art works found in various locations in Igboland and in many other places outside Igboland. **Igbo** culture can be found in books, lectures, magazines, newspapers and other documented works of the **Igbo**, their visitors and their friends. **Igbo** culture is strongly enshrined in various social and religious ceremonies in Igboland. An **Igbo** born and bred in Igboland is a culture bearer and creator. His behavior makes cultural statements about the **Igbo** and distinguishes him from other people.

> *Clyde Kluckhohn, (1963: 24) defines culture as: that part of the environment that is the creation of man, a way of thinking, feeling, believing; a theory that helps us to understand a mass of otherwise chaotic(social) facts; a store-house of the pooled learning of the group found in the*

memories of old men and women, in books and material objects created by man, and the learned experiences by individuals as the result of belonging to some particular group. Cultures produce needs as well as provide a means of fulfilling them; every culture is a precipitate of history; culture throws up to history social facts which the sieve of history can hold, in changed or unchanged form but always with altered meanings to maintain the cultural and ideological integrity of a living people. Culture is like a map, an abstract but an approximate representation of a particular cultural entity which enables the young and the stranger to find their way in particular cultures; and all culture bearers are creators and carriers of culture as well as consumers of culture and its products.

Based on the foregoing, we can safely maintain that **Igbo** history is the record of important past issues in **Igbo** culture, and that if there was no **Igbo** culture there would be no **Igbo** history. In view of this position every **Igbo** should endeavor to preserve **Igbo** culture for the continuity of their cultural identity and the preservation of their oriented values.

Some **Igbo** people might want to ask why the need for culture preservation and learning now that they are Christians, especially those who now live outside the **Igbo** culture area or those who have citizenship rights of other countries. Those people should remember that no matter whatever height they have achieved or wherever they live, they have ancestral roots that can only be identified and maintained through their cultural links. These links help us to understand why we believe, think, feel, and behave the way we do.

The saying that history repeats itself is apt in this situation. Culture, like history, has a canny way of repeating itself in culture bearers and their offspring no matter where they go. Such acquired or inherent traits like music and athletics of the **Igbo**, for example, project themselves in the offspring of the **Igbo** irrespective of the location of their birth or residence. Secondly the **Igbo** is a very religious person and this religious trait goes with him and his offspring to wherever they decide to live whether as traditional worshippers or as Christians.

In my effort to take the **Igbo** culture to readers, I shall delve into the historical links and social formation of **Ihe Shikeaguma** of **Ntuegbe** clan in Enugu State of South Eastern Nigeria which is a sample core **Igbo** culture community. I shall also take readers to their various social and religious concepts, sociocultural institutions, symbolisms and human work, where **Igbo** culture is strongly but beautifully exhibited.

The **Igbo** community is the second largest language group in Nigeria, covering the whole of **Abia, Anambra, Ebonyi, Enugu, Imo,** and parts of

Cross River, Delta, Kogi and Rivers States of Nigeria. This community is tied together by one language with mutually intelligible dialects, belief in God the Creator (**Chukwu Okike**), intermediary spirits **(Ndi nmụọ)**, numerous deities (**Alụsi**), Ancestors (**Ndi ichie**) and other sociocultural identities.

b: Elders as Culture Store House
In 1955, when I was in a Teacher Training College, we were taught that there were forty-two generations between Abraham and Jesus Christ:

14 Lay generations, Abraham to Jesse;
14 Royal generations, Jesse to Jeconiah;
14 Lay generations, Jeconiah to Joseph.

At the end of the lesson, I decided to ask my father who our forefathers were and how many generations of our lineage he could remember. Many other questions came up in my mind, such as: "Where did my forefathers come from"? "Are we actually related to the white men through Adam"? "When did man actually start life on Earth"? Etc.

As soon as I came home on midyear holiday in August of that year, I approached my father and asked him; "who were your grandfather, great grandfather and his forefathers"? He laughed and asked me why I wanted to know. I told him that it was a school assignment for the holiday period. He paused awhile, then gave me the names of his father, grandfather and great grandfather, and stopped there. When I pressed further for more names, he promised to think about it and answer the question the following day. Early in the following morning he woke me up and sang for me an **Igbo** song which he called his father's praise song:

> **Eneze Ude, Ojinwagụ,**
> **Nwa Nevo Anioke, Ọnyia Uba.**
> **Amụlụ n'Ebe n'Amagu**
> **Nwa Agu Ekwe, Agu Igwe, Ọnyia Ovu.**
> **Nna nwụlụ agu n'eke, etc.**

He explained that the twelve names in the song are in the order of seniority, starting from **Eneze** and ending at **Ovuokolo**, the eldest. He could not go further than that. He explained the meaning of the praises to me thus:

Ojinwagu, is a short form for **Ojinwagu alata nne ya**, which in English is: "He (a hunter) who held a young tiger and made it cry in order to attract the mother". **Amulu n`Ebe n`Amagu** means that his father was born at **Amagu** Village, the owners of **Ebe** village square. **Nna nwụlụ agu n`eke,** means that his father caught a tiger with his hands.

After that revealing song, he answered other questions on the genealogy of the family, the village, the kindred, and the **Ntuegbe** clan. He then referred me to his peers and elders for further questions on the issue. I was delighted and put all the oral information down in a new exercise book. I consulted some elders from other villages and communities later to verify the authenticity of some of the information obtained.

In 1988, I was opportuned to come by the 1987 **Ahiajoku** lecture by Professor Michael **Angulu Onwuejeogwu,** on the "Evolutionary Trends in the History of the Development of the **Igbo** Civilization in the Culture Theatre of Igboland in Southern Nigeria". This lecture sharpened my curiosity once more and I got interested in the **Ahiajoku** Lectures. The lectures led me to other books and further inquiries relating to **Igbo** origin, culture, religion and philosophy. The other book that inspired this work was Rev. Dr. S. **Onuigbo's** "The History of **Ntuegbenese**".

In doing this work, my main objectives were:

(I) To satisfy my own personal desire to know and record what I could collect on the history and culture of my people: their family, their village, their town, their clan and their tribe in Nigeria, because I had to start somewhere to record our oral history and culture before the facts faded away completely beyond the reach of my children.

(II)   To collate, translate and pass on in a

written form the oral history of our roots and culture which I collected from my father and his peers; to **Igbo** youths and historians, so that they can do future scientific and historical studies on the information so recorded.

(III)   To try to confirm the authenticity of some of these oral stories by making references to expert study and conclusions on the subject.

(IV)   To raise questions on our oral history and culture that shall be needing scrutiny and answers by historians, anthropologists and archaeologists, so that more accurate scientific and historical records shall emerge for the benefit of posterity.

(V)   To strive to answer some questions that have not yet been answered in any written form known to me before now, especially on my sample core **Igbo** culture communities; "**The Shikeaguma** town and **Ntuegbe** clan," the main focus of this work.

(VI)   To explain to our youth some aspects of **Igbo** culture and philosophy in order to show how our culture and philosophy have been affected by subsequent cultures of our neighbors in Nigeria and by other foreign and European influences and civilization.

27

(VII)   To inform the young ones that we of **Ihe Shikeaguma** in particular, and the **Waawa** Speaking people of South Eastern Nigeria come from the epicenter of the birthplace of **Igbo** culture and philosophy and have contributed in no small way to the evolution of the **Igbo** Community.

(VIII)   To bring to their knowledge the fact that our **Waawa** dialect is indeed the mother dialect of **Onitsha, Owerri**, and Western **Igbo**.

(IX)   To highlight the fact that our native religion, which is the **Igbo** traditional religion was in its purest form, "God-centered and humane," before it got polluted by other influences, and that it was in place for several centuries ever before the birth of Christianity and Islam.

(X)   To stress the need for our youth to be proud that they are **Igbo**, because the **Igbo** have a rich historical past and an enviable cultural heritage that should guide our future growth, in all aspects of human endeavor and in maintaining our oriented values.

(XI)   Since the main purpose of this book "**Igbo** Culture," is to pass on to the youth of **Igbo** origin, a recorded brief history of our roots and culture, I shall be as practical as possible. I shall use specific samples of events, people and places, and adopt a time frame from when my ancestors wandered about on the high lands of East, Central, and West Africa, for several millions of years, to the time when they settled at:

Ugwuele Okigwe and environs about, 200,000 - 2,500 BC. The Scarp lands **(Enugwu)** of South Eastern Nigeria, 2,500- 500 BC. **Ntuegbe** Clan, 700 BC. – AD. 600, **Ihe Shikeaguma** town, AD.600-AD 700, **Enugwuoke** Kindred, AD.700- AD.1100, **Amagu** Village, AD.1100-AD.1200, **Umuaguekwe** Family, AD 1200- AD.1800, **Eneze Ude** Compound, AD 1800- AD. 2000.

(XII)   Another purpose for using specific communities, places and people in recording the details of **Igbo** culture and history, is to ensure that the records are easily verifiable for the purpose of correcting any possible cultural or historical errors that may arise since some of the stories recorded were handed down orally by elders, apart from quotations from books written by experts on the subject.

(XIII)   To give life to the oral stories collected without dates, it became necessary that an approximate dating formula should be adopted by using the twenty six known generations of our ancestors to represent two thousand six hundred years of our history, at an average period of one hundred years for each generation.

c: Building Childhood Memories

After celebrating my seventieth birthday on the twentieth of August 2007, I felt more obliged than ever to do what old men of **Igbo** tribe of my age do for their children. This includes the handing down of **Igbo** culture to the youth. I still remember vividly how my father, a traditional worshipper and farmer imparted the various aspects of our culture to us – his children, directly, by way of his own day- to - day life and through stories, folk tales, music and art. In Igboland, this handing down of culture to the youth is like a relay race. Based on this belief, I wish to do my bit of the race as fast and as far as I can go.

Today times have changed. Children spend a greater part of their day in school away from their parents. Some parents of my age in various towns in Igboland spent their entire school days in towns or villages far away from their homes, where their parents lived. They did not have the opportunity of learning their culture from their parents like I did. Also, Western Education that introduced foreign cultural values and Christian religious teaching, reduced emphasis on the teaching and learning of **Igbo** culture in school and at home

After the British colonial masters took over the government of Nigeria in 1914, employment opportunities for white collar jobs and vacancies in other commercial activities became available in locations far away from home. These opportunities and the eventual hiring of **Igbo** youths denied thousands of **Igbo** children who were born far away from Igboland the opportunity of learning **Igbo** culture directly in their **Igbo** culture area. In view of the above reasons, and my aforementioned objectives, I decided to write down some aspects of our culture in this book, so that those youths who live far away from home can study some aspects of **Igbo** culture from the book, with other children from different culture areas. Even **Igbo** youths who were born and bred in Igboland will use the book as a handbook in their study of **Igbo** culture. It will also serve as a reference book for parents, teachers, historians and researchers in their study, and teaching of **Igbo** culture to the youth. Here, we should call to mind the words of General Colin Powell, founder of America's Promise – (The Alliance for Youth)

All children need a laptop; not a computer, but a human laptop; moms, dads, grannies and grandpas, aunts, uncles - someone to hold them, read to them, teach them; loved ones who will embrace them and pass on the experience, rituals and knowledge of a hundred previous generations; loved ones who will pass to the

> *next generation their expectations of them, their hopes and their dreams.*

In studying the **Igbo** culture, we should remember that culture is dynamic. It changes its outer coat with time and locality and makes room for alternatives. Culture is like **Igbo** language that changes its dialects from one locality to the other without changing its meaning and essence. As no one can speak all the dialects of **Igbo** language, so also can nobody master all the aspects of **Igbo** culture. Readers of this book should use the issues discussed in this book as pointers to their own cultural version of the same topics.

Following from the above position, I shall trace the more than twenty six generations – deep lineages, beliefs, concepts, customs and history of **Ihe Shikeaguma in Ntuegbe** clan of Enugu State in Southeastern Nigeria, as a sample **Igbo** culture community, and write briefly on those aspects of **Igbo** culture that are obtainable in that community and in many other communities of the **Igbo** Scarp lands area which is the birth place of **Igbo** language and culture.

Chapter one
IGBO Roots in West Africa

1.1: THE ORIGIN OF MAN

In the effort to find **Igbo** roots in West Africa let us briefly look at the origin of man on Earth. Anthropologists and Archaeologists agree that human life might have started on Earth between thirteen and one million years ago. Recent archaeological work showed that there were evidences of human life in the Omo Valley of Ethiopia and the Lake Chad Basin of West Africa at least three million years and seven million years ago respectively.

As Archaeological work continues on Earth, we hope to be able to place the exact place and date of the origin of man. So far, experts agree that man started life on the continent of Africa, before moving to other parts of the World, in search of food, shelter and safety from man-made and natural disasters. We are told that God made man and gave him the power and the endowments to increase and multiply, and to cover the face of the Earth.

This assignment by God made man inquisitive about himself and his neighborhood and gave him the desire to discover and conquer his surroundings. The desire made him wander from one place to the other, discovering new places, new things and new situations; increasing and multiplying in his trail. He moved from high land to high land as these high lands were visible from long distances. These high lands were also relatively drier, safer, cooler and healthier. He finally settled in the fertile river or lake basin on, or near one of the high lands. Historians suggest that man moved from the high lands of East and Central Africa to the rest of Africa, Asia, Europe and America many millions of years ago. Archaeologists and Anthropologists, through empirical observations and analysis of fossils and artifacts have come to agree that man truly originally inhabited East, Central and West Africa as the following references show.

M. A. **Onwuejeogwu** (1987) states that:

All existing evidence points to the calculation that Africa particularly East Africa was the major center for the physical and technological development of man. East Africa was the Garden of Eden of mankind and from there the spread started[1]

---

[1] M.A. **Onwuejeogwu, Ahiajoku** Lecture 1987, page 14.

Michael Brunet of the University of Poitiers, France, in E. N. **Onwu** (2002) asserts that:

> *We find the recent Archaeological findings of earliest ancestors of modern homo sapiens named, Toumai (hope of life), with the scientific name, Sahelanthropus Tchadensis (Sahel hominid from Chad) dated about seven million years old in the Lake Chad region. That man first settled in Africa is no longer an Archaeological statement but a historical fact.*[2]

Recently, Rick Weiss, (2005) in his work on a DNA change on white skin suggests that:

> *The skin whitening mutation occurred by chance in a single individual after the first human exodus from Africa when all people were brown skinned. That person's offspring apparently thrived as humans and moved Northwards into what is now Europe, helping to give rise to the lightest of the world's races.*[3]

The fact that many ancient African families produced albino babies and treated them as abnormal babies gives credence to the above suggestion by Weiss.

---

[2] E.N.**Onwu, Ahiajoku** Lecture 2002, page 6

[3] Rick Weiss, Dec. 2005, Washington post, page A1.

M. A. **Onwuejeogwu** (1987) brings the issues nearer home thus:

> *The Sangonans were forest dwellers occupying the great lakes of Central Africa, the present-day Congo and Angola, and around the Zambezi River. They probably spread into different areas in the forest zone of West Africa. This resulted in the development of variants of stone cultures found in West Africa of different ages, as shown by the Archaeological findings in, Ugwuele, 55,000BC (Anozie 1980); Nsukka, 2,555BC. -(Hartle 1967 and 1972); Iwo Eleru, 9,250BC (Shaw 1965).[4]*

1.2: WEST AFRICA AND IGBO CULTURE

In his "Time Chart of Events: Africa and **Igbo** Culture Area", (**Ahiajoku** Lecture 1987, figure 1) M.A. **Onwuejeogwu** showed that:

I. The **Ugwuele** culture, (Early Stone Age to Middle Stone Age) covered the period, about 200,000BC – 2,500BC, within which the Proto Igboid period 100,000BC – 5,000BC, flourished. On page 12, he also showed that **Anozie,** (1981), dated the onset of **Ugwuele** culture to as far back as 750,000BC.

II. The proto Igboid Period (Early Stone Age to

---

[4] M.A. **Onwuejeogwu, Ahiajoku** Lecture 1987, page 15.

Middle Stone Age) mentioned above in (I) started at **Ugwuele** about 100,000BC and continued till 5,000BC.

III. The **Okigwe, Afikpo**, **Udi**, **Nsukka** era, an offshoot of **Ugwuele** culture, which is also called Scarp lands civilization, (Middle Stone Age, through Late Stone Age to Early Iron Age), started about 2,500BC and continued till AD 800, when the **Nri** era started.

IV. The **Nri** era, (Iron Age), started about AD 800 and lasted for about nine centuries to AD 1700.

V. The **Aro** civilization (Slave Trade to Colonialism) started from about AD1700 and continued to about AD 1900. This era was contemporaneous with other less popular Iron Age **Igbo** cultures.

From the above record, one can suggest that, in addition to the three **Igbo** Stone Age cultures, (I, II and III) mentioned above (200,000BC – AD 800) there were also the Saharan and other West African cultures that existed simultaneously with the above Stone Age cultures; having overlapping periods between them and producing "the variants of Stone Age cultures found in West Africa" at the time, as above shown by **Onwuejeogwu**. As the Stone Age period was wearing out (100,000BC –

5000BC) and the Proto Igboid culture was taking root at **Ugwuele** and environs, population growth and accompanying need for more food and shelter sparked off population movements from this culture area to other settlements in the Lower Niger area and beyond. The period 5000BC – 2,500BC was an important period in the history of West and North Africa because it was marked by the drying up of the Saharan region which was blooming with vegetation and the Saharan cultures. This situation and the resultant loss of pastures and arable lands to dry conditions, triggered the movement of its inhabitants, herdsmen and farmers, to greener and wetter parts of West and North Africa, carrying with them their livestock, crops and craftsmanship, to boost the existing cultures and economy of the equatorial forest of West Africa and the Mediterranean lands of North Africa. This situation created the need for the Trans Saharan caravan trade between the Mediterranean region and the West African settlements.

The Scarp lands civilization (2,500BC – AD800) which became the immediate yield of the **Ugwuele** culture probably got a cultural boost through interactions with the Saharan culture after the movements that followed the drying up of the Saharan lands. **Eri**'s (Ancestor of **Nri)** movement to the **Anambra** river basin is a case in point.

Considering the ages of archaeological findings in **Ugwuele Okigwe,** 750,000BC, (**Anozie** 1981) and 100,000BC, Igboid period, (**Onwuejeogwu** 1987), one could ask; why did it take so long for the **Igbo** to develop into a modern civilization?

Let me attempt an answer:

1. **Ugwuele** in **Okigwe** of South Eastern Nigeria is situated in the Equatorial rain forest region of West Africa. The earliest **Igbo** ancestors who lived here during this period as hunters and gatherers of forest roots, fruits and vegetables lived in makeshift settlements, and were often forced to change their settlements as a result of inter settlement disputes, epidemics, famine, natural disasters or other environmental reasons.

2. The traditional **Igbo** political structure and allegiance to ancestral heads and local community, led to the absence of a well-developed pan **Igbo** political organization that could have enhanced the development and spread of a modern **Igbo** civilization.

3. Lack of any developed form of writing by the **Igbo** at this time, which could have been used to record their movements, experiences and innovations, hampered the development and continuity of their innovations and the

transfer of these developments to subsequent generations.

4. Safe and fast comunication with other settlements in West Africa at that time were non-existent as there were no roads and bridges over the many rivers and dry valleys in those equatorial rain forest settlements.

5. The drying up of the Saharan lands by climate change due to persistent drought (5,000BC – 2,500BC) and the consequent loss of pastures and settlements cut off closer contacts of the West African region with the North African and Arab civilizations of that time.

   When the Arabs first learned of West Africa, its civilization was already centuries old. Although the land from the Atlantic to the Nile had enjoyed limited contact with other civilized portions of the World, much of the culture that the Arabs found was indigenous to the area.[5]

6. The limited North African and Arab Trans-Saharan caravan trade routes into West Africa did not penetrate the forest zone due to the region's high humidity and exposure of camels

---

[5] Franklin and Moss Jr., A history of African Americans, 2000, Volume 1, page 2.

and the caravans to insect pests that transmitted deadly diseases through their bites in that zone. The only outside contacts with residents of the forest zone, through bush paths were made on foot by local middlemen and vendors who carried their merchandise on their heads or shoulders. This means of transportation and interaction continued till the 18th Century.

7. The strongest and most recent external influence on **Igbo** culture was the European influence. The Europeans met and traded with an existing **Igbo** civilization but cared little about the **Igbo** socio- political welfare and their innovative spirit. They were more interested in the looting of **Igbo** cultural artifacts and in the reduction of **Igbo** human resources by slavery.

8. But for a change of heart by European governments on Transatlantic slave trade in the 19th Century due to protests in America by individuals and groups against the evil trade, the possibility of any growth in **Igbo** civilization by now could only be imagined because the transatlantic slave trade hit **Igbo** civilization hard on the head at a time when it was evolving into a regional civilization in West Africa. Most of the **Igbo** sold in the evil trade came from the Scarp lands area of **Igbo** land which was then a major center of iron industry in West Africa.

PERIOD		ERA	CIVILIZATION
B.C.	100,000		
B.C.	90,000		
B.C.	80,000		
B.C.	70,000	EARLY STONE AGE	
B.C.	60,000		
B.C.	50,000		
B.C.	40,000		
B.C.	30,000		
B.C.	20,000		
B.C.	10,000		
B.C.	9,000		
B.C.	8,000	MIDDLE STONE AGE	UGWUELE OKIGWE
B.C.	7,000		
B.C.	6,000		
B.C.	5,000		
B.C.	4,000		
B.C.	3,000		
B.C.	2,000		UGWUELE OKIGWE / SCARPLANDS (ENUGWU)
B.C.	1,000		
B.C.	100	LATE STONE AGE	
A.D.	100		
A.D.	200		
A.D.	400		
A.D.	600		
A.D.	800		ANAMBRA
A.D.	1,000		
A.D.	1,200	IRON AGE	NRI
A.D.	1,400		OWERRI
A.D.	1,600		NGWA
A.D.	1,800		IKA / NDIOSI-MIRI / ENUANI
A.D.	2,000		ARO / NIG.

Time Chart of civilization in Igbo Culture area
100,000 BC - AD 2000

42

1.3: THE SCARPLANDS (ENUGWU) CIVILIZATION

In the chapter on the origin of man, I put together the expert conclusions of Archaeologists and Historians on the origin of man; the probable routes in his wandering days on the high lands of Eastern, Central and Western Africa; and how some of his offspring settled at **Ugwuele Okigwe** on the Scarplands of South Eastern Nigeria. The Scarplands cover the areas around **Afikpo, Agbonta**, and the high lands of **Okigwe, Awgu, Udi, Nsukka** and **Igboukwu. Onwuejeogwu** (1987) states that:

> *Four of the Archaeological finds in Igboland became very relevant: the Ugwuele, Afikpo, Nsukka and Igboukwu. These four sites have produced abundant and irrevocable evidence of the fact that at least between 100,000BC and 5,000BC. Man has started his cultural drama in what I refer to as the theatre of Igboland.*[6]

The **Ugwuele Okigwe** settlement was able to grow into a culture community and remained so for centuries because the land provided stone shelters and caves in the **Okigwe** hills and dolerite intrusions on the hillsides near **Ugwuele** for stone tools and weapons. The hillsides which had fertile soil for farming and livestock rearing also had good

---

[6] M. A. **Onwuejeogwu, Ahiajoku** Lecture 1987, page 8

clay for pottery, which flourished at **Isiagu** in the vicinity of **Ugwuele**. **Onwuejeogwu** (1987) also has it that; **Anozie** after his Archaeological work concluded that:

> *Ugwuele is dominantly a hand-axe culture with tons of hand-axes and large quantities of cleavers and mini flake tools. This culture might have flourished any time between 750,000BC and 55,000BC.*[7]

Since Armstrong suggested that the Bini and Yoruba languages separated from the **Igbo** around 7000 years ago (about 5000BC) and that both Bini and Yoruba languages have words that are cognates with **Igbo** words, it is possible that **Ugwuele** was probably the birthplace of the ancestors of some of the other West African tribes before their ancestors moved to their various present day settlements.

This scenario is based on the possibility that by 55,000BC the **Igbo** had developed at **Ugwuele** as a distinct people with a tribal identity, one religious concept, one language and a cultural philosophy within the several thousands of years of settlement at **Ugwuele** and its environs, before small dispersals to other settlements. These small dispersals were on the Scarp lands as well as other places on the Lower Niger area.

---

[7] M. A. **Onwuejeogwu, Ahiajoku** Lecture 1987, page 12.

The **Ugwuele** culture which evolved into the **Okigwe, Afikpo, Igboukwu**, **Udi** and **Nsukka** culture or simply the Scarp lands (**Enugwu**) civilization, had a common economy based on yam as a main crop; production of stone tools and weapons during the Late Stone Age, and iron tools and weapons during the Early Iron Age. The stony nature of the Scarp lands made the use of iron tools diggers and hoes, necessary in the cultivation of the land for food, and construction of stone shelters for habitation.

Afikpo which is on the Cross-River basin was one of the various contemporary settlements that sustained the **Ugwuele** civilization because of the food from the environs of **Afikpo**. The farming at **Afikpo** created a major market for the stone tools made at **Ugwuele** and small iron tools and weapons made at **Achi**, **Udi** and **Nsukka**, while pots were supplied from the pottery industries at **Isiagu, Inyi, Nsukka**, etc. **Afikpo** might have served as a dispersal route for stone technology to **Abakaliki** which also has dolerite deposit used for making tools and weapons. Stone tools were used as far away as **Aba** and **Ikot Ekpene** at the time.

On the economy of the Scarp lands civilization, M.A. **Onwuejeogwu** (1987) writes:

The Nsukka – Udi civilization is hereby referred to as the civilization of furnace. In its earliest form about 4000 years ago (2000 BC), it is contemporaneous with the Afikpo and both might have evolved from the Ugwuele forms. The late Stone Age evolved into the Iron Age and Nsukka area was foremost in the development and diffusion of this culture which gave rise to a rich civilization characterized by iron industry, agrarian and commercial economy based on the marketing of iron implements, elephant tusks, ivory bracelets and horses from the North[8]

Having dealt with the role played by **Ugwuele, Okigwe, Afikpo** and **Nsukka** in the development of the historical and economic growth of the Scarp lands civilization, let us look at its religion. The Scarp lands people had strong belief in God (**Chukwu Okike**) and great respect for human life as the work of God (**Ọlụchi**). They believed that God gave life to man (**Chinenyendụ**) and commanded him to preserve and nurture it. They honored the living and dead members of their families who lived worthy and honorable lives, according to the oral code of natural and the peoples' laws (**Nsọani**). God was recognized as the father of humanity. It was abomination punishable by man and God, to destroy any human life of any

---

[8] M. A. **Onwuejeogwu, Ahiajoku** Lecture 1987, page 45

age, because human life was held sacred by the **Igbo** traditional religion of that age.

From about 2000BC, during the early Iron Age, population of the Scarp lands people had grown. The discovery of iron which resulted in the manufacture of iron farm tools coupled with the need for the production of more food-crops, made the movement of people from the high lands to low and more fertile lands necessary. Consequently, the rapid dispersal of people from the center began in earnest. From the northern part of the Scarp lands, movements were made from parts of what came to be known as Greater **Udi** and **Nsukka** divisions, westwards and southwest-wards into the alluvial plains of the **Anambra** River basin and to the vicinity of **Awka**, carrying with them, the art of blacksmithing and divination. Small groups moved at different times from parts of Greater **Okigwe** and **Awgu** divisions into **Igboukwu, Ezira, Oreri**, down to **Ibusa** across the Niger.

Another group moved from **Okigwe** to Orlu and **Owerri**; and from **Owerri** to **Oguta** and **Aba**. On the eastern and south eastern fronts of the Scarplands, movements from Greater **Nsukka**, **Udi**, **Awgu**, **Okigwe** and **Afikpo** divisions settled at different times and in different parts of the upper flood plains of the Cross-River basin. The Cross-River basin settlements were later joined by small movements of the border peoples.

Tertiary movements in different directions were made within the **Igbo** culture area later, especially in the western, eastern and the Niger Delta areas of Igboland. Some of the new settlements were later joined by other movements from outside the **Igbo** culture area. These fusions resulted in the cross fertilization of different cultures that gave birth to hybrid cultures within the **Igbo** culture area. **Eri** came down the **Anambra** River with his theocratic philosophy and spread a ritualized kingship system among the people of the **Anambra** River basin and their neighbors on both sides of the River Niger.

Further west, the Bini influx brought the **Iduu** culture into the Western **Igbo** culture area. From the coastal seaboard came the already mixed cultures of the trading peoples of the Atlantic seacoast, which influenced the **Aro** civilization and the cultures of the Rivers people. The culture influence from the East affected the cultures of the people of **Abakaliki, Afikpo** and **Arochukwu**, while the **Igala, Idoma** and **Tiv** influx took its toll on Northern **Igbo** communities. This situation of cross-border mutual fertilization of cultures resulted in the fact that the oldest and purest sample of **Igbo** culture and philosophy is traceable only at the center of **Igbo** culture area which incidentally is the Scarp lands culture area.

Earliest Igbo Culture Centres And Population Movements

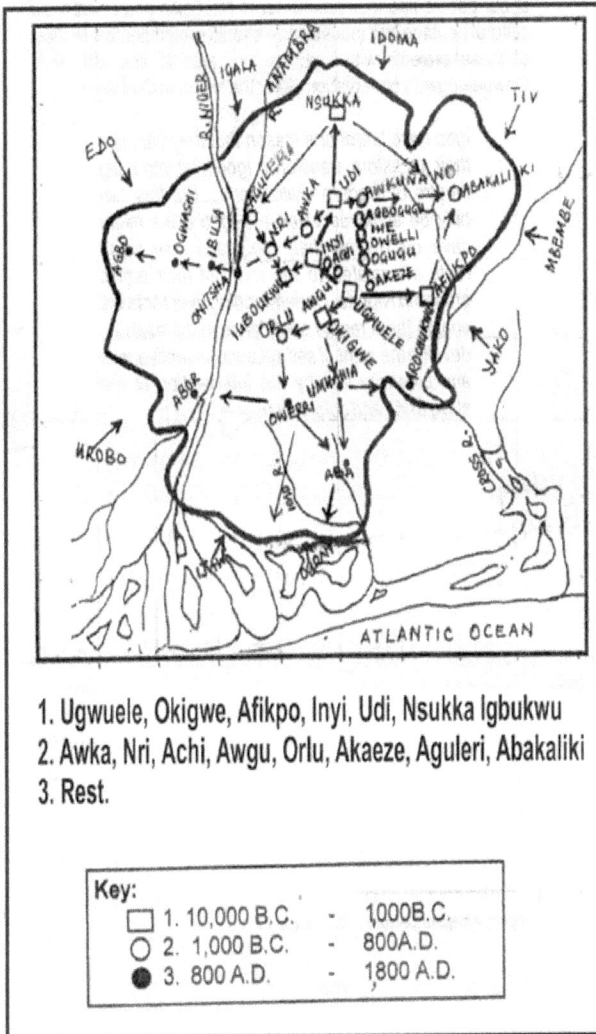

1. Ugwuele, Okigwe, Afikpo, Inyi, Udi, Nsukka Igbukwu
2. Awka, Nri, Achi, Awgu, Orlu, Akaeze, Aguleri, Abakaliki
3. Rest.

Key:
☐ 1. 10,000 B.C. - 1,000 B.C.
○ 2. 1,000 B.C. - 800 A.D.
● 3. 800 A.D. - 1,800 A.D.

Chapter Two

Cultural Background of Author

2.1:THE GENEALOGY OF NTUEGBE CLAN

The five **Ntuegbe** towns live close to each other along the **Awgu – Enugu** old road, starting from **Ogugu** and ending at **Enugu**. **Ozalla,** a non **Ntuegbe** town lives between **Agbogugu** and **Akagbe Ugwu**. On the western hillsides of **Ntuegbe** clan, starting from the South, are **Maku, Ugbo, Amoli, Umabi, Agbudu, Isuawa, Ituku, Obioma, Nsude and Ngwo.** On the Eastern side, are **Ogbaku, Amuri, Agbani, Akpugo and Emene.** We have **Nenwe** on the South and **Nike** on the North, while **Enugu** state capital is between **Awkunano, Ngwo**, **Nike** and **Emene** towns.

The elders unanimously agreed in their stories that our earliest ancestor, **Ajaka Uba** was a great hunter from **Akeze,** a border town in Greater **Afikpo** Division and one of the neighboring towns of **Uturu Okigwe** in the vicinity of **Ugwuele.** **Ajaka** Uba settled at a valley resort at **Ezioha** in **Ogugu (Ogwugwu)**, about 700 BC. His residence at **Ogugu** grew from a hunters' makeshift village to a town, and later to **Ntuegbe** clan.

The name **Ntuegbe** which means: "Gun powder" is not the name of a person. It is a hunting title assumed by the descendants of **Shike Oke**, to indicate their talents in hunting as a profession. This hunting expertise is still celebrated today by the five towns of **Ntuegbe** clan during the **Ani** Festival on the days of **Mgbaji Nkwu** in **Ogugu, Mgbaji Ichikele in Owelli, Igbanta** in **Ihe Shikeaguma,** gun presentation and maneuver at **Ihe Shikeaguma, Agbogugu** and **Awkunano (Akagbe).** This hunting proficiency is indicated in several hunting names given by **Ntuegbe** people, such as **Ojeneguegwu, Aguma, Agwede, Akegbe, Ubagu,** and in hunting gestures made during the dancing of **Ikpa** and **Nkwa** war-dances in the five towns of **Ntuegbe** clan.

Before the major dispersal of **Ntuegbe** clan from **Ogugu,** after about one thousand years, **Ajaka Uba's** lineage, starting from the youngest, was in this order: **Shike Oke, Ani Mkpume, Uba Ojene, Ajaka Onwe, Ajaka Uba.** This order of names shows that before the dispersal of **Ntuegbe** clan, **Ajaka Uba's** lineage had grown to about ten generations within about one thousand years in **Ogugu**, since one name represents one generation.

Shike Oke, the youngest of the ten generations, married **Uzunma,** the daughter of a migrant **Mgbowo (Aliechara)** barter trader and had five sons and one daughter. The first son was **Ani**

Shikeoke, the father of **Shike Ani** who settled at **Ogugu**. The second son was **Eze (Ebe) Shikeoke,** the father of **Ubagu Eze,** who settled at Enugu Owelli. The third son was **Aguma Shikeoke,** the grandfather of **Ihe Shikeaguma** who settled at **Ụmụọgbee** Ihe. The fourth son was **Akulu Shikeoke,** who begot **Oshie Akulu,** the grandfather of **Oshie Aneke,** who settled at **Amofia Agbogugu.** The fifth son was **Wiwa (Nwaiwa) Shikeoke,** who begot **Osa (Oshie) Wiwa,** the grandfather of **Osa Agwede,** who settled at **Akegbe Ugwu.** The sixth child was a woman, **Mgbọkwọ Shikeoke,** who was married to **Toke** who begot **Uba Toke (Ituku)** and **Ukpa Toke (Ozalla).**

The latest significant movement of **Ntuegbe** origin from the clan was that of **Aninta Anieze,** a professional hunter from **Uhuahu Amanabo** in **Ogugu.** He moved from **Ogugu,** through **Agbogugu** to **Amuri** as a hunter. He moved again from **Amuri** to **Nome** where he settled as the ancestor of the **Unateze** clan made up of **Nome, Naara** and **Amagunze** in **Nkanu** Local Government Area. The distance from **Ogugu** and the muddy terrain of the land between **Ogugu** and **Nome** cut off the **Aninta Anieze** family from close cultural relations with **Ogugu** and the rest of their kinsfolk in **Ntuegbe** clan.

The five towns of **Ogugu, Owelli, Ihe, Agbogugu** and **Awkunano** are culturally and traditionally treated as equal in status irrespective of the differences in population. The cultural ties which had existed between the five **Ntuegbe** towns in the past are still growing from strength to strength irrespective of the incursion of European culture imposed on us by the white man who colonized our land and overhauled our way of life.

However, the colonization of Nigeria by the British, has helped in the development of the **Ntuegbe** clan in several ways:

The construction of the **Enugu-Awgu** old road which passes through the five **Ntuegbe** towns has greatly enhanced the communication and the socio-cultural relations of the clan. From this road, many other roads have been made to connect other villages and towns in **Enugu** State. The Europeans who colonized Nigeria, also came with the Church Missionaries who built schools and healthcare institutions; and opened trade relations and evangelization with the natives. The various primary and post primary institutions built by the Government and private institutions in the clan have helped to bring formal education and economic development to the clan. These educational and commercial institutions on both sides of the **Enugu-Awgu** road have placed the five **Ntugbe** towns many years ahead of their **neigbors** in physical development.

PERIOD		ANCESTOR	SETTLEMENT
B.C.	700	UBA	AKEZE/OGUGU
B.C.	600	AJAKA	OGUGU
B.C.	500	ONWE	v
B.C.	400	AJAKA	v
B.C.	300	OJENE	v
B.C.	200	UBA	v
B.C.	100	NKPUME	v
A. D.	100	**ANI**	v
A.D.	200	OKE	v
A.D.	300	SHIKE	v
A.D.	400	AGUMA	OWELLI/IHE
A.D.	500	SHIKE	UMUOGBEE-IHE
A.D.	600	IHE	v
A.D.	700	NWAGUMA	UHUEZE-IHE
A.D.	800	OVU	v
A.D.	900	ONYIA	v
A.D.	1000	IGWE	v
A.D.	1100	AGU	AMAGU-IHE
A.D.	1200	EKWE	v
A.D.	1300	AGU	v
A.D.	1400	UBA	v
A.D.	1500	ONYIA	v
A.D.	1600	ANIOKE	v
A.D.	1700	NEVO	v
A.D.	1800	UDE	ENEZE COMPOUND
A.D.	1900	ENEZE	v
A.D.	2000	EKOUDE	v

GENEALOGICAL AND SETTLEMENT TIME CHART OF NTUEGBENESE CLAN 700 B.C. – A.D. 2000 (ENEZE ROOT)

PERIOD		ANCESTORS				
BC	700	UBA				
BC	600	AJAKA				
BC	500	ONWE				
BC	400	AJAKA				
BC	300	OJENE				
BC	200	UBA	**NEW SETTLEMENTS**			
BC	100	MKPU				
AD	100	ANI				
AD	200	OKE				
AD	300	SHIKE	EZE	AGUMA	AKULU	WIWA
AD	400	ANI	UBAGU	SHIKE	OSHIE	OSA
AD	500	SHIKE			ANEKE	AGWEDE
AD	600				OSHIE	OSA
AD	700					
		OGUGU	OWELLI	IHE	AGBOGUGU	AWKUNANO

TIME CHART OF THE DISPERSAL OF NTUEGBENESE CLAN 700 BC – AD700

1. ANI SHIKEOKE, THE FATHER OF SHIKE ANI, REMAINED AT OGUGU.

2. EZESHIKEOKE, THE FATHER OF UBAGU EZE SETTLED AT ENUGU OWELLI.

3. IHE SHIKEAGUMA, THE GRANDSON OF AGUMA SHIKEOKE SETTLED AT ỤMỤOGBEE-IHE.

4. OSHIE ANEKE, THE GREAT GRANDSON OF AKỤLỤ SHIKEOKE SETTLED AT AMAOFIA-AGBOGUGU.

5. OSA (OSHIE) AGWEDE, THE GREAT GRANDSON OF WIWA (NWIWA) SHIKEOKE SETTLED AT AWKUNANO.

2.2: THE MEANING OF IGBO NAMES

The language of a people largely constrains their thoughts. Its words, concepts and syntax, out of all the signs that people use, are the most important determinants of what they are free and able to think.[9]

2.2a: Concept of God as Revealed to Our Ancestors

In **Igbo** language, which is as old as the **Igbo** Community, (100,000 BC.), among other meanings, the word, **chi, (ti)** is, "hit", as in the **Igbo** words, **chigọ** or **chisa**, ("bend or design" by hitting). Also, the **Igbo** word, **chi**, is, "install or establish", as in **chie eze**, (install a king). The **Igbo** word **ukwu**, among other meanings, is, "first establishment", as in the **Igbo** name, **Ezi ukwu** (first home or compound before new ones). The name **Chiukwu,** coined from the above words, means, "First Spirit Design and Establishment" The **Igbo** word, **Okike,** means, "creation", as in **Chukwu Okike** (God of creation) The word, **waa,** in **Igbo**, is, "design or make", as in **waa ọgụ** (make a hoe) or **waa nma** (make a knife).

---

[9] M.A. **Nwachukwu, Ahiajoku** Lecture, 2003, page 20

Through our ancestors' earliest interactions with spirits in dreams and trances, they came to the conclusion that God (**Chiukwu)** created what was created and made what was made (**Awụwa walụ ihe na Okike kelu ihe**), and they called what He made, the sky and the land (**Enu na Ani**). In later usage, the word, **Chiukwu** was shortened to **Chukwu**.

Precisely, our ancestors believed in the existence of the Spirit-world that originated through the wisdom of an original powerful and skillful spirit-designer of what is created. They perceived him as a loving protector of all that is created (**Chukwu Okike Obiọma**); who made the sun, an undying eye (**Anyanwụ**), to continuously watch over the earth; and who allows His guiding spirit (**Chi**) which manifests in every individual, to direct each person through life on Earth.

This clear concept of God through our earliest ancestors as far back as at least 100,000 BC., takes us to St. Thomas Aquinas' argument, later in the 13th Century A.D, that: "Wherever there is a complex design, there must be a designer". It should be clear to any doubting Thomas that **Igbo** ancestors who were the inhabitants of the core **Igbo** culture theatre that flourished as far back as 100,000 BC, believed in no other deity or spirit as the creator of the universe and its contents, physical and spiritual. Since our ancestors had the concept of God as the great and invisible designer of the universe but imagined him in human form, they interacted with him in practical human ways through created intermediaries or natural phenomena such as, the sky and the land (**Enu na Ani**), the physical and the spiritual (**Anyanwu na Agbala**), the living and the dead (**Madụ na Mụọ**). In traditional worship, in **Ihe Shikeaguma,** apart from (**Eze Enu**) King of the most high offering, which is usually a thanksgiving sacrifice with a white cock raised up alive on a tall stick and offered directly to God, as King of the universe, all other offerings to him are made through created intermediaries or natural phenomena.

Our ancestors who held God as a just but merciful creator (**Chukwu onye ebele**), believed that when a person's good deeds or those of his parents find favor with God and put him under the guidance or possession of the spirit of God (Chi), the person is said to have good luck (**Chi ọma**). If a person's bad deeds or those of his parents anger God or his intermediaries and the person is abandoned by the spirit of God (**Chi**), to the guidance or possession of evil spirit (**Ajọ Nmụọ**), the person is said to have bad luck (**Ajọ Chi**).

Our ancestors believed that when a person is so abandoned by the spirit of God, he should appease God through those intermediaries directly offended, such as, persons (**Ikwu n'ibe**), ancestors (**Ndi ichie**), the deities (**Alụsị ukwu m'ọbụ Alụsị**

nta). To remain in the favor and love of God and the ancestors, it was mandatory on every traditional **Igbo** male family-elder to pray every morning during the **Ọjị Ụtụtụ** rite, to reaffirm belief in God, on behalf of his family and community, for the accomplishment of the five realizable aspirations of the **Igbo**: Good health, Love, Peace, Wealth and Children. In order to entrench these aspirations in the memory and life of the family, **Igbo** children are named after these five aspirations as:

I. **Ndụbụisi** (May God grant good health before other gifts.)

II. **Ihụnanya** (Child given by God to show his love.)

III. **Udokanma** (May God grant peaceful solutions to our problems)

IV. **Chinenyeaku** (God gives wealth)

V. **Nwabụisi** (Childbearing is man's principal physical assignment on earth)

2.2b: The Ancestors of Ntuegbe Clan

In **Ntuegbe** clan, our ancestors' lives mirrored their very concept of God, and the sanctity and love of the family, as we shall see in the meaning of the prayer forms of their names; and in the foster names of their parents, given to their children and grandchildren. Our oral history has it that the **Ntuegbe** ancestor, **Ajaka Uba** came from **Akeze in Afikpo** Division about 700 – 600 BC. and settled at **Ezioha** (Home of the people) **Ogugu**. He and his descendants were great hunters hence the title, **Ntuegbe**, which means, "Gun powder". Also, in his book, "The history of **Ntuegbenese**", Rev. Fr. Sylvernus N **Onuigbo** confirms the myth of **Ntuegbenese** as a historical fact, in the long list of names of our ancestors; **Shike Oke, Ani Mkpume, Uba Ojene, Ajaka Onwe, Ajaka Uba**. In **Igbo** culture, every man bears his father's name. Sometimes he gives his son his own father's name as a patron name, as can be seen in the following names; **Ajaka Onwe Ajaka Uba, Shike Aguma Shike Oke, Nwaguma Shike Aguma, Shike Ani Shike Oke, Enezenta Eneze, Ekwenta Ekwe, Agunta Agu, Oshie Aneke Oshie Akulu, Osa Agwede Osa Wiwa.**

If we trace the **Eneze** lineage from **Ajaka Uba**, down to the present generation as explained above on the genealogy of **Ntuegbe** clan, and in my time chat, we shall see that from **Ajaka Uba** to **Shike Oke**, there are five double names or ten generations, as one name stands for one generation. If we take one generation to be an average of one hundred years, we can comfortably maintain that from **Ajaka Uba** to **Shike Oke**, was a period of about one thousand years. From **Aguma Shike Oke** to **Agu Igwe**, we have eight generations or a period of about eight hundred years. From **Agu Igwe Onyia** down to the present generation of my father- **Ekoude Eneze** is nine generations or a period of about nine hundred years. On the whole, the period from **Ajaka Uba** to **Ekoude Eneze** (my father) is twenty-six generations or about two thousand six hundred years. This period in history will be from, about 700 BC-A.D. 2000.

In the ancestral area of **Ntuegbe** clan, names denote our concepts and are rich in meaning, as follows:

*Agu is a name given to a male child born after a tiger is killed in hunting.

*Aguma, (sharp as razor) is a title for a warrior who killed a tiger with a sword in hunting.

*Ajaka, is short form for **Ajakanma** (sacrifice is more effective than other measures in getting God's solution of our problems.)

*Ani, is the short form for **Anieke (Aneke)** (good judgement of **Ani** deity) **Ani**, is also the name given to a child born during the month of **Ani** festival.

*Ekwe has its full meaning as **Ekwengba** (name given to a male child born on the day or month of the wrestling festival.)

*Igwe is the short form for **Igwenagụ** (plenty of children are desirable). It is also short form for **Nwigwe,** (child born after a visit to the oracle, or during the establishment of an oracle, or whose birth was foretold by the oracle).

*Nkpume is the name given to a child born on the day or month a sacrifice is made at **Nkpumenese** shrine.

*Ojene has its full meaning as **Ojen'ẹgụ egwu** (a fearless warrior).

*Oke is a short form for **Okechukwu,** (God's gift or portion to a family).

*Onwe is a short form for **Nwaonwe,** (child given as a consolation or as a replacement by God for a lost relation.

*Onyia is the name given to a child born after an epidemic, famine or war.

*Ovu is a short form for **Ovuokolo**, (powerful wrestler who carries other men on his shoulders).

***Shike** is a short form for **Ụmụshike,** (may my children be plentiful).

***Ụba** is a short form of the **Igbo** concept of wealth, **Nwakaụba** (children are more precious than riches).

In **Igbo** culture every person's name has a meaning as can be seen from the few examples shown above.

2.2c: Settlements in Ntuegbe Clan

Apart from **Ntuegbe** and **Akagbe,** which are hunting titles in the list of names of **Ntuegbe** settlements, the other names, **Ogugu, (Ogwugwu), Owelli (Owele), Ihe (Iheanụ) Agbogugu (Agbogwugwu**) are names of settlements. Some of the names of **Ntuegbe** settlements are used with the names of the founders of such settlements, as in **Owelli Ubagueze, Ihe Shikeaguma, Agbogugu Oshieaneke, Awkunano Osagwede.** Before **Ntuegbe** title-taking, all the settlements from **Ogugu** were taken as **Ogugu** settlements hence **Owele** (**Ogugu**), **Agbọ Ogugu**, and **Akegbe Ogugu**. The **Ihe** ancestor **Aguma Shike**oke, originally moved to **Enugu Owele** with his brother, **Eze Shikeoke,** before he moved again to a shelter at the **Ugwuenyi** wilderness **(Iheanụ or Ih'egu).**

The name **Ogugu**, is the white man's pronunciation of **Ogwugwu**. The actual meaning of **Ogwugwu** is, "valley settlement, surrounded by hills". It was in this well protected and well-watered location that **Ajaka Uba** settled and established a hunting shelter which has become the ancestral seat of **Ntuegbe** clan. While **Ajaka Uba** and his descendants settled at **Ogwugwu**, most of their social and spiritual needs were still supplied from **Akeze** and environs.

By about AD. 300, (after about nine centuries or nine generations at **Ogwugwu**), the population of **Ajaka Uba's** descendants increased to the extent that the available land at the small village of **Ezioha Ogwugwu** and environs became too small for the population. The surrounding hills are stony and were covered with huge forest trees. **Shike Oke** decided that his other children should move out of **Ogwugwu** while his first son should live at home.

Based on this decision it became traditional in **Ntuegbe** clan that first sons live at home in their father's house while other male children build new houses or move out of their father's compound and sometimes outside their ancestral land. Nowadays, this order of movement is reversible on agreement by members of some families.

Shike Oke begot his first son and gave him the patron name of his grandfather, **Ani**, who begot

Shike Ani Shikeoke, who settled at home to become the ancestor of **Ogwugwu**. His second son was **Eze** (short form for **Chibụeze or Nwabụeze**) who begot **Ubagụ Eze**. His father, **Shike Oke** asked him to move to an area behind his settlement (**Azụ owele**). His father also asked his third son **Aguma Shike**oke, to accompany **Eze** in the movement. **Eze** chose a hillside position (**Enugwu Owele**) and settled there as the ancestor of **Owelli.** It was from here that **Aguma Shikeoke** moved to the wilderness of **Ugwu enyi** (Elephant hill). **Aguma Shikeoke** was a brave professional hunter. His name **Aguma** is a hunting title which means: "sharp as razor".

This title was given to a hunter who killed a tiger with a sword. **Aguma** had a hunting shelter at **Ugwuenyi** while still living at **Enugwu Owele**. He was accompanied to the shelter by his son, **Shike Aguma** and it was there in the shelter at **Ugwuenyi** hillside that **Shike Aguma**'s son was born and nicknamed **Nwa Iheanụ Shikeaguma**. Till today, **Owelli** people still call the farmland or Wilderness **Iheanụ** or **Ih'egụ** Also till today, if an **Owelli** man is angry with an **Ihe** man, he will call the **Ihe** man, **Nwanụẹbọ** (man born in the bush). The **Ihe** man would retaliate by calling the **Owelli** man, **Owelli iduegu (Owelli** of the forest), because **Enugu Owelli** was in a thick forest when it was newly inhabited by **Owelli** people. **Owelli** town today, has patches of thick forest. The present day

Ihe and **Owelli** people who crack these jokes may
not know that they are relating to the history of the
origin of both towns.

Nwa Iheanu Shikeaguma was later shortened to
Ihe Shikeaguma. He moved to a cave on the
Ugwuenyi hill side. When he refused to return to
Enugu Owelli with his family, **Enugu Owelli**
people called them, **Ụmụọgba** (cave people). Till
today, this village is still called **Ụmụọgbee**. The
actual name of this village, which is the ancestral
seat of **Ihe Shikeaguma**, is **Ụmụngene Ugwunta
Aniugwu**. Later, **Ihe Shikeaguma's** descendants
moved out of the cave and settled by the river side
where they live today as **Ụmụọgbee** village. **Ihe
Shikeaguma** got many children at **Ụmụọgbee**,
from where some of them moved out to
Enugwuoke, **Enugwuẹgụ** and **Enugwuechi**
kindreds otherwise called **Enugwunatọ Ihe or
Ihenatọ**. **Ihe Shikeaguma** was nicknamed,
Aguma Aniugwu because of the hills, **Ugwu** in
the three clans (**Enugwuoke**, **Enugwuẹgụ** and
Enugwuechi); and also because of the name of the
ancestor of the eldest village in **Ihe- Aniugwu
Shikeaguma.**

Ihe Shikeaguma's first son, **Ugwu,** was named
after the place of his birth, **Ugwuenyi**. He settled at
Ụmụọgbee and begot **Ani Ugwu**, who begot
Ugwunta, the father of **Ngene Ugwunta
Aniugwu Shikeaguma:**

*Ihe Shikeaguma gave his second son, his grandfather's patron name, **Nwaguma** and he moved out of **Ụmụọgbee**, to a place now called, **Ụmụekwenta Alọ** in **Uhueze** village of **Enugwuoke Ihe**. **Nwaguma's** first two sons, (**Ọkpala Nwagụma**, father of **Uhueze** village and **Ovuokolo Nwagụma,** father of Amagụ village) founded the **Obunọ** kindred of **Enuguoke Ihe**.

* **Agu Igweọnyịa,** the great grandson of **Ovuokolo Nwagụma Shikeagụma**, moved out of **Uhueze** and settled at a place called, **Nkwabokobo** in **Amagu** Village. There were other settlements apart from the **Obuunọ** and **Ụmụọgbee** settlements in **Ihe Shikeaguma** at that time.

* **Anebe Chimeonwo Anebeaguma,** the ancestor of **Ụmụanebe,** founded the **Umuanebe** village.

* **Ebeke Chimeọnyia and Oji Ọnyịangene,** cousins of **Anebe Chimeonwo,** founded **Ebekenọjị** village.

*Shike Ajanaonwo, the ancestor of **Umusike** village and his first cousin, **Anebe Chimeonwo**, the ancestor of **Ụmụanebe,** with the ancestors of **Ebekenọjị,** founded the **Obuegu** kindred of **Ihe Shikeaguma**.

*The latest significant movement into **Enugwuoke** kindred, of **Ihe Shikeaguma**, was the movement of **Chime Igweǫnyi,** from **Awkunano Osagwede**. He settled close to **Ụmụǫgbee** village and became the ancestor of **Awkunano Osagu** village in **Ihe Shikeaguma.** This movement was one of the secondary movements within **Ntuegbe** clan.

***Aligwe Ọnaka**, who moved from **Ụmụǫgbee**, settled at **Ụmụnukpu Enugwuẹgụ** and founded the **Enugwuẹgụ** village.

***Ọnyiaja Anugwọaji**, founded **Umuonyia** village, while his brother, **Ọlụaja Anugwọaji**, founded **Umuọlụ** village.

***Ogodo Igweonwo Amanakụlụ**, the ancestor of **Ụmụogodo**, who moved from **Ụmụamana** in **Isuawa** as a refugee during the **Agbogugu and Isuawa** war, was one of the last significant movements into **Enugwuechi** kindred of **Ihe Shikeaguma.**

***Onwo Eneagụma,** the ancestor of **Ụmụonwo** village, made the last significant movement from **Ụmụogbee** hence it is the sixth and the youngest of the six major kindreds in **Ihe Shikeaguma.**

These kindreds in the order of seniority are:

i. **Ụmụọgbee (Awkụnanọ** settled close to **Ụmụọgbee)**

ii. **Obunọ (Uhueze** and **Amagụ** villages)

iii. **Obuegụ (Ụmụanebe, Ebekenọjị** and **Ụmụsike**)

iv. **Enugwuẹgụ**

v. **Enugwugwu (Ụmụọnyia, Ụmụọlụ** and **mụogodo)**

vi. **Umuonwo.**

Oshie Aneke Oshieakụlụ, a great grandson of **Shike Oke,** and the ancestor of **Agbogugu,** moved from **Ogugu** through **Enugu Owelli** and **Ihe,** down to a place called **Amaọfịa,** (forest settlement) in **Agbogugu.** The town **Agbogugu,** which means, lower village or settlement of **Ogugu,** at the time of settlement was called **Agbogwugwu.** At the time of this settlement, **Oshie Aneke** was more attached to **Ogugu,** his former home, and his great grandfather's settlement than to **Ihe** or **Owelli,** his cousins' settlements hence his settlement was called **Agbọ Ogwugwu** instead of **Agbọ Ihe** or **Agbọ Owelli.** Another great grandson of **Shike Oke, Agwede**

Ọsawiwa also moved from **Ogugu** to **Akegbe** and his settlement was then called **Akegbe Ogwugwu**. **Agwede** was a brave hunter hence his nickname, **Agwede** (wild cat). His descendants were sharp shooters hence their settlement was called **Akegbe**, which means, those whose trade, (**Aka**) was the use of the gun, (**Egbe**). **Akegbe** the settlement of **Osa Agwede** which is the youngest settlement of the five **Ntuegbe** towns is now called **Awkụnanọ Ọsa Agwede** and is the largest in population.

The various **Ntuegbe** towns that moved from **Ogugu** to their present-day settlements have lived in peace with other **Ntuegbe** towns for centuries. Populations have increased and there have been improvements in their physical developments. The cultural relationships with the other **Ntuegbe** towns have remained good for centuries to the extent that there is no history of war among the **Ntuege** towns, apart from inter person and inter village land disputes, that were usually settled by the elders.

The good and brotherly relations among **Ntuegbe** people can be seen in the timing of the celebration of their biennial **Ani** festival, and in the observance of one traditional legal system (**Omenani Ntuegbe**). The traditional legal system was not coded but was orally passed on from father to son, by elders who were respected as judges and representatives of the ancestors.

PERIOD	ANCESTORS							
400 AD	AGUMA							
500 AD	SHIKE							
600 AD	IHE							
700 AD	NWAGUMA							
800 AD	OKPALA							
900 AD	EGWU							
1000 AD	NJOKU							
1100 AD	ALOZO				EZE			
1200 AD	EGHUCHI				EKWESU			
1300 AD	OYO				INEM	ONWO		
1400 AD	ENENTA	EGWU	EKWENTA		EZE	EKE	OYO	
1500 AD	EMENTA	NGENE	ONWO	EGWU	ONWO	UKWU	OYONTA	
1600 AD	UCHEAGWU	ANUOKE	IGWESHI	ENENTA	ENENTA	NWEKE	ANU	
1700 AD	EKO	ONAA	OKOLONKWO	UDE	UGA / ONATA	OGWUGA	CHIME	
1800 AD	OKOYE	EGBO	EKO	NWEKWE	OBAZI / IGWESHI	EKO	OTUSA	
1900 AD	OKOLO	IJEOMA	CHUKWU	OGBUU	OKELEKE / NEVO	ANEKE	AGU	
2000 AD	NWOSU	NZEKWE	EKONTA	NWIKE	CHUKWU / OKAFO	ONUIGBO	ENEWE	

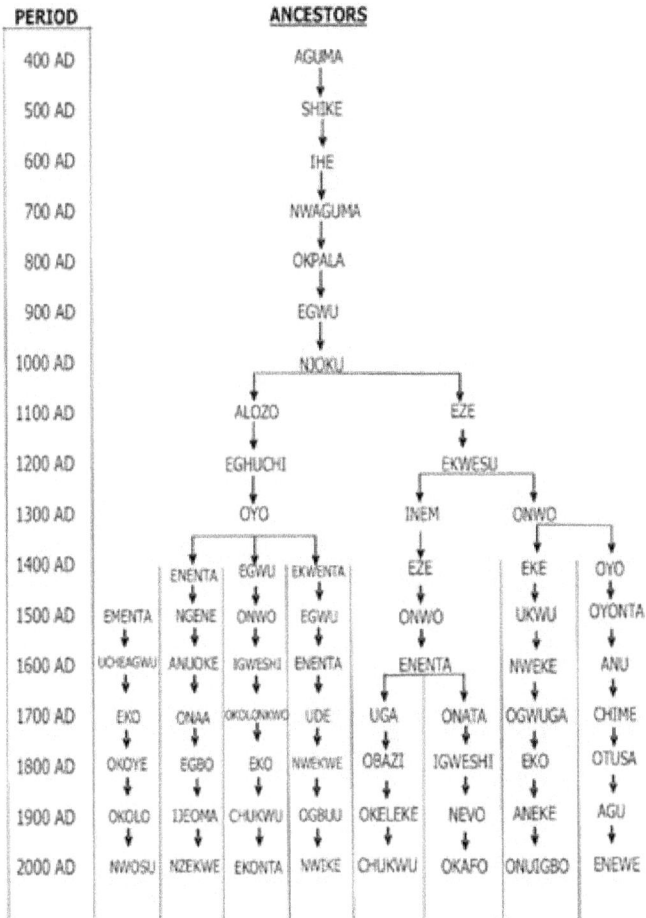

GENEALOGICAL TIME CHART OF SOME LINEAGES IN UHUEZE VILLAGE IN OBUNỌ KINDRED OF IHE SHIKEAGỤMA

PERIOD	ANCESTORS
400 AD	AGUMA
500 AD	SHIKE
600 AD	IHE
700 AD	NWAGUMA
800 AD	OVUOKOLO
900 AD	ONYIA
1000 AD	IGWE
1100 AD	AGU
1200 AD	IJE — EKWE
1300 AD	CHIME (IJE) ; AGU, EKWENTA (EKWE)

PERIOD	AGUMA	INEM	INEM	UBA	AGUNTA	ONWO	AGU	NWOKE
1400 AD	AGUMA	INEM		UBA	AGUNTA	ONWO	AGU	NWOKE
1500 AD	CHIME	EZUNU	ANI	ONYIA	UDE	AGU	ONYIA	ANEBE
1600 AD	ANIEGU	ONAGA	CHIME	ANIOKE	NEVO	UGAA	EKWE	IGWE
1700 AD	MBA	ONWO	IYOVO	NEVO	CHIME	AGU	ONYIA	ONWO
1800 AD	IGWESHI	IGWESHI	ANIOKE	UDE	NWEKO	ONUOHA	AGU	IGWESHI
1900 AD	OYIWA	IBE	EKO	ENEZE	NWEKENTA	CHUKWUANI	NEVO	NEVO
2000 AD	CHUKWU	NWEKE	AGANIGBO	EKOUDE	NWANKWO	UDEONU	EKO	OFO

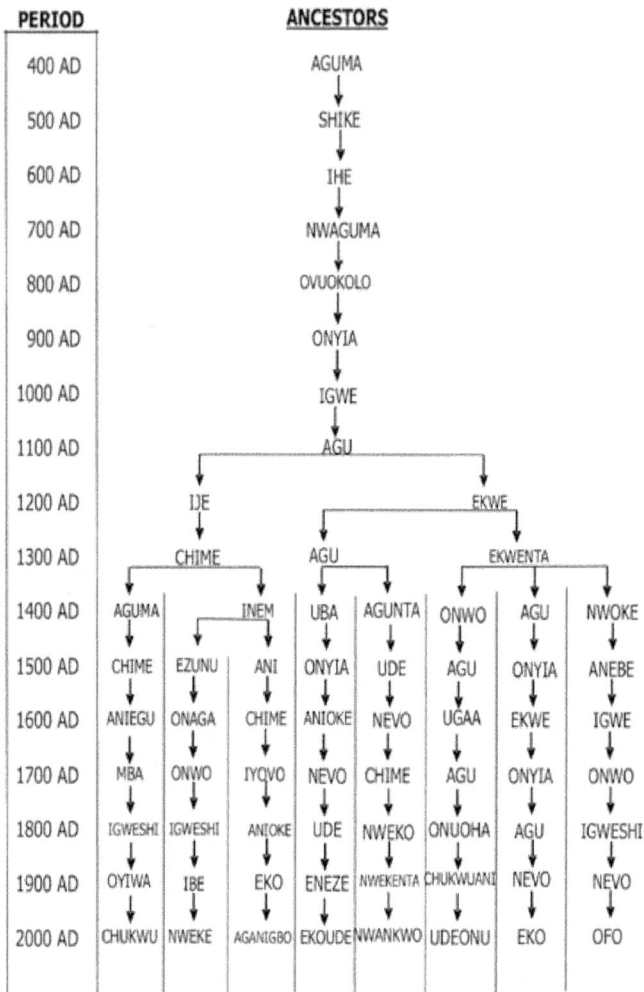

GENEALOGICAL TIME CHART OF SOME LINEAGES IN AMAGŲ
VILLAGE OF OBUNŲ **KINDRED OF IHE** SHIKEAGŲMA

2.3: IHE SHIKEAGUMA: A CORE IGBO CULTURE COMMUNITY

2.3a: Historical and Geographical Evidences

To establish the fact that **Ihe Shikeaguma** is a core **Igbo** culture community, I shall firstly quote Professor Michael **Angulu Onwuejeogwu** (1987)

> *Between 3000 and 2000 BC; In the theatre of Igbo culture area, the Igbo speaking people seem to be concentrated in the Nsukka, Okigwe, Afikpo triangle. In my opinion, considering the present Archaeological and linguistic evidence before us, this is the major core of Igbo culture. It is from here that the second major dispersal might have started.[10]*

Secondly it is established from today's Geography of **Enugu** State of Nigeria, that **Ihe Shikeaguma** community in **Mbanabo** North of **Awgu** Local Government Area, is inside the said **Nsukka, Okigwe, Afikpo,** triangle. Among the five towns of **Ntuegbe** clan, **Ogugu**, **Owelli**, **Ihe**, **Agbogugu** and **Awkunano**, **Ihe** is by age, number three and by Geography, resident at the center of the five towns of **Ntuegbe** clan, along **Enugu-Awgu** old road, which is inside the said **Nsukka, Okigwe, Afikpo** triangle.

---

[10] M.A. **Onwuejeogwu, Ahiajoku** Lecture, 1987, page 17

2.3b: Linguistic Evidence

The linguistic evidence of the evolutionary history of the earliest cultures in the theatre of Igboland can be provided by looking at the relationship of the **Igbo** language with the other Lower Niger languages otherwise called the Kwa languages that extend along the Guinea Coast from Liberia to Cross River of Nigeria.

> *Linguists seem to agree that the best known of the group includes Kru, Twi, Ga, Ewe, Urhobo, Isoko, Fon, Yoruba, Edo, Nupe, Igbo, Ijo, Idoma, Igala and Gwari. It is hypothesized that those languages have a common stock, because they have common basic words which are cognates. Inspecting Armstrong's sample of list of words that are cognates, one will easily note the astonishing relationship of those languages. (Armstrong 1964).[11]*

Armstrong suggests that **Igbo**, Bini and Yoruba languages derive from a common stock.

> *Igbo separated from the stock between 7000 and 6000 years ago while Yoruba and Bini separated between 6000/5000 years ago.[12]*

[11] M.A. **Onwuejeogwu, Ahiajoku** Lecture, 1987, page 9
[12] M.A. **Onwuejeogwu, Ahiajoku** Lecture, 1987, page 11

If we go back to the migration of the lower Niger people, we shall see that Armstrong's conclusion, suggested that the Igbo ancestors lived with the ancestors of the other tribes at this Igbo culture triangle before their ancestors moved to their present settlements, or that the ancestors of the various lower Niger tribes lived together somewhere as a distinct people with one language, from where they separated to their various settlements. Therefore, by about 7000 years before the separation of the languages, there was no Bini or Yoruba language but Igbo, or at least a language more Igbo than Bini or Yoruba.

Looking closely at the **Igbo** meaning of the words, three, four and say, for example, from Armstrong's list of words, in comparison with the Bini and Yoruba meaning of the same words, one will see that the words in **Ihe Shikeaguma** dialect are more cognate to words in the two other languages, Bini and Yoruba, than the words in central or **Onitsha-Igbo** dialects. This simply means that the **Ihe-Igbo** dialect and many other dialects of the Scarp lands **Igbo** culture area are older than central, Western and **Onitsha-Igbo** dialects; and that the three dialects derive their origins from the dialects of the core-**Igbo** or **Waawa** speaking people, as can be seen in these three examples:[13].

---

[13] M.A. **Onwuejeogwu Ahiajioku** Lecture 1987, Pg. 9

THREE

(Ihe) **Igbo** *Dialect*	Ẹtọ	(Atọ or Itọ)
Bini language	Ẹha	
Yoruba language	Ẹta	

FOUR

(Ihe) **Igbo** *Dialect*	Ẹnọ	(Anọ or Inọ)
Bini language	Ene	
Yoruba language	Eri	

SAY

(Ihe) **Igbo** *Dialect*	Kaa-si	(Kwuo)
Bini language	Khaa	
Yoruba language	Ka sọ	

Note that the word (**Ihe**) in brackets at the beginning of (**Igbo** dialect) in each group of words, lays emphasis on the similarities with a particular **Igbo** dialect while the words in brackets at the end of the first lines of the three groups of words point to the dialects of central **Igbo** and **Onitsha Igbo** language.

2.3c: Genealogical Evidence

My time chart on the dispersal of **Ntuegbe** clan shows that our ancestor **Ajaka Uba** left **Akeze**, in greater **Afikpo** Local Government Area about two thousand six hundred years ago (about 700BC) and settled as a hunter at **Eziọha Ogugu** in **Mbanabọ**. South of **Enugu** State. His descendants, generations of hunters and farmers, have grown into five towns of **Ogugu**, **Owelli**, **Ihe Shikeaguma**, **Agbogugu** and **Awkunanọ**, and are the constituents of the **Ntuegbe** clan. From **Ajaka Uba's** settlement at **Ogugu**, our ancestral base, (about 700BC) to the present generation, we of **Eneze** root for example, have about twenty-six generations (about 700BC – AD 2000). This period of twenty-six generations is divided into four historical periods of settlement at:

i.   **Ogugu**: **Ajaka Uba** to **Shike Oke**, for nine generations or 900 years.
ii.   **Ụmụogbee Ihe**: **Shike Oke** to **Nwaguma Shikeaguma** for 4 generations or 400 years.
iii. **Uhueze Ihe**: **Nwaguma Shikeaguma** to **Igwe Onyia,** for three generations or 300 years.
iv.   **Amagu Ihe**: **Igwe Ọnyia** to **Ekoude Eneze**, for ten generations or 1000 years.

2.3d: Cultural Evidence
Under the heading, genealogical evidence, it was stated that **Ihe Shikeaguma** of **Ntuegbe** clan is a native of the core **Igbo** culture area through our ancestor, **Ajaka Uba** of **Akeze,** who settled at **Ogugu** as a hunter. The material and immaterial elements of growth of **Ajaka** Uba's family since his settlement about 700 BC resulted in the emergence

of the **Ntuegbe** people as a recognizable clan, and as a historical entity. The **Ntuegbe** culture grew out of the core **Igbo** culture, during the Scarp lands **(Enugwu)** civilization or what **Onwuejeogwu** (1987) called the **Okigwe, Afikpo, Nsukka** Era. The **Igbo,** between 100,000 BC and 5000 BC., had inherited a keen awareness of God and a well-developed concept of human life.

This awareness of God which started as far back as about 100,000 BC in **Ugwuele Okigwe** was reaffirmed and expressed every morning by the **Igbo** family elder during the traditional morning-prayer (**Ọjị Ụtụtụ**) as handed down to us by our earliest ancestors. Traditionally, it was ritually mandatory on every **Igbo** family- elder to say the traditional morning prayer and carry out the meal rite of (**Ịtụ Aka**) offering food to God and the ancestors for as many times as the family sat together for meals.

The traditional morning prayer (**Ọjị Ụtụtụ**) has no specific form or length but contained or implied the following affirmation of faith in God and the intermediary elements who were believed to deliver prayers to God or act as his agents, as handed down orally to us by **Igbo** ancestors.

Traditional Morning Prayer (Ọjị Ụtụtụ)
i.   God of creation and of tender heart;

(**Chukwu Okike obi ọma**)

ii. Who made what was made and created what was created; come and eat our kola. **Awụwa walụ Ihe, n'Okike kelu Ihe; bia taa ọjị**)

iii. The sky and the land; (**Enu n'Ani**);

iv. The sun and the oracle; (**Anyanwụ n'Agbala**);

v. Major and minor deities; (**Alụsị ukwu n'Alụsị nta**);

vi. Four market days; (**Mbọsi afia ẹnọ**)

vii. Our Ancestors, and you the intermediary forces of God, come and eat our kola. (**Ndi Ichie, na ndi ozi Chukwu; bia taa ọjị anyi**).

viii. We pray with this kola for, good health (life), love, peace, wealth, and children; for our family and our community. (**Anyi ji ọjị a, n'ayọta ahụike (ndụ), ihụnanya, udo, akụ n' ụba; nke ezi n'ụnọ anyi**).

In numbers (i) and (ii) above, our ancestors called on God to partake of the kola nut. In numbers (iii) to (vii) they called on intermediary forces and spirits to also take their share of the kola nuts, since they were believed to be the messengers of God on earth. In number (viii), the family head then prayed for his family and his community for the gift of the five realizable aspirations of the **Igbo**: life, love, peace, wealth and children. The use of intermediary elements at that time in history was not peculiar with the **Igbo** or the African. These intermediary forces and spirits were also used in worship in Egypt, Babylon, Greece and Rome.

The traditional **Igbo** concept of God and the use of intermediary spirits in the worship of God predate some very powerful religions of today by several centuries. These concepts developed into what we know today as the earliest **Igbo** culture and philosophy. The concepts created a very closely woven fabric of family life with extended family ties and God-conscious community life, which became the **Igbo** traditional religion. This religion made it a sacred duty of everyone to protect the life and property of members of the family and the community. One was not allowed to destroy any human life of any age except in self-defense. Even in self-defense, the killer of a human being needed ritual cleansing.

Ajaka Uba came to **Ogugu** about 700 BC, well vested in these concepts and imparted the same culture and philosophy to **Ntuegbe** ancestors. In **Ihe Shikeaguma**, manual labor needed for important community projects such as, the erection of market stalls, construction of new settlements, clearing of village and farm roads, and construction of shades for marriage and burial ceremonies, were communally handled, free of any charges.

Everybody was bound to defend the community in case of any attack, and to protect the good image of the community. The **Ihe** man held the **Ihe** community at a very high esteem, hence the saying: **Ihe amaka (Ihe** is very good) and would go to any length to prove that belief. Every child born in **Ihe Shikeaguma** was seen as a gift, not only to the parents but to the whole community, hence the name: **Nwadụlụọha**, (the community owns the child). It was a sacred duty of every **Ihe Shikeaguma** person to protect the life of every other **Ihe** person, especially outside **Ihe Shikeaguma** or in the hands of a stranger. This protection tendency of **Ihe** people is still alive today in places as far away as Europe and America among natives of **Ihe Shikeaguma** community.

2.3e: Traditional Ancestral Government Structure in Igboland

The traditional government in most of Igboland, which has the ancestor as a focal point of origin, set forth and administered the public policy and affairs of the four segments of the **Igbo** community.

i. The mega family (**Ụmụnna**)
ii. The village (**Ama, Ụmụ or Uhu**
iii. The town (**Obodo),** and
iv. The clan **(Mba)**

The ethnic **Igbo** government was prehistoric in origin but purely democratic and meritocratic in nature and was as old as the earliest **Igbo** community (at least 100,000BC).

The Ancestral Government Structure in Ihe Shikeaguma:

(i) **Ụmụnna**: A mega family unit, having one ancestor and its eldest male as its titular head. The **Ụmụnna** is constituted by several micro families, of husband, wife and children. It is the first level of government in Igboland, and has such names as: **Ụmụagụ**, **Ụmụigwe** and **Ụmụchime**.

(ii) **Ama, Ụmụ or Uhu**: The second level of government is the village unit which has several mega family units **(Ụmụnna)**. It usually has one ancestor with the ancestral name attached to the name of the village e.g. **Amagụ, Ụmụshike** and **Uhueze.**

(iii) **Obodo**: The third level of government is the town which is constituted by several villages **(Ama, Umu or Uhu),** having one ancestor, with the ancestral name, title, place of birth or residence attached to the name of the town e.g. **Ihe Shikeaguma**, and **Ogugu Ntuegbe**.

(iv) **Mba**: The fourth level of government is the clan with several towns **(Obodo),** usually having the ancestral name or the number of its towns attached to the name of the clan, e.g. **Umuojebo Ogene**, **Ntuegbenese**, **Mbanabo,** and **Mbaise.** The clan as in **Ntuegbenese** is more of a cultural body than a political unit. Its cultural meetings are most of the time, based on representation from the towns of the clan.

These clans of the **Igbo** Community have some common identities based on a common language, one traditional religion and other common cultural patterns. They were never organized as one political entity under one ruler or government. In all matters of government each of the towns of the **Igbo** community, existed and functioned as an autonomous entity in no way subject to political control by its neighbors, but was culturally tied to the **Igbo** community. As the population of a clan increased, it was further split into smaller autonomous sub clans within the mega clans. This ancestral government structure which started centuries BC, are still very much in use today in **Ntuegbe** clan and many other **Igbo** communities, with some added coloration due to European influence.

From time to time, as the need arises, adult members of each of the first three levels, family, village or town meet at the village or town square, or at an agreed place to discuss both internal and external affairs of each segment of the community; and take decisions by consensus, with voice votes or acclamation. Every adult male present in such a meeting, has the right to contribute his opinion on all the matters under discussion. The eldest man on each level, who is usually a titular head, or a titled man appointed by him, usually leads in the opening prayers and controls the proceedings in the assembly. For the purposes of efficiency and speed in the execution of decisions of the assembly, councils or committees are created for specific assignments. The selection of appointees for councils or committees is based on merit, age or experience. Standing committees whose members are assigned such jobs are appointed by the assembly of each level. In some cases where there are no volunteers, individual members of the community are appointed to lead the councils or committees. Sometimes committees are limited to specific qualifications or to existing associations such as the elders council (**Ndi Okenye** or **Ikenye),** title-holders council **(Ndi Eze),** Age grades **(Ndi Ọgbọ** or **Ndi Uke);** and professional groups like, hunters **(Ndi Nta**), Diviners (**Ndi Dibia**), Black smiths **(Ndi Ụzụ**), Artists **(Ndi Nka**) etc.

All services to the community by an individual volunteer and each member of a council or committee are honorary as everybody contributes his best services for the good of the community. Leaders, whose appointments are based on merit, serve for a given period or for a particular assignment and for as long as they are effective in office. It is a great honor to be given an assignment by the community. Functionaries compete among themselves for meritorious services in order to show appreciation for their appointments.

Ọfọ Stick as a Staff of Office to Elders

In a traditional **Igbo** setting, the **Ọfọ** stick is a symbol of truth and fair play. The **Igbo** believes that truth gives life to any society and sustains good relationship with God, the deities and fellow men hence the **Igbo** saying: "Truth is life" (**Eziokwu bụ ndụ**). This **Igbo** concept also points to the philosophy of the **Igbo** founders of the University of Nigeria, **Nsukka**: "Seek the truth; teach the truth; and preserve the truth." **Ọfọ** is a staff of office inherited by the elders of each community who are also the titular heads. These titular heads of the **Igbo** community are expected to be the custodians of truth and fair play. This is why the **Igbo** reserve their important traditional functions of marriage rites, funeral rites, kola nut rites, libations, communing with the ancestors, sharing of inheritances, deciding the ownership and boundaries of land; in the hands of elders, who are also treated as representatives of the ancestors. These elders in the discharge of their titular jobs believe that they are accountable to God, the deities and the ancestors; and not to any temporal ruler or force.

Democracy in Igbo Land

For purposes of effective commitment and

consensus, majority of families (**Ụmụnna**) are required to be represented in the village assembly while the town (**Obodo**) assembly needs many villages. The same majority-representation of towns takes decisions in the cultural meetings of the clan. No one person, even the titular head, can take a unilateral decision that is expected to be binding on all the segments of the community without prior consultation and approval of the people concerned.

Democracy which the civilized world cherishes and advocates as the best type of governance thrived in Igboland many centuries BC, before the advent of Europeans in Igboland. This system of democratic governance with its many adhoc leaders, made it difficult for the British to get protection treaties signed with the **Igbo** in the nineteenth century, because getting such a treaty from the **Igbo** involved so many people and needed a lot of negotiating time. In **Aba** Division alone, it took a period of seven years 1892 – 1898 to sign treaties with the various big towns in the division:

> *Kings and Chiefs of Akwete in 1892, Chief Ananaba of Obegu 1895, Chiefs of Osusu, Obeaja, Oza, Ohuru and Ohanko, Abala, Ogwe, Umuiku Iko and Obohi 1896, Chiefs of Asa and Obote 1897, Chiefs of Ohabiam and Abeyi 1898.*[14]

---

[14] East-central State Census Commission events list 6/7/1973.

After the British got treaties of protection negotiated and signed with the big kings of the Hausa, Yoruba, Bini and the other neighbors of the **Igbo**, they resorted to swift military expeditions in Igboland, to silence the small units of poorly armed but effective **Igbo** insurgency.

C.A **Onwumechili** (2000) captures this incident:

In Southern Nigeria, the British swiftly imposed their rule by overthrowing King Jaja of Opobo in 1887, and easily conquering Ijebu in 1892, Nana of Itsekiri in 1894, Benin and Ilorin in 1897. The events were similar in Northern Nigeria. Sir Frederick Lugard easily captured Bida and Kontagora in 1901, Bauchi in 1902, Kano and Sokoto in 1903. In Eastern Nigeria there was no single state or power whose defeat would put the whole region or any large part of it into British hands. Although Arochukwu was captured in 1901-1902, it was not until about 1920, after 20 years that the whole of Igboland was subdued in a series of small military expeditions.[15]

Michael Crowder also noted the **Igbo** resistance to British rule:

---

[15] C.A. **Onwumechili, Ahiajoku** Lecture, 2000, page 23 and 24

Since each village offered its resistance, there was no identifiable army to defeat among the Igbo as there was, say, among the Tukulor, the emirates of Nigeria or Samoris' Mandingo Empire. Each village or federation of hamlets had its own war leader. These societies conducted what was in effect guerilla warfare against the invading armies, quite the best tactic that could have been adopted in the circumstances.[16]

From the foregoing, one can see that the **Igbo** traditional system of government was purely democratic and meritocratic in nature but derived its origin and credibility from the ancestor. Minus the debilitating effect of the slave trade which weakened the **Igbo** before the military onslaught and economic exploitation by the British Colonial Government, this type of democratic government, might have developed with time, into a bigger democracy with its influence over the whole area of the emerging **Igbo** economic influence, in the Lower Niger Area of Nigeria.

---

[16] Michael Crowder, West African Resistance to Colonial Rule, 1971

2.3f: Law Enforcement and the Ihe Movement

In **Ihe Shikeaguma**, our earliest ancestors had traditional laws (**Nsọanị**) that maintained community peace. Traditional laws were not coded but learned orally by all and sundry and were handed down from father to child. These laws were enforced by the community courts of, father's family (**Ụmụnna**), the village or town (**Ọha**), who often handed down stiff penalties and fines, such as death or banishment. Offences that were concealed by the offenders were usually left for God, the deities and ancestors to enforce in their own way.

Every able-bodied **Ihe Shikeaguma** man was expected to play the role of soldier and police in the community when necessary, for the enforcement of the community laws (**Nsọanị**). Also, every elder was a judge bound by traditional laws (**Nsọanị**), to be fair and fearless in his judgement of others. In the courts of the community, the elders with reference to traditional laws (**Nsọanị**) announced the sentences passed on offenders after consultations (**Igba Izu**) for consensus, where necessary. Some punishments for offenders were required to be executed by the offenders themselves without delay, to avoid exposing the offenders and their relatives to public shame and ridicule. Some of these offences were murder, defilement or theft of yam or sheep.

Murder: If an **Ihe Shikeaguma** person intentionally killed another **Ihe** person for any reason whatsoever, the murderer became ritually unclean because he/she had committed an abomination and was no longer ritually fit to live in **Ihe Shikeaguma**, or even enter any house or touch any **Ihe** person, including his/her closest relations. Such a person had the option of being banished from **Ihe** and **Ntuegbe** clan forever or taking his/her own life by hanging. If the killing was accidental, he/she also remained ritually unfit to live in **Ihe** or any **Ntuegbe** town until he/she was made clean ritually.

Defilement: If an **Ihe** man had carnal knowledge of a close relation such as mother, sister or daughter, both man and woman were banished forever from **Ihe**, but they had the option of hanging themselves.

Yam, the Sustainer of Life (Ji ji ndụ): Yam was the main crop of **Ihe Shikeaguma** and was treated as being next to life. Anybody who stole yam was banished from the town but had the option to hang himself. During the slave trade, such an offender was sold as a slave.

In any of the above life sentences, if a man chose the option of banishment, he remained ritually unfit to live in **Ihe Shikeaguma** all his life but could continue to bear his **Ihe** name in his exile. He was denied all his citizenship rights except the right to be called an **Ihe** man. This law made it possible for banished **Ihe** men to go to other distant towns, faraway from **Ntuegbe** clan, to establish settlements, some of which grew into new **Ihe** towns or villages far away from **Ihe Shikeaguma** town. Towards the end of the 18th Century, the children of banished men, freed or run-away slaves of **Ihe** origin, were not allowed by traditional law (**Nsoani**) to return to **Ihe Shikeaguma** as free men, in order to avoid revenge actions. Once a man became a slave, he and his descendants remained slaves during the slave trade. Consequently, freed slaves and banished **Ihe Shikeaguma** men established settlements outside **Ihe Shikeaguma** town. Some of the following settlements might have been established by **Ihe Shikeaguma** diviners, hunters, migrant farm workers, craftsmen, inter town (**Isu and Ewho**) war-refugees, banished **Ihe** men or freed slaves.

Ihe Movements:

1. **Ihe Achi**, Oji River Local Government Area of **Enugu** State
2. **Ihe** Aka, **Nsukka** Local Government Area of **Enugu** State.
3. **Ihe n'Owele**, **Nsukka** Local Government Area of **Enugu** State.
4. **Ihe Mbosi, Ekwusigo** Local Government Area of **Anambra** State.
5. **Ihe Ichida, Aniocha** Local Government Area

91

of **Anambra** State.

6. **Ihe Mbawsi**, Northern **Ngwa** Local Government Area of **Abia** State

7. **Ihe Ukwu**, Northern **Ngwa** Local Government Area of **Abia** State.

8. **Ihie Chiowa**, **Arochukwu** Local Government Area of **Abia** State.

9. **Ihe Obegu, Ugwunagbo** Local Government Area of **Abia** State.

10. **Ihiagwa, Owerri** West Local Government Area of **Imo** State.

11. **Iheoma, Orlu** Local Government Area of **Imo** State.

12. **Ihe Umuakpu, Ohaji** Local Government Area of **Imo** State.

All the settlements that originated from **Ihe Shikeaguma** must have been established after **Shikeaguma** settled at **Ihe Shikeaguma** of **Ntuegbe** clan in **Enugu** State, about AD.500. Some of the **Ihe** settlements may have been of secondary or even of tertiary movements.

2.3g: Defense

The production of iron tools and weapons as early as the 14th century at the Scarp lands settlements in **Achi**, **Udi**, and **Nsukka** areas, provided badly needed weapons, such as sheathed swords (**nma ọbọ**), machetes **(obejili),** daggers **(opio)** and spears **(alọ)**, for the protection of crops and livestock from rogues and wild animals. At that time farmers, hunters and tradesmen lived in relative peace in small autonomous village units.

By the 15th and 16th Centuries, the Portuguese who traded along the West African Coast, exchanged flint guns (**Ọkwụlụọka**) for palm produce, elephant tusks, hides and skin, and other farm and forest produce. About the beginning of the 17th Century, other European traders joined the Portuguese in the West African trade and opened slave trade routes in the West African hinter land. These new imports of guns, in addition to locally made hand weapons, prepared fertile grounds for inter settlement wars and slave raids along the West African coast and its hinterland.

The resultant inter settlement wars and slave raids were facilitated by the European slave traders who instigated inter settlement wars and equipped local hirelings for raids within the West African hinter land, for the purpose of procuring slaves. These wars and slave raids chased farmers away from their farms to the battle fields and watch posts. Communities mobilized their entire population to defend their towns and villages that were torn apart by inter community wars and constant slave raids. All their able-bodied men were trained to defend the villages and few remaining nearby farms from wild animals and bandits well-armed by the white traders to carry out slave raids. Each community or settlement had its own army, defense anthem and war songs. Their war leaders specialized in guerrilla war tactics but did not have enough and appropriate arms and ammunition to effectively fend off slave raids. In **Ihe Shikeaguma**, the defense anthem was made up of several established historical statements, recited by one of the people's leading heroes to an audience for their reaffirmation. The recital of each historical statement was originally followed with a question: "Is that right"? (**Ọkwẹ-ẹ nụ**) The audience reaffirmed with another statement: "Yes" (**Iya-a**) The question, **Ọkwẹ-ẹ**? (Is that right?) and the statement: **Iya-a** (Yes) are from the dialect of **Ihe Shikeaguma** and other Scarp lands or **Waawa** speaking people of what is now **Enugu** State, **Ebonyi** State and parts of **Abia** and **Imo** States of Nigeria.

After many years of usage, the question, **Ọkwẹ-ẹ nụ** (Is that right), was reduced to a statement, **Kwe-enụ** (Reaffirm), while the reply, **Iya-a** (Yes) is still in use till today. Also in **Ihe Shikeaguma**, the anthem was recited by heroes (experienced hunters and warriors) only, and usually at the beginning or end of important meetings such as deployment or redeployment meetings held in a village square or shrine by men before a battle, a hunting expedition, and recently before an inter town or inter village wrestling match. Men who were not heroes and women were not qualified traditionally to recite the anthem before an audience of men. The anthem could only be recited in a village square, village shrine or marketplace but never in a person's compound. It was believed before the advent of Christianity in **Ihe Shikeaguma** that when this anthem was recited and concluded with a war song in front of **Ngwu** shrine, spiritual and physical protections were given to men in action during fighting, hunting expeditions and wrestling matches.

The movement of migrant farmers into the fertile river basins of the Scarplands area for the production of more foods, gave rise to the demand for more land from the original settlers in the area, for habitation and for the grazing of livestock. This demand for more land resulted in inter settlement disputes and the manufacture of locally made iron tools and weapons.

The arrival of European traders in the 17th century with better iron tools and weapons strengthened the defense capabilities of the Scarp lands people but also armed some Arab hirelings for slave raids. The local people with their locally made weapons and few cap guns could not contain European fire power. As a result of this position thousands of able-bodied men and women were killed or carried away into slavery by the European slave traders.

DEFENSE ANTHEM IN IHE SHIKEAGUMA

REAFIRMATION

1	**Ihe: Kwe-e nu?** (We are the sons of **Ihe**: Is that Right?)	**Iya-a** (Yes, we are.)
2	**Aguma Aniugwu: Kwe-e nu?** (We are the sons of Aguma Aniugwu?)	**Iya-a** (Yes, we are.)
3	**Ọgụ n'akọlụ Igbo: Kwe-e nu?** (We are great farmers in Igboland: Right?)	**Iya-a** (Yes, we are.)
4	**Ama onye, kulu onye: Kwe-e nu?** (We are generous to strangers: Right?)	**Iya-a** (Yes, we are.)
5	**Oje n'ẹgụ egwu: Kwe-e nu?** (We are fearless in battle!)	**Iya-a** (Yes, we are.)
6	**Nnekwu ọkụkụ ije, ụmụ ya n'ọsọ?** (As the hen, we protect our kin?)	**Iya-a** (Yes, we do.)
7	**Kpakpayi gbalụ ọfịa nkụlụkụ: Kwe-e nu?** (In hunting or battle, we are thorough: Right?)	**Iya-a** (Yes, we are.)
8	**Ọbọlụ enyi ọkpa n'atọ: Kwe-e nu?** (We fearlessly claim what is ours: Right?)	**Iya-a** (Yes, we do.)
9	**Kwe ndụnụ, kwe ndụnụ agha: Kwe-e nu?** (We successfully fought two towns at same time?)	**Iya-a** (Yes, we did.)
10	**Ihe: Kweshie n'ike** (Sons of Ihe: Give loud affirmation.)	**Iya-a-a-a** (Yes Yes Yes)

Many more historical statements could be added to the above.

The message of the Anthem:

1. **Ihe Shikeaguma**'s sons shall live up to their tradition and be as brave as their forefathers.
2. Being the descendants of **Aguma**, his kin shall be as rugged and as fearless as **Aguma**, who killed a tiger with a sword.
3. **Ihe Shikeaguma**'s sons (a hoe of the **Igbo**) are great farmers like their ancestors.
4. **Ihe Shikeaguma** people are not hostile to law-abiding strangers.
5. Sons of **Ihe Shikeaguma** shall be fearless in battle.
6. Sons of **Ihe Shikeaguma** shall learn from the hen that continues fighting back, when attacked, while its chicks disappear into cover.
7. **Ihe Shikeaguma**, in battle or hunting, is likened to the thorny creeping vines (**Kpakpayi)** that spread their branches under forest trees.
8. Sons of **Ihe** should remember that **Ihe** hunters killed an elephant, long ago, in a forest and covered it with leaves, and left to reinforce. When they came back to the elephant, hunters of that town had removed one of the elephant's

legs. **Ihe** hunters fought them and recovered the elephant with one leg missing.

9. **Ihe Shikeaguma** sons should remember that their ancestors successfully defended **Ihe** town when attacked at two fronts by two towns at the same time.
10. The historical statements are true; we shall fight!

After reciting the anthem, the leading hero or elder started a war song to raise the spirit of his men and to inform them of the seriousness of the situation. He then informed them through the song that they had to fight (**Anyi awalụ je ọgụ**). In **Ihe Shikeaguma**, "He-e or He-i" is an exclamation uttered when something grave happens, such as the death of a person or attack from the enemy. If the happening is very grave, the "He-e" is repeated in accordance with the seriousness of the incident.

War Song:
    Refrain:
    He-e! He-e! He-e! Awalụ je ọgụ

    Okụlo enwẹghi egbe: Awalụ je ọgụ
    He-e! He-e! He-e! Awalụ je ọgụ
    (Any man who has no gun; we must fight)

    Ele-e ya Aro: Awalụ je ọgụ…
    He-e! He-e! He-e! Awalụ je ọgụ

(Will be sold to **Aro** slave traders,
because we must fight)

Ewelu ya kpọlụ egbe: **Awalụ je ọgụ**
He-e! He-e! He-e!... Awalụ je ọgụ
(The proceed will be used to buy a gun,
because we must fight)

Okolo enwegh alọ: Awalụ je ọgụ
He-e! He-e! He-e!... Awalụ je ọgụ
(Any man who has no spear) …

Okolo enwegh nma: Awalụ je ọgụ
He-e! He-e! He-e!... Awalụ je ọgụ
(Any man who has no sword) …

The above war song reminded the men that it was
mandatory on every able-bodied man to have at
least one of the three weapons in use at the time,
with which to fight. If any man failed, he would be
sold after the battle to **Aro** slave traders and the
money used to buy weapons. It was a clarion call to
action by the hero. It portrayed the determination
of the men to defend their community.

Song Before a Battle:

Refrain:
He-e-e! He-e-e! Ude agha egbuna anyi (May
we not die in battle)

E welụ ọkụkụ gba aja, Ude agha egbuna anyi,
He-e-e! He-e-e!... Ude agha egbuna anyi,
(If the enemy sacrificed a fowl, may we not die in battle)!

E welu ebini gba aja, Ude agha egbuna anyi,
He-e-e! He-e-e! Ude agha egbuna anyi
(If the enemy sacrificed a ram, may we not die in battle)!

E welu efi gba aja, Ude agha egbuna anyi,
He-e-e! He-e-e! Ude agha egbuna anyi
(If the enemy sacrificed a cow, may we not die in battle)!

This second song is a prayer by the battle leader that he and his men shall not die in battle whether the enemy sacrificed a fowl, a ram or a cow.

2.3h: Igbo Lunar Calendar:
Igbo Market Day
The original belief of the **Igbo** during those prehistoric years, when the sun was given the **Igbo** name **Anya-anwụ** (undying-eye), was that God created the sun to continuously guide the day and night, the four market days of the native week, seven native weeks in the lunar month, and twelve lunar months of the year. The **Igbo** believes that God provides man with every livelihood for every

day before it breaks in the morning. The day continues its life from morning through the noon (**Efifie**) to the evening (**Mgbede**) before the sun goes home into the horizon. As soon as the sun deeps into the evening horizon, it starts nourishing the next market day through the evening (**Anyashi**) and night (**Uchichi**) till the next day is born in the morning at cock's crow.

Since the **Igbo** translate their live experiences in practical human ways, the life of the market day is likened to the life of a human being. The life of **Eke** market day is believed to start after **Nkwọ** day's sunset (**Mgbede Nkwọ**), when the market closes for the day; **Eke** lives through the night (**Uchichi**) and is born in the morning at cock's crow. **Eke** lives through the noon (**Efifie**) and expires at sunset (**Mgbede Eke**). The same life cycle applies to the other market days: **Oye**, **Afọ** and **Nkwọ**. This market day life cycle explains why a baby born in **Ihe Shikeaguma**, after **Nkwọ** market day sunset (**Mgbede Nkwọ**), is named after **Eke**, as **Nweke, Okoloeke**, or **Mgbọeke**. It is to be noted here that every day in **Igbo** year is a market day and every baby is born on one market-day or the other. Traditionally every baby is named after the market- day, at the moment of birth, before any other name is given during the naming ceremony after cutting the first tooth.

The life span of the **Igbo** market-day is divided into

five periods:

> **Anyasi**: (Evening after sunset, when the **Igbo** day starts life)
> **Uchichi**: (Nighttime, which is the expectancy period of the market-day)
> **Ụtụtụ**: (Morning time, which is the birth and childhood period of the day)
> **Efifie:** (Noon, which is the adult age of the day, when the market is full)
> **Mgbede**: (Evening time before sunset, which is when the market day expires).

Igbo Native Week (Izu)

Igbo native week is made up of four market days: **Eke, Oye, Afọ** and **Nkwọ**. In **Ntuegbe** clan, every town has its own market. Although each market is situated in a town, it is usually attended by the people of other **Ntuegbe** and non **Ntuegbe** towns within and outside **Enugu** State of Nigeria.

Igbo Lunar Month (Ọnwa)

Igbo lunar month is made up of seven native weeks of twenty-eight market-days. All the twelve lunar months of the year have twenty-eight days each. This lunar calculation which was based on moon sighting is as old as the earliest **Igbo** community which flourished at least as far back as 100,000BC.

Igbo Lunar Year (Afọ)

Igbo lunar year is made up of twelve lunar months,

eighty-four native weeks or three hundred and thirty-six days.

Seasons in Igboland
One lunar year in Igboland is divided into two seasons of farming and harvesting, or rainy and dry seasons. The rainy season, which is the farming season, is from May to October, while the dry season which is the harvest season is from November to April. The lunar year is shorter than the calendar year by one month. This is why the annual adjustment of the **Igbo** lunar year by one month to agree with the planting and harvest seasons of the year is necessary. This forward movement of the year by one month is carried out annually by each clan or community in Igboland, for the fixing of its local festivals or ceremonies. An example is the **Ani** festival in **Ihe Shikeaguma**, which comes up between November and January of the festival year, depending on the moon counting and adjustment of the year by the **Ntuegbe** clan. The new yam festival (**Fiajioku**) takes place in **Ihe Shikeaguma** in the month of May or June yearly.

Traditionally the **Igbo** are a farming people but some of them are traders while others are government and company workers. The craftsmen and traders among them do part-time farming. Most of the important festivals, title taking and marriage ceremonies in Igboland, take place during the harvest season which incidentally is from November to April.

103

Traditional Festivals in Ihe Shikeaguma:

August	1st month (Ọnwa mbụ):	Mgba Aja Nwafia (At 2nd native week)
Septemb.	2nd month (Ọnwa ebọ):	Ọgbụlụgbụ (At 3rd native week)
October	3rd month (Ọnwa etọ):	Nwangene (At 3rd native week)
November	4th month (Ọnwa enọ):	Igwu nkwụ **Ani Ihe** (at 3rd w. biennially)
December	5th month (Ọnwa ise):	**Ani** Ihe (At 5th native week biennially)
January	6th month (Ọnwa isii):	Ọmụ and Ọfia (At 3rd & 5th week)
February	7th mt. (Ọnwa esaa):	Nmanwụ & Ajụ
March	8th mt. (Ọnwa esatọ):	Farm-work
April	9th mt. (Ọnwa itenani):	Farm-work
May	10th month (Ọnwa ili):	Fiajiokụ & Farm work
June	11th month (Ọnwa ili n'ofu):	Farm-work
July	12th mt.(Ọnwa ili na ẹbọ):	Mgba Aja **Eke**

2.3i: Yam, the Sustainer of Life (Ji Ji Ndụ)

Igbo mythology has many versions of the history of the origin of yam. **Nri** mythology has it that yam was given to **Eri** after he sacrificed his first son to God, who also advised him to distribute yam to the **Igbo**. The same mythology also has it that God gave **Eri** the right and power to officiate as a priest in the establishment of **Fiajioku** altars in **Igbo** villages and towns. Another **Igbo** mythology has it that yam was the reincarnation of the first son of an **Afikpo** woman sacrificed on the orders of the **Ibunu Ukpabi** oracle.

> *The woman first sacrificed a slave and the community quite appropriately got a bastard yam (Ji Abana). When however, she sacrificed her own son, (Amadi Ji) a man's yam sprouted up.*[17]

Recent studies on the origin of yam show that:

(i)   Yam was in Igboland before **Eri** came to **Anambra** river basin (AD. 800) and before **Ibunu Ukpabi** was established in Igboland.

(ii) Yam is not planted and eaten only in Igboland where these yam myths apply.

(iii) Yam is believed to be native to most of the West African countries, and this belief brings us to what is known as the West African Yam-belt which stretches from the Cameroons to the Ivory Coast.

(iv) *The yam-belt of the world stretches through the equatorial tropics with the edible yam clustered around four distinct centers of*

---

[17] M.J.C. **Echeruo, Ahiajoku** Lecture, 1979, page 9

origin; the Indo-Chinese peninsula, Southern China, the fringe of the West African forest and the Caribbean area.[18]

(v) *The large-scale introduction of iron in West Africa dates from about AD. 300. At least four hundred years before that (100 BC.) several species of yam and oil palm were already firmly established in the forest and woodland regions of West Africa.*[19]

Ajaka Uba, the ancestor of **Ntuegbe** clan of **Enugu** State of Nigeria, came to **Ogugu**, **Mbanabo** South, as a hunter and part time farmer, about 700BC. His main crop then was yam, and yam was used in worship rituals especially in the worship of **Ani** and **Fiajioku**. In **Ihe Shikeaguma** today wild yams can still be found in the forest. Many varieties of wild yams such as, **Jiagọ, (Jiọfia) Ekpukpu, Okpulu, Ngeyinge, Edụẹgbẹ, Ezeọgwu**, and **Okolo ọcha**, can still be seen growing luxuriantly in the virgin forests and wood lands of, **Apa, Ọfia Ag'ụdụ, Ọfia Ugwuegbe and Ọfia Uke**.

These wild species of yams are not yet domesticated anywhere that I know of today. One can only identify the wild yams by their young shoots that usually sprout with the first rain every

---

[18] V.C. **Uchendu, Ahiajoku** Lecture, 1995, page 70
[19] M.J.C. **Echeruo Ahiajoku** Lecture, 1979, page 9

year. If the shoots grow beyond human height into the trees, identification of the yams becomes difficult. If even they are identified, the tubers lose their quality as edible food. At this time of the year, harvested yams are tied in the barns and some families use the wild yams as supplement food. In **Ihe Shikeaguma** it is believed that apart from **Chukwu Okike**, who lives in the Sky and **Ani** who lives on the land, the next deity in age is **Fiajioku** who is the deity that controls the growth and fruition of what is planted on the land, especially yam. Yam (**Ji ji ndụ**) is called the sustainer of human life and the food of the gods and the ancestors.

Having the above in mind, one can conclude that yam is as old as the earliest **Igbo,** or earliest West African, some of whose ancestors passed through Igboland on their way to their present-day settlements. Yam was among man's first foods, apart from meat, fruits and vegetables and was usually roasted when there were no pots. It is this early roasting of yam that the **Igbo** try to relive and celebrate during the **Fiajioku** festival.

In **Ihe Shikeaguma**, our own mythology on the origin of yam has it thus: Long ago there was a long period of famine on the land. Many people died of hunger. A man called **Ekweke** lost his wife and children to hunger. In desperation he ran into the forest at night, calling his personal guiding spirit (Chi) to take his life, but he did not die. He continued running into the forest until he became tired. He fell down and slept under a tree. In his dream, the spirit of his dead father took him to the base of an oil-beam tree and showed him a small bulge on the ground near the tree and told him to dig up the content of the bulge and eat it.

When he woke up the following morning still in desperation, he looked round and noticed that he was under an oil-bean tree that resembled the one that his father's spirit took him to in his dream. He looked round and saw the small bulge on the ground. He got up and dug the bulge out with a stick and found out that it contained a tuber. He ate it as he was instructed by his father's spirit, believing that he was going to die and join his dead father, but he did not die. On the following morning he woke up and found out that he had more energy. With this new energy and good health, he understood that his father wanted him to live.

He changed his mind about wishing to die. He searched for and collected more of the tubers in the forest. As he ate the tubers, he became more and more strong and healthy. After three native weeks (12 days) in the forest, he was able to retrace his way back home, carrying some of the tubers. On his arrival home, his brothers who thought that **Ekweke** had killed himself in the forest were very happy to see him still alive and strong. He told them his story and showed them the remaining tubers. They also ate the tubers and called the tuber; "sustainer of **Ekweke**'s life" (**Oji ndụ Ekweke**). When the tuber became popular in the settlement the name was later shortened to; "sustainer of life" (**Ji ji ndụ**). Today in **Ihe Shikeaguma**, any yam that bulges out from the yam mound or ridge, is called; **Ji Ekweke** or **Ji gbalụ Ekweke** as a memorial of that dream event. This myth on yam suggests that yam was discovered in the forest by the **Igbo** and domesticated by the earliest residents of the core **Igbo** culture area.

The various developed species of yam, through careful cultural development, might have grown to their present-day status and spread in West Africa, following the movements of the ancestors of the various tribes of W.Africa. This spread of yam was possible considering the ease with which yam is propagated; starting from the tip of the tale which can break off during harvest and start growth again in the bush during the next season; to a small piece of yam thrown away into the bush with domestic refuse, that can sprout on the top of the ground in the bush, send down roots into the soil and start off again after the first rain in the year.

2.3j: Fiajioku Festival in Ihe Shikeaguma:

The New Yam Festival is celebrated throughout the countries of the West African Yam-zone in different ways and at different times of the year.

> *In an area where yams were ennobled about*
> *4000 – 3000 BC it is no wonder that the*
> *yam-zone is regarded by some authors as*
> *the home of the highest cultures and*
> *civilization.*[20]

In Igboland, the celebration takes place between May and August, depending on soil type and amount of rainfall in each area. In **Ihe Shikeaguma**, special yams for the new yam festival are planted in specially selected, tilled and well manured pieces of land, called, **Ani Igwugwu**. The yams, **Ekpe, Egaa, Nw'agba** and **Alafu**, are planted in December or January, so that an early harvest in May or June will be used for the **Fiajioku** festival ritual. By May or June, only professional farmers are able to have mature yams for the celebration of the **Fiajioku** festival but they are ritually bound to sell some of their yams, so that nonprofessional farmers or farmers who do not have good harvest can take part in the rituals, and in the celebration of **Fiajioku** festivities.

Professional farmers look forward to **Eke Fiajioku**; the day of the sale of new yams for the roasted yam ritual. They make deliberate effort to come to **Eke Fiajioku** market with the biggest and most mature yams in their farms. When most

---

[20] B.N. **Okigbo, Ahiajoku** Lecture, 1980, page 20

people were farmers, **Eke Fiajioku** was usually a yam- show day in **Ihe Shikeaguma**. It was believed that any professional farmer who refused to sell or bring his new yams to **Eke Ihe** market on **Eke Fiajioku**, had starved the ancestors and would have poor yam harvest in that year. Buyers of new yams came from **Ihe Shikeaguma** and all the neighboring towns.

Every year, when the 10th lunar month appeared in the sky, the **Fiajioku** priest came to **Eke Ihe** market and announced the appearance of the new moon and the day of the festival. The festival usually took place eight or twelve days from the first **Eke** day after the new moon. The festival usually started on **Nkwọ** day when new yams were harvested, and ended on the following **Eke** day, which is the day of the sale of new yams for the roasted yam ritual.

Any professional farmer who had taken a yam-title was bound to offer a black ram on the **Fiajioku** shrine in his barn. Small farmers were free to offer black cocks on their fathers' **Fiajioku** shrines during the festival. My father was a professional yam farmer, with two yam-titles of, **Ọfiaẹkụ** and **Ogbuuji** meaning, a rich farmer who fed many people with yams. He usually bought a mature black ram, a week or so before the new yam festival, if he did not have a black mature ram in his flock of sheep.

Early in the morning, on **Nkwọ-Fiajioku** day in 1945, while we were still asleep, my father went to the farm with my mother to harvest the new yams. On his return, he summoned our kinsmen (**Ụmụnna**) for the usual morning prayers (**Ọjị ụtụtụ**). During the prayer, he highlighted special thanks to God for sparing the lives of members of his family and of his kinsmen. He also included thanks for good new yam harvest for the festival. He did not forget to include prayers for God's continued kindness in future new yam festivals, before going into the year's roasted new yam ritual. The new yams, usually four in number, were then roasted in a woodfire set up at the center of the compound.

When the roasting was completed, the yams were presented by my mother, with accompanying shredded oil bean meal (**Akpaka**), usually prepared with red palm oil, fresh red pepper and salt. My father and one member of the kin took some pieces of the roasted yams in a wooden bowl (**Ọkwa**) and went to the **Fiajioku** shrine in the yam-barn. He took a piece of the roasted yam in his right hand, and thanked God, the land deity, and the yam deity for the harvest of the new yam and for the preservation of the lives of members of the family and of the kin, for the new yam festival. Then he put some pieces of the roasted yam into the shrine bowl. He also offered the oil bean food into the shrine. He took some of the food with his assistant in front of the shrine before they returned to the compound.

When he came back to the kin, they greeted him by his yam titles: **Ọfiaẹkụ** or **Ogbuu**. The roasted new yams were shared by all the people in the compound. After asking of the harvest of other members of the kin, my father gave out some of his own tubers of yam to those whose harvests were poor, or those who returned from other towns for the festival, so that members of their immediate families might also take the new yam. He also invited his kinsmen and their wives to the next stage of the new yam festival.

In the evening, the kinsmen came back with their wives. My father presented eight big tubers of new yams, a big black ram, two jars (8 gallons) of palm wine and kola nuts for the ceremony. Two of his kinsmen who had taken the yam title, carried the ram and the yams, with a cup of palm wine and a kola nut, and went with him to the **Fiajioku** shrine in the barn. The eight yams were placed side by side in a line in front of the shrine. The ram's legs were tied up with a rope.

The usual prayers were said, giving thanks for the preservation of life and for a good harvest of the new yams. The kola and the palm wine were offered, and the ram was slaughtered by my father.

The ram was held by the other two titled men as it struggled. Most of the blood was poured into the shrine-bowl, while some of the remaining blood was sprinkled lightly on the eight tubers of yams, before the ram was dropped on the ground in front of the shrine.

After the ritual, the slaughtered ram and the eight tubers of new yams were brought back to the compound. The yams were given to the women who peeled and cut them into small pieces for cooking. The men cut the ram into the usual traditional parts after singeing off the hair on an open woodfire, in preparation for cooking. Then the meat and the yams were put into two big clay pots, followed by the addition of salt and palm oil. When the food was ready, women presented the cooked yam in two big baskets and the meat also in two baskets while the gravy was in two clay bowls.

My father and the two titled men took the upper part of the heart of the ram, and two pieces of the yam and cut both meat and yams into small pieces; and mixed the pieces with red palm oil and salt in the small wooden bowl. They took the food to the shrine in the barn. Prayers were said by my father, and the food was offered as he prayed, putting some of the food in the shrine-bowl in small portions, one after the other.

At the end of the offering, the three men took

small portions of the sacrificial food in front of the shrine before they joined the kinsfolk, who were waiting in the compound for the ritual to come to an end. When my father and the other two titled men came out from the barn, both the men and the women greeted my father again by his yam titles. The women shared the food in small clay bowls, while the two titled men shared the meat.

After the meal, the palm wine was shared with native cups (**Oko**) and everybody took his or her fill. As they were drinking, the women were singing praises to God for the year's successful new yam festival. In their song they also praised my father for his usual generosity and asked God to bless him. The other two titled members of the kin carried out the same rituals and ceremonies earlier in the day like my father, according to their means. The above new yam festival rituals took place in all families according to each person's means, among traditional worshippers in **Ihe Shikeaguma**.

The following day was **Eke** market day; the yam-sales day; the day of thanksgiving for the gift of the yam, and the day each farmer entertained his immediate family members in the house. It was a yam-show day and the day that farmers' wives came out colorfully dressed in their best. It was a day of drumming and dancing for various age groups and village dance-troupes. It was a day that farmers who were successful showed off their yam harvest in the market and entertained in-laws, extended family members and friends with palm wine in **Eke** market.

After the sale of new yams, people sat in small groups in the market stalls, sharing jokes, exchanging greetings, drinking palm wine and discussing the yam sales of the day. They compared the new yam sales of the year with the sales of previous years by the various villages in **Ihe Shikeaguma**. Each village had its own dance troupe in front of its market stall. Singing and dancing, accompanied with the spraying of coins on dancers, continued till the evening. The new yam festival originated when every **Igbo** practiced the **Igbo** traditional religion and when yam farming was the main profession of the **Igbo**. This festival reflects some of the cultural values of festivals by the **Igbo**, such as:

* Thanksgiving to God after good fortune;

* Sharing our harvest with our relations;

* Respect of the mega family (**Ụmụnna**) as a cultural and political unit;

* Artistic, religious and recreational values of dance music;

* Use of the market as a cultural center.

These values are attributes of our people handed down to us by the ancestors. They are assets preserved for our own good which we as **Igbo** people should protect because these values have projected the **Igbo** as a distinct people. Today in **Ihe Shikeaguma** as in many other places in Igboland, we have more Christians than traditional worshipers, and we have less than half of the population as yam farmers. All of us still eat roasted and cooked yams and are still natives of Igboland. We still worship God, some as Christians and some as traditional worshipers. Christians thank God for the gift of the yam with Christian prayers during the new yam festival and uphold the other aspects of our Christian festival-culture because our culture is about our existence and identifies us as a recognizable people with specific oriented values.

Yam was believed to be discovered in the forest and domesticated by our earliest ancestors. It enjoys great respect by the Igbo as king of all tubers. It is also called the food of the gods and sustainer of life, as a result of the ease with which the yam is prepared for food. The new yam festival which is one of the most popular festivals of the Igbo nation is celebrated in many ways in various parts of Igboland.

A RESIDENTIAL COMPOUND IN IHE SHIKEAGUMA IN 1945

2.3k: A Family Compound (1945) in Ihe Shikeaguma

The compound was very large. It was enclosed with about six feet mud-walls reinforced with broken stones and covered with layers of palm fronds. It had a main entrance gate with a carved door and an exit gate with another small carved door at the rear. The compound floor was of gravel and there were altogether ten building structures and six shrines in it. Some of the roofs were conical and were framed with strong bush poles. The roofs were thatched with palm fronds and dry grass while their walls and floors were finished with red mud-plaster.

Houses

Nkolo, Ụfụ, or Agbara: This residence of the family-head was a round house about fifteen to twenty feet in diameter with two opposite entrances and six to seven feet mud-walls. Each of the two entrances had no doors and one of the entrances was facing the compound main entrance. **Nkolo** had two mud beds and many mud seats, usually covered with animal skins or, straw mats. The ceiling, which was partial and above one bed, was made of palm wood planks plastered on the top with mud. This ceiling was used as a shelf for personal effects and weapons. There was a fireplace in front of this bed, and the fireplace was used during the rainy season, May, June, July, August and September. It was also used during the

Harmattan season, December, January and February. **Nkolo** served as a watch post and a living room cum bedroom for the family head. It was also used as a meeting place for the family at mealtimes and for consultations with nonmembers of the family. The other bed was a sleeping place for any of his teenage sons, old enough and able to keep the watch with his father. As a titled man, his seat, which was always covered with white ram-skin, was at the entrance of the house and facing the compound gate. In his presence, no other member of the family or a guest sat on this seat.

Ụnọ Nta: (Guest house): This two-room house also belonged to the family head personally. It had two rooms, each measuring about ten feet by ten feet, and had eight feet walls, two small windows, three doors and two mud beds. The two beds were covered with mats and had no pillows, as the use of pillows was not popular then in **Ihe Shikeaguma**. The outer room was used as a guest room while the inner room was used by his younger sons. The inner room was sealed with palm wood planks plastered on the top with mud. This plastered ceiling was used for the storage of the man's work implements and sundry goods. There was a fireplace in the outer room in front of the bed.

Ụnọ Nwanyi (Wife's House): Each of his two wives had a separate oblong house of two rooms with a door between them. The inner room had two mud beds with a small window above each bed. The ceiling was made of palm wood planks but not plastered to allow hot air circulation in the ceiling as dried food items were stored there in pots, bowls and baskets. The hot air coming from the fireplaces under the beds, kept the room warm at night during the rains and during the Harmattan season. This room was used by his wife and her female children. The outer room which had an open front was used as a veranda with a fireplace at one corner for cooking. Above this fireplace was a drying shelf (Ukonta) made of split bamboo. The veranda had three long mud seats by the three walls for the use of the wife and her children, and female guests, especially during her maternity periods.

Ụnọ Ekwu (Kitchen): Each of the two wives also had an additional house used as a kitchen and for the storage of cooking utensils and food stuff. This house had two rooms with a door joining them. The outer room measuring about ten feet long by eight feet wide and eight feet high was used as a veranda and had a fireplace at one end for cooking. The entire two rooms of this kitchen were sealed with palm wood planks, except for a small access opening in the inner room along the innermost wall. The top of the ceiling was not plastered to allow smoke and hot air to spread to the drying items of food stored in the ceiling. There was also a bowls-shelf (**Ukonta**) along one side of the kitchen-wall below the ceiling. The bowls-shelf which was made of split bamboo sticks projected about two feet from the wall. The inner room of the kitchen was used for the storage of water and fresh food items such as yams, oil-palm seeds and vegetables. Cooked food and cooking utensils were also kept there. The chicken house was an attachment to the outside of the back of the kitchen.

Ọba (Barn): There was a yam barn walled into the compound. Inside this barn was a small one room seed-store house (**Nkpuke**) used for the storage of small seed yams, tenia and cocoyam. The barn also housed the shrine of the yam deity (**Fiajioku**) said to be responsible for the growth and preservation of yam and other crops.

Nkwụ Efi (Cow Stable): Beside the yam barn, was the cow-stable about thirty feet long and fifteen feet wide with six feet walls. This stable also housed sheep and goats. One end of the stable was covered with thatch. Under the thatch was the trough for cow, sheep and goat food. The walls of the stable were made of large broken stones laid with mud and covered with layers of palm fronds like the compound walls.

Shrines:
Ọnụ Egbo (Gate Shrine): On the main entrance gate of the compound was the shrine of the gate

deity, believed to keep off evil spirit or neutralize enemy charms on entry into the compound.

Ani Obu (Ani Family Shrine**):** Beside the house of the family head was the family shrine of (**Ani Ihe** deity). Certain offerings for **Ani Ihe** deity could be made here instead of going to the main shrine at **Eke Ihe** market. All deities in **Ihe Shikeaguma** were believed to receive their power and legitimacy from **Ani Ihe** hence **Ihe** people would talk of: "**Ọgbụlụgbụ Ani Ihe**, **Ngwu Ani Ihe**, **Nze Ani Ihe** etc".

The same status was given to every **Ani Ntuegbe** shrine in each of the five **Ntuegbe** towns. It was believed by **Ntuegbe** people that **Ani Ntuegbe** received his power from God to direct all the deities and ancestors in **Ntuegbeland**. Our ancestors also believed that God created (**Ani**) the land deity and gave it both power and resources to look after the minor deities that existed on the land for the efficient running of the land; He also created the sun; gave it power and majesty and commanded it to perpetually rule over the heavens and warm the face of the earth so that the land can produce food for man and animals.

Agwụ (Ẹgwụ): On one side of the guest house was the **Agwụ** shrine. This deity was believed by our ancestors to be responsible for the consultation of other spirits and for the guidance of men during warfare, hunting, wrestling and other male activities. The **Agwụ** deity which is a no-nonsense deity was worshipped by men only and sacrifices were made to it with the left hand.

Chi Nwanyi (Woman's Guardian Spirit): In **Igbo** culture it is believed that every person is given a guardian spirit (Chi) by God as expressed in: **Onye na chi ya** (Everyone has a guardian spirit), **Onye kwe, chi ya ekwe**, (what one wills, is what his guardian spirit wills). Based on the above belief, the **Igbo** holds it that every woman's guardian spirit accompanies her from her father's house on her way to married life and guides her away from all evil especially childlessness. Consequently the ancestors directed that at death a woman's relations should receive the last bit of her bride price and destroy the shrine of her guardian spirit (Chi) so that her spirit can accompany the woman's relations to commune with her ancestors for twelve days before returning to her children in her husband's home.

Each of the family head's two wives had her own guardian spirit's shrine between her house and the kitchen. The shrine had a fig tree (**Ọgbụ**) and a small bowl by the side of the tree with a ring of stones surrounding the bowl.

2.3l: Eke Market Day
Eke day in **Ihe Shikeaguma** to date, is a work-

free day and people are expected to come to the market to sell farm produce or livestock; to buy provisions brought in by traders from **Ihe** and the neighboring towns; or to meet with friends or in-laws. **Eke Ihe** market is a big market patronized by the eleven towns in **Mbanabọ** and traders from as far away as **Imo** State, **Enugu**, **Udi** and **Agbani** Local Government Areas. The market square is also used as the civic center of **Ihe Shikeaguma** community. Important historical meetings with the earliest colonial adventurers and missionaries were held there.

A Day When Elders Handle Social Issues (Eke market day)

On that Harmattan day in December 1945, the family head woke up early in the morning; took his machete and went out to the toilet **(Ije ogwe or Ije idu)**. There was blazing fire in the fireplace stuffed with choice **Akpaka** wood which kept his house warm. Some elders from the village came in, one after the other, to bask in the wood-fire warmth; to have some discussion; to share the usual morning kola (**Ọji Ụtụtụ**) and sometimes palm wine with the family head.

They were enjoying morning jokes in his absence but greeted him by his titles as he returned. He exchanged pleasantries with them and welcomed them after inquiring about the health of their various family members. At this stage the elder's palm wine tappers brought in two kegs of palm wine and went out to continue their morning rounds. He sat down on his usual seat covered with white ram-skin and brought out a bowl of kola nuts and a snuff box. He presented a kola nut to the elders for their usual morning prayer. Since he was a titled man and an elder, the other elders asked him to break the kola nut and lead them in the prayer. The elders gave their affirmative input of, **Ise-e-e**! to indicate their support in the prayer. The elder then threw the kola nut bud outside and took one of the lobes of the kola nut. The other elders then greeted him by his titles. He gave the wooden bowl containing the kola nut lobes to the elders.

After eating the kola, he took a pinch of snuff from his snuff box and offered it to God and the ancestors by throwing the pinch outside. He took another pinch and snuffed it with relish after which he gave the snuff box to the elders for their turn. He presented a keg of palm wine and gave it to the youngest of the elders to share. The sharer gave him the first cup of the palm wine which he also offered to God and the ancestors by pouring the libation outside before he received the second cup which he drank. He then advised the sharer to give the wine to the others, one after the other. As the elders were rounding up the palm wine, his senior wife presented a steaming bowl of cooked yam, prepared with vegetables, fresh pepper, and plenty of red palm oil. He took a piece of yam, offered it

to God and the ancestors and threw it outside.
He took another piece of the yam and ate it before
the other elders joined him in taking the food. The
above food rituals handed down to us by our earliest
ancestors, were carried out as a way of thanking
God and sharing with the minor deities, our
ancestors, and our neighbors, the bounties of God.

After the morning prayers and the yam breakfast,
the elders talked about the coming **Ani Ihe** festival
and how to provide gunpowder and meat for the
occasion. They discussed other issues for which
the men visited him. When the elders left, he called
his two wives to his house and they talked about
provisions needed by the family for the festival.
They agreed that some yams would be sold that
day at **Eke** market to get money for the purchase
of food items for the family and clothes for the
children. Each of the two wives carried a basketful
of yams to **Eke** market. His elder son carried a keg
of palm wine while his younger son carried a small
basketful of tomatoes for the mother. On their way
to the market, he prayed to all the deities that had
their shrines in view as they passed. He prayed for
good sales and protection from evil people and
evil spirits that were believed to also come to the
market.

While his wives were selling the yams as he had
instructed, he went around and called his in-laws
and friends to his village market stall where he had

told his sons to stay with the keg of palm wine. When they came together, he reminded them of the date of the festival (**Igba nta Ani Ihe**) and invited them to his house. He presented the keg of palm wine to them and asked his elder son to share it. He received the first cup of the palm wine, prayed over it and poured it outside as a libation. He received the second cup and drank it before he asked his first son to serve the wine to his in-laws and friends. His two wives who had just finished selling their yams, joined in the drinking. When the palm wine drinking ended, his sons left their parents and went home with the empty wine keg. After buying new clothes for all his children, the elder and his wives left the market for home.

2.3m Ẹwhọ War

The origin of **Ẹwhọ** people was unknown to the elders. Their culture was completely new to the surrounding settlements. They had no **Ani** deity, but their major deity was **Ọgba Ẹgbẹlẹ** whose shrine was at **Oye Ẹwhọ** market. Their ancestors came from an unknown place and they settled at **Apa**, a woodland between **Ihe**, **Amoli**, **Achi** and **Ụmabi**. The **Ẹwhọ** had no cultural relations with any of the surrounding settlements. They were good craftsmen and blacksmiths and spent all their time making iron tools and weapons. They were professional blacksmiths but had no professional hunters. The surrounding settlements had professional hunters and part-time farmers. The **Ẹwhọ** survived on food bartered in exchange with their crafts, iron tools and weapons.

Some of them lived on other people's crops, stolen or taken by force from the farms of the neighboring towns. They had no respect for human life and were hostile to themselves and their neighbors. They terrorized other people with their weapons. Such neighbors were often threatened and intimidated with their huge stature and large population. Their population which increased rapidly was more than twice the population of **Ihe**, **Amoli** and **Umabi** put together, but they were not united as a people. They often fought one another over trivial issues relating to marriage ceremonies, cultural rites and idol worship rituals.

Some **Ẹwhọ** youths often laid ambush and kidnapped women and children whom they used as domestic slaves. Any man found in the company of the women or children, was killed and his head was cut off and presented to their **Ikolo** war dance. They also kidnapped some men for human sacrifice to their principal deity, **Ogba Egbele**. Sometimes they skinned their captive and presented his skin and skull to another war dance, called **Obune**, at their **Oye** market. The **Obune** did not sound unless a man was killed in an ambush or during human sacrifice to the **Ogba Egbele** deity. During the burial of their titled men and leaders the **Obune** war dance could be heard very early in

the morning by the surrounding villages. This
early morning sound of the **Obune** war dance was
a warning to their neighbors, that anybody going to
the farm was doing so at the risk of losing his head
or being kidnapped.

Due to **Ẹwhọ** terrorism, **Ihe** and **Amoli** negotiated
a truce in their border skirmishes, to be better able
to fight their common enemy, the **Ẹwhọ**. The
surrounding towns, **Ihe**, **Amoli**, **Achi** and **Umabi**,
who suffered the excesses of **Ẹwhọ** people, formed
an alliance and contributed resources for a show
down. The influence of the **Ẹwhọ** extended to such
towns as **Ugbo** and **Ụmụaga**, who also joined later
in the war effort. Before the beginning of the attack
of **Ẹwho**, powerful diviners were consulted by a
committee of the allies.

All the major deities in the four towns were
appeased and pledges were made to them for a
successful prosecution of the struggle. Sacrifices
were also offered separately by each of the four
towns at their homes to the minor deities.
Influential people from the four towns donated the
sacrificial materials needed, such as yams and
animals. Also, weapons were donated according
to each person's means. An example was a man
called **Ọnyia Ụba** from **Amagu Ihe**, who donated
a cow for which he was given a large piece of land
(**Ani Ụmụọnyi Ụba**) at **Ụpata** area of **Amagu Ihe**,
after the war.

A plan to reduce the large population of the **Ẹwhọ** was made by a committee, made up of experienced diviners and hunters from the four towns, who usually met at **Afọẹgụ** market.

The committee opened the attack spiritually with the sacrifice of ripe pumpkin seeds to the god of vengeance (**Ọbọ**). An old woman whose only son was kidnapped by the **Ẹwhọ** was commissioned to scatter the pumpkin seeds at the base of the large cotton tree in **Oye Ẹwhọ** market. The pumpkin seeds germinated and spread their vines over a large area in the market and bore many fruits. The fruits which were seen by the **Ẹwhọ** as a gift from their market deity were shared by the villages and eaten by many people. The pumpkin meals sparked off an outbreak and the spread of a plague that claimed many **Ẹwhọ** lives. There was wailing and mourning in every **Ẹwhọ** home.

While in this mourning mood, a shadow diviner was sent to the **Ẹwhọ**. The diviner foretold that an attack from an unknown town would be made against their town in the near future. He suggested that they take a title (**Ovuakpụ n'ogwe**) that would show the surrounding towns that the **Ẹwhọ** caught and carried away a falling cotton-tree before it could touch the ground. The shadow diviner further explained that such a feat would show the might of the people and scare away any town from attacking the **Ẹwhọ.** He promised to offer sacrifices for the success of the exercise. He further suggested that they cut down the huge cotton-tree in their market which was known to strangers who came to their **Oye** market; and carry it away from the market square. The leaders of **Ẹwhọ** town happily accepted the diviner's suggestion and started planning for the title taking exercise. They instructed the town crier to go around and announce that all able-bodied men should come to **Oye** market for an important meeting.

On the next **Oye** market day, the market was full of able bodied hefty young men. The leaders explained what was required of them and stressed that the diviner said that they would do that or face a brutal war soon. The young men shouted their acceptance of the suggestion and started singing their war songs which shook the market. Other people in the market were cleared from the area and the young men were arranged in four lines along a track road by the side of the cotton tree.

Tree cutters were instructed to cut the tree to fall along the track road where the young men were standing. As the cutting was going on, the men were singing, with their hands raised up above their heads towards the tree, to catch it before it touched the ground. As the tree came down to the ground, the weight of its trunk and branches crushed most of the young men to instant death.

Those who did not die on the spot had serious injuries. The entire **Ewho** town went into serious mourning. The diviner had disappeared when the tree was being cut down, pretending to go for a sacrifice.

While **Ẹwhọ** was in this mourning mood, the allied soldiers surrounded **Ogwono** village, which was the largest village in **Ẹwhọ** town. **Ogwono** was maltreating the smaller villages before this war because of its large population. These smaller villages refused to assist **Ogwono**, because of the past hostilities of **Ogwono** who sent messages of assistance to the smaller villages. It was a matter of days before **Ogwono** village was overrun by the allied forces of **Ihe**, **Amoli**, **Achi** and **Umabi**, because most of the **Ẹwhọ** able- bodied men, who formed the bulk of their fighting force, died after the pumpkin meal or during the ill-fated title-taking exercise.

Many of the inhabitants of **Ẹwhọ** ran away as war refugees to various directions. The smaller villages were also attacked after **Ogwono** and defeated one after the other until the whole of **Ẹwhọ** town was subdued. Their people were either killed or taken away as captives by the allied forces. The **Ogba Egbele** shrine where men were sacrificed was burnt down and the priests were carried away by **Amoli** men. The **Ẹwhọ** war dance (**Obune**) instruments were captured by **Ihe** men and brought to **Ụmụigwe** in **Amagu** village where **Ẹwọ** refugees lived. The **Ikolo** dance instruments went to **Umabi** men. Their blacksmithing tools were captured and carried away by **Achi** and **Umabi** men. All **Ẹwhọ** villages were looted and their houses destroyed.

Today there is no **Ẹwhọ** town. Their descendants who became assimilated into the various villages of the surrounding towns live peacefully with their neighbors. Their lands; **Apa, (Ọnụ Nwangene)** and **Ọfia Ẹwhọ,** or **Ẹgụ Ewe (Ẹwhọ)** and the economic trees there are now the common property of the surrounding villages. The **Ẹwhọ** story is used today to warn any dissenting community that disunity can bring down any community, village or family, no matter their wealth, strength or population.

2.3n: Isuawa (Isuewe) War

The exact origin of **Isuawa** could not be ascertained from the elders, but they said that **Isuawa** settled after **Ihe** and **Agbogugu.** The elders said that the **Ihe** ancestor, **Shike Aguma,** settled at **Ụmụọgbee, Ihe,** about AD.500. By about AD.700 and 800, there were already settlements at **EnugwuOke, Enugwuegu and Enugwuechi.** It was also said that **Oshie Aneke,** great grandson of **Akụlụ ShikeOke,** settled at **Amọfia Agbogugu,** about AD. 700. Some elders suggested that the enterprising ancestors of **Isuawa** might have migrated as hunters from **Isukwụatọ** or **Isuochi** which are also Scarp lands towns in **Okigwe**

Division as early as between AD.900 and 950. They probably settled in and assimilated into the small **Ẹwẹtokẹ** community of the **Toke** clan, said to have ancestral relation with **Ituku Ubatoke**, and **Ozalla Ukpatoke**. They settled for four centuries before they started the **Isuawa**, **Ihe** and **Agbogugu** encounters which took place sometime between AD.1300 and 1400.

By AD.1300, the population of the three towns had increased. Locally made iron farm tools and iron defense weapons had been introduced. The need to produce more food crops for the growing population of the three towns increased. This need for more food resulted in the desire for more farmland. The growing population also needed more land for habitation and for the grazing of their livestock.

The **Isuawa** war started as border skirmishes between **Ihe** and **Isuawa** farmers. **Ihe** which settled before **Isuawa** and which had a bigger population, repressed the **Isuawa** move for more land across the **Iyiakwa** River. Having been repressed on the **Ihe** side of the banks of the **Iyiakwa** River, **Isuawa** farmers moved further down to the other side of **Iyiakwa** River and towards the banks of the headwaters of the **Ọtụọgụ** stream and confronted the **Amọfia** settlement. This border struggle was intermittent and lasted for many years. Crops were destroyed or stolen. There were ambushes in the farms and people were kidnapped or killed. There were attacks and revenge attacks. Subsequent villages that grew out of **Amọfia** village were forced to look for settlements farther east of **Amọfia** village while those of **Isuawa** who needed expansion space more could not expand eastwards towards **Ugwuọnwụ** or southwards across the **Iyiakwa**.

On the other hand, farmers from **Ihe** found it difficult to cross the **Iyiakwa** River. Crops planted at the riverbanks were at a risk. Machetes, swords, spears, clubs, stones, bows and arrows were used during the border skirmishes. There were few flint guns (**Ọkwụlụọka**) owned by warriors and men of substance in the three towns and their neighboring towns.

During the skirmishes, **Isuawa** escalated the struggle into a major conflict by importing flint guns from **Udi** with which they drove **Amọfia** village eastwards into the other villages of **Agbogugu**. Some refugees crossed the **Iyiakwa** River into **Enugwuechi** villages of **Ihe Shikeaguma**. **Agbogugu** felt threatened and sought assistance from **Ihe** to help defend **Amọfia** which is the ancestral base of **Agbogugu** town. **Ihe** which previously had border skirmishes with **Isuawa** joined in the struggle to contain the **Isuawa** moves against her neighbors. **Isuawa** was attacked at two fronts at the same time by **Ihe** and **Agbogugu**, till

it was pushed out of the **Ọtụọgụ** and **Ugwuọnwụ**
areas by **Agbogugu** and the disputed lower banks
of the **Iyiakwa** River by **Ihe**. They were pursued
until they were driven out of their villages to the
wooded hills and caves. Their belongings were
looted, and their homes destroyed.

At this stage of the struggle, **Ihe** withdrew some of
their men from the **Isu** front to take care of incursions
from **Amoli** on the **Amagu** side of **Ihe** town,
hence the **Ihe** title of: **Kwe ndụnụ, kwe ndụnụ
agha** (Defender of its two war fronts successfully
at the same time against two communities). It was
believed by the elders that **Amoli** in sympathy
with **Isuawa** attacked **Ihe** at this time to reduce
the pressure on **Isuawa** who reorganized in the
hills, went back to **Udi** with some slaves, males
and females, got more flint guns and gun powder;
and engaged **Agbogugu** again.

Agbogugu withdrew to her previous position at
Amọfia. **Isuawa** returned to her villages and dug
the defense trenches (**Ekpe**) to slow down a
possible resurgence of **Ihe** warriors across the
Iyiakwa River. A truce was negotiated and declared
between **Ihe** and **Isuawa**; and between **Agbogugu**
and **Isuawa**, on the other hand. Unfortunately, the
truce was broken from time to time. There were still
small scattered border skirmishes among farmers
on all the sides because there were no agreed clear
boundaries apart from the **Ekpe** and **Iyiakwa**.

The effects of the war were devastating on the three towns. All the land on both banks of the **Iyiakwa** River, between **Ihe** and **Isuawa**, and all the area extending from **Isuawa** to **Amofia** village became a battlefield and unhabitable as a result of constant attacks, both by day and by night. Subsequent expansions by **Agbogugu** were directed eastwards towards **Amuri** and northwards towards **Ozalla** while the people of **Ihe** moved towards **Owelli** and **Amoli**. **Isuawa** was the worst hit by this situation because their settlement was helmed in on the north by **Ituku** town, on the east by the disputed land, on the west by rugged and wooded hills, and on the south west by the **Ekpe** defense trenches between **Isuawa** and **Ihe**.

The border villages of **Isuawa**, **Ihe** and **Agbogugu**, found it difficult to farm on the land between them, as crops such as yams and coco-yams were uprooted after sowing by thieves. Those crops that escaped from being stolen were either destroyed or harvested prematurely by night marauders. The situation of no peace and no war in the area continued for long after the truce and forced population movements out of the areas worst hit.

As **Ihe** was fighting on two fronts at the same time, some refugees moved out of **Ihe** and settled as hunters, craftsmen, diviners or farm laborers within the **Igbo** culture area. The ever enterprising **Isuawa** hunters moved hill wards into **Udi** area and from there westwards to the vicinity of **Awka** (Oka) They probably settled at **Isu Aniocha** from where their descendants joined the religious trail of the **Nri** in the fifteenth century. They moved farther west and south west to become secondary and tertiary **Isu** movements. Probably also there were movements southwards from **Isukwuato**, a Scarp lands community, to the vicinity of Orlu, thereby complicating the **Isu** movement within the **Igbo** culture area, as noted by M. A. **Onwuejeogwu**,

> *The Isu movements are curious movements of people from the East Igbo because the movement followed the religious trail of the* **Nri**. *They are also secondary movements which deserve special attention because of their consequences in founding new autonomous settlements This movement ended in the foundation of over a dozen Isu towns in the Igbo culture area.*[21]

Recently the **Isuawa** and **Agbogugu** border erupted again in the 1934 land dispute and the 1949 road dispute.

---

[21] M.A. **Onwuejeogwu, Ahiajoku** Lecture, 1987, page 2

Chapter Three

IGBO THOUGHT

3.1 FREEDOM OF THOUGHT

From prehistoric times, the **Igbo** have lived together as republicans under titular leaders in crowded village settlements, for the purposes of thinking together, acting together and socializing together, to enhance and protect the well-being of their extended families. Their culture guaranteed freedom of thought, freedom of speech and freedom of pursuits to every adult but demanded absolute observance of the tenets of **Igbo** tradition which was the product of the intellectual activity of their ancestors.

Since the **Igbo** have great respect for ancestors, the fruits of their thought are valued and preserved for posterity. Among these products of **Igbo** thought are their cultural artifacts and their belief in the imperishable nature of spirits. Their encounters with spirits in dreams and trances led them to believe in the ancestral spirit (**Ichie**), the guardian spirit of God (**Chi**), and God the creator (**Chukwu Okike**). This thought influenced **Igbo** belief and rituals in connection with birth, life, work, relationships, death, burial, and after-life. In order to dedicate the products of their thought to public service, **Igbo** ancestors established their institutions of marriage, extended family system, social status structure, title system, informal education system, traditional legal system, community service, ancestral republicanism, health care system, traditional religion, festivals etc., in order to ensure the existence of a culture of self-improvement through hard work, fair play and the worship of God.

3.2: BELIEF SYSTEM

3.2a God
At least as far back as 100,000 BC., **Igbo** ancestors of the core **Igbo** culture area on the Scarp lands of South Eastern Nigeria, believed in one supreme God the Creator who made what was made (**Awụwa walụ Ihe na Okike kelụ Ihe**) They imagined him in human form and worshiped him in practical human ways through created intermediaries, such as the Sun and the Oracle (**Anyanwụ na Agbara**) minor deities and the ancestors. The above concept led the **Igbo** to believe that God created human life into a physical but spiritually controlled world, guided by the guardian spirit of God (**Chi**). This concept manifests in the **Igbo**, either as a traditional worshiper or Christian, and portrays him as having religion as a central issue in all his endeavors; giving rise to the existence of numerous deities, diviners, worship houses and clerics in Igboland.

3.2b Self

Amid any difficult situation the **Igbo** believes first and foremost in himself. He is very confident in his ability as a person fully endowed by God to solve his own problems and to achieve success in life. He assesses himself as a special person. This belief gives him the impetus to reach the highest goals in all competitive ventures, be it sports, learning, commercial activities or community service. He also knows that at the end of the day he will be assessed as a person by **Igbo** culture for his personal contributions towards the development and progress of his family and his community.

This stimulus drives him towards becoming a very aggressive and enterprising individual. His orientation makes him appear to be proud and selfish; and excites fear and resentment in other less enterprising people. Unfortunately, this same orientation drives the **Igbo** towards individualism and sole proprietorship in his business enterprise. The situation is an issue which modern **Igbo** education has started to address; but Ben. **Nwabueze** has this to say about the orientation and attributes of the **Igbo**.

> *In their enterprising spirit and aggressive individualism, the Igbo may appear to be exploitative, grasping and greedy, but these are attributes which characterize all*

> *aggressively   enterprising   people*
> *everywhere.   These   attributes   are   not*
> *therefore   proper   grounds   on   which*
> *resentment   can   justifiably   be   nursed*
> *against the Igbo by other Nigerians.*[22]

Though the **Igbo** may be aggressively enterprising, he still believes that he needs God's protection and guidance in all his endeavors, hence the **Igbo** name, **Chinedu**. God leads the way.

3.2c: Family

The **Igbo** believes that the family is a sacred institution crafted by God for the procreation and protection of humanity. In **Igbo** culture, the family is the first unit of government; an opinion pool; and a spiritual power source which every **Igbo** must refer to before taking important decisions of his life, be it on his career, residence or marriage. Culturally it is incumbent on every **Igbo** whether at home or abroad, to contribute to the physical and spiritual development and wellbeing of his immediate and extended families. This contribution channeled through the various **Igbo** town unions at home and outside the **Igbo** culture area; is seen in the pouring of heavy financial and material investments into various educational, religious and cultural projects, undertaken by the **Igbo** at home and abroad.

---

[22] Ben **Nwabueze**, 1985, **Ahiajoku** Lecture, page 8.

Every micro or mega family unit makes deliberate and sustained effort towards the preservation of the lives of all its members at home and abroad, through the morning prayers (**Ọji Ụtụtụ**) of its elders and through their offering of sacrifices to their various deities and ancestors. These efforts are made to ward off the evil effect of the negative forces of retribution and the anger of evil spirits. Among the **Igbo** of the Christian persuasion, the same deliberate effort is made towards spiritual protection of the immediate and extended family members in Christian ways, with due regard and reference to the family unit.

3.3: HUMAN LIFE

3.3a: Source of Life

> *In traditional Igbo society, human life is considered sacred. It cannot be taken away with impunity. Suicide is considered a most abominable crime...The rural Igbo had very great respect for life (Ndụ) because it comes from God. It is greater than money or wealth. It cannot be foundered by a blacksmith.* [23]

Our ancestors, as far back as at least 100,000 BC., believed that God created all things including human life. He loved it and assigned his guardian

---

[23] E. N. **Onwu**, 2002, **Ahiajoku** Lecture, page 25

spirit (**Chi**) to guide it through its existence here on earth and hereafter, to its final destination, based on its own performance on earth. Since our ancestors believed in God, loved and worshiped him every morning during the **Ọji Ụtụtụ** ritual, they valued and protected human life as God's most important gift to man (**Ndụ bụ isi**). The **Igbo** knows that when life is destroyed, it is God's property that is destroyed. He knows also that a most abominable sin is committed against **Igbo** culture and that the punishment for murder is death.

3.3b: Preservation of Life

Traditionally the **Igbo** places a lot of importance on human life, hence his belief that life is to be preserved before other valuables (**Ndu bu isi**). For this reason, every stage in the life of an **Igbo** person, from pregnancy to birth, and finally to death, has one religious ritual or the other. The rituals usually start with prayers of thanksgiving and go on to petitions for protection and guidance.

The **Igbo** believes that God who created life is the only one who can preserve and nurture it. In his morning prayers (**Ọji ụtụtụ**), he places life (Good health) first before the other four realizable aspirations of the **Igbo** (love, peace, wealth, and children). The traditional **Igbo** will go to any length to preserve his life and the lives of members of his immediate and extended family (**Ezi n'ụnọ**). This he usually does with prayers, the use of protective charms, the wearing of amulets, and initiations into secret cults. In addition to the above he consults diviners, oracles, and herbalists to ascertain the way forward on thorny issues surrounding his life and the lives of members of his family. After the consultation of spiritual experts, he resorts to traditional prayers (**Ịgọ ọfọ**), and sacrifices to the ancestors, deities, and malevolent spirits. All these measures are his efforts to ward off uncertainties of life.

After Christianity came to Igboland with the white man, the **Igbo** still did not change his inherent religious attitude towards the preservation of his life, and the lives of members of his immediate and extended families. He swapped the consultation of traditional religious practitioners, with the consultation of pastors and priests for prayers. The usual **Igbo** morning prayers (**Ọji ụtụtụ**) changed places with Christian morning prayers and morning church services. The honor previously reserved for **Igbo** ancestors had to go to patron saints while initiations into traditional secret cults were replaced with initiations into various Christian religious societies and knighthoods. Some sects of the Christian faith resorted to the wearing of medals and scapulars in place of amulets, as a means of protection or as a sign of devotion to particular saints. All these are done in a bid to ensure that both physical and spiritual health are secured.

3.4: BIRTH

3.4a: Preparation for Birth

The age-old belief in **Igbo** culture that God is the owner of life (**Chi nwe ndụ**) establishes the strength and depth of **Igbo** concept that God creates life and gives it to whoever He pleases. **Igbo** ancestors in their wisdom built meticulous precautions into the marriage institution because it is the avenue through which God's gift of a child (**Onyinye**) comes to the family and the community.

In a traditional **Igbo** setting, as soon as a woman's pregnancy, especially the first one becomes noticeable, the family of the husband and her own family start preparing for a safe delivery of the baby. These preparations include prayers and the consultation of diviners. Sacrifices are made to the deities and the ancestors, to ward off the anger of evil spirits; to appease the gods; and to pray for protection against all evil effects of retribution associated with reincarnation from both families. Among Christians, all the above spiritual consultations and sacrifices have given way to ante natal and post-natal medical attention in hospitals, in addition to Christian prayers and services.

3.4b: Thanksgiving Offering

In **Ihe Shikeaguma** tradition, the seventh lunar month of a pregnancy is the month of a thanksgiving sacrifice to the ancestors, known as, **Enunu mbọka**. This sacrifice is offered with a she-goat,

147

kola nuts, eight tubers of yams and about eight gallons of palm wine, in the home of a pregnant woman's parents. During this sacrifice, kola nuts, goat-meat, cooked yam, and palm wine are shared among all the people present, hence the name, **Mbọka** which means, shared to all and sundry.

After this sacrifice, the two families start preparing for the arrival of the baby. The husband prepares a room for the twenty-eight days of confinement of the wife and her expected baby. He equips the room with all the materials that will give the mother and her child maximum comfort. He also saves food items and money for the twenty-eight days. On the other hand, the mother of the pregnant woman also starts saving food items and money for the maternity period. During the period of a woman's confinement in her home, she does not do any house or farm work. She is given good food by her mother and allowed to rest. In **Igbo** culture, the birth of a baby is likened to the arrival of a very important personality (The baby), and the return of a valiant victor (The mother).

3.4c: Delivery

In the olden days, the midwife or nurse-practitioner went to the house of a pregnant woman and delivered her. If the baby was safely delivered, the midwife gave the baby a name after the appropriate market day. During this delivery, experienced mothers in the family assisted the midwife and took care of the delivered mother and baby until her own mother arrived. The midwife prescribed required herbal medicine and food for the delivered mother and left for home with her fee of four tubers of yams, or some money in place of the yams. If the baby was malformed or dead, the midwife usually left without taking any fee.

The news of a normal delivery spread very fast from woman to woman. In one hour, the news spread round the whole town. There was joy in the community. Women neighbors ran to the family that was blessed with a baby, to dance and sing praises to God. The husband of the delivered woman served kola nuts and palm wine to all the people who came to rejoice with the family on the safe delivery of the baby. After the birth of a baby, it was traditional in Igboland, to send a messenger to break the news of a safe delivery to the parents of a delivered woman. As the bearer of good news, the messenger was entertained with food and drinks. Presents of money were also given to her by the parents and relations of the delivered woman.

3.4d: Confinement (Ọmụgọ)
Confinement in **Igbo** culture was always a period of celebration for the arrival of a new life and the survival of the mother. After the birth of a baby, the mother of the delivered woman left her own home to look after her delivered daughter during

the twenty-eight days of maternity confinement. The mother usually carried some food items with her for the confinement. Neighbors, friends, and relatives visited the woman in confinement with gift items and food stuff.

On the 4th day (**Izu mbụ**) of her delivery, if in the village, she went to the stream in the company of another woman to take her first bath in the stream because since her delivery she had received only hot water massages by her mother or another woman. The stream bath gave her some exercise and sunshine. On the twelfth day (**Izu n'atọ**) of the delivery, she went to the stream again in the company of another woman to take her second bath. After this bath a prayer session (**Itụnyị any'ọkụ**) was conducted. If the baby was a boy, the prayer was conducted by a boy-child but if the baby was a girl, it was conducted by a girl-child. The prayer was conducted to terminate the use of wood fire which was used in those days to keep babies and their mothers warm when there were no blankets or sweaters. A wood fire was kept in the fireplace in the maternity room for twelve days. After this period the baby was weaned from the wood fire warmth; and prayers of thanksgiving were said for the survival of the baby for twelve days.

The child conducting the prayer brought out the wood from the fire place; he poured water on the fire and prayed that the anger of evil spirit would not affect the baby, that he would have good health, that he would have good behavior and be obedient to his parents. On the 20th day (**Izu ise**) of the birth of the baby, the mother was escorted again by another woman to the stream to take her third stream-bath. Another prayer session (**Igụ izu**) was held to thank God for keeping the child alive for the period of twenty days. The prayers also asked God to protect the baby from evil spirits and direct him to be a good citizen. This prayer session could be postponed to later in the baby's life if either the baby or mother was not well on that day or if the father was not ready with the materials for the prayers.

The outing ceremony took place on the 28th day of the birth of the baby. It was the final celebration of the birth by the family. It entailed the provision of a cock, eight big tubers of yams and some gallons of palm wine, for the entertainment of relatives and neighbors for their cooperation during the delivery of the baby and the confinement of the mother. Early in the morning on the outing day, the woman in confinement shaved her head, collected the hair, all the clothes and mats used during the confinement, domestic trash and sweepings, and threw them into a refuse grove. She was accompanied again by another woman to the stream to take the last bath of that confinement. On her return from the stream, she changed into new clothes. The cleansing ritual by a traditional priest took place since she unavoidably shed her own blood on the land. After this cleansing ritual, she was then free to cook, go to the farm or market and enter other peoples' homes. Before the wife's mother left for home, the son-in-law provided her with new clothes, other gift items and money as a show of gratitude for her own gifts and assistance to his family during the confinement of his wife.

In recent times among some Christian sects, all the above traditional rituals and prayers during and after confinement, have given way to church ceremonies and infant baptism during the presentation of the baby to the church. The period of confinement has been reduced for those who cannot afford house-help or subsistence during this period. Other sociocultural aspects of birth with the joy and celebrations associated with the delivery of a baby have been maintained.

3.4e: Birth Taboos (Nsọ Ani)

During the **Nri** civilization of nine centuries AD 800 – 1700 and the **Aro** civilization of one and a half centuries, AD. 1700 – 1850, it was abomination in Igboland, for a baby to be born with the legs coming out first; for twin babies, albino or malformed babies to be born; and for a child to cut the first tooth on the upper jaw. **Nri** agents and priests preached that if such babies were left in their community, the abomination would bring some evil and the anger of the gods onto the town. They recommended that such babies be thrown away or be given out to **Nri** agents for the disposal of such babies. Parents who refused to give away their baby were usually driven out of their town with their baby. **Nri** agents used these taboos to secure babies who grew up in **Nri** settlements to eventually become their domestic slaves or commodity for the slave market during the **Aro** civilization.

These **Nri** agents were secretive about the future of the abandoned babies they collected. Parents of such babies were traumatized by the loss of their babies and were haunted by the fear of the unknown. In addition to their loss, they were expected to have a cleansing ritual in their home where the abomination was committed, to forestall a future recurrence. This ritual was also conducted by **Nri** priests at a big cost to those who invited them. Based on the foregoing, pregnant women and mothers of babies lived in great fear of losing their babies even after they were safely delivered and lived with their mothers till the cutting of the first tooth.

Consequently, babies that appropriately cut the first tooth on the lower jaw were treated as victors coming from the war front. First toothing from the lower jaw was celebrated hence the name, **Ịnụ agha**. During this celebration other children from the mega family (**Ụmụnna**) were called together in the evening. The family elder in the presence of the children put one of his fingers inside the baby's mouth to feel the tooth. He announced the appearance of the tooth from the right place. The elder hugged the baby in congratulation and gave the baby a present such as tubers of yams or money. Based on this ritual the **Igbo** have the saying that: "No one sees the first tooth of a baby with empty hands". After the declaration by the elder, the children shouted with joy, carried the baby on the shoulder like a victor and went around the mega family, singing victory songs. Elders gave tubers of yams or money to the baby as a well-deserved prize for its bravery. At the end of the ceremony the children were entertained with food. The yams and money given to the baby become its first property as it has qualified through right toothing as a member of the family.

Both the recognition of these issues as abomination and the punishment meted out for them in Igboland today have been consigned to history and pregnant women and mothers no longer have the fear of losing their babies. Most babies today are delivered in hospitals and health clinics under the watchful eyes of the law.

3.5 DEATH

3.5a: Preparation for Death
Dating from many centuries before Christ, the **Igbo** believed that life comes from God (**Chi nwe**

ndu), and that it is guided by God's guardian spirit (**Chi**). They also believed that death on earth for man, though inevitable, is not the end of life. The **Igbo** have been farmers from prehistoric times and their understanding of life on earth has been conceptualized in the terms of sowing and reaping. Based on this concept, **Igbo** culture prepares every child from the moment of conception, for this life of sowing on earth and reaping partially here on earth but fully hereafter in reincarnation or in spirit land. This preparation is indicated in the various prayer sessions and sacrifices held from the period of pregnancy to the day of burial of every traditional **Igbo** person; to absolve him of the evil effect of retribution arising from reincarnation or sins committed here on earth. These prayers include petitions for God's guidance of the person through life.

3.5b: Unworthy Death (Ajọ Ọnwụ)
Certain deaths were seen by **Igbo** culture as punishment from God for sins committed in this life or in reincarnation by the person involved or any of his predecessors. Such deaths manifested in:

Death before puberty
Death by drowning/fall from a tree
Death by fire, leprosy, ulcer, hernia or edema
Death by suicide
Death by manslaughter
Death by murder

People involved in these types of death (**Ajọ ọnwụ**) were not ritually entitled to normal burial rites in **Ihe Shikeaguma**. They were entitled to ordinary burial without any burial rites or ceremonies. Traditionally, if the death of a child occurred before puberty, the corpse of such a child was buried outside his or her parents' compound without burial rites. A circle was made with wood-ash around the grave to stop its reincarnation into the family. If a person died by drowning, the corpse if found, was buried by the river or lake side without any burial rites. If the death was by fire or any of the other unworthy deaths mentioned above, the person was buried in a burial ground for unworthy death.

Today in Igboland Christian teaching and research work in medicine have thrown some light on **Igbo** thought towards death and burial. These traditional burial practices have been thrown into the trash-bin of history by Christians who bury their dead members with Christian burial rites.

3.5c: Murder (Igbu Ọchụ)

During the precolonial days in **Ihe Shikeaguma**, the punishment for willful murder was suicide by hanging or banishment for life; in addition to an angry demonstration (**Inụ ọchụ**) by the relatives of the murdered person, to destroy the house of the murderer. After the hanging, the murderer was buried in the bush under the tree where he hanged himself without any burial rites. The same type of burial was given to any person who hanged himself or herself for any reason whatsoever.

Traditionally, in an accidental killing of any **Ihe Shikeaguma** or **Ntuegbe** person by another **Ihe Shikeaguma** person, the killer culturally committed an abomination and became ritually unworthy of eating any food or entering any house in **Ihe Shikeaguma**, including his own house. He became an outcast. If he entered any house before his ritual cleansing (**Ịlọ Ani**), that house also became unclean and was cleansed at the expanse of the killer's family. The same cleansing rite applied to anybody touched by the killer before his cleansing, including his closest relatives such as wife and children.

Even after the cleansing rite, he still observed some abstentions all through his life such as; not sleeping in **Ihe Shikeaguma** on the day **Ani Ihe** festival was announced, and on **Eke Ani Ihe** day. He did not receive normal burial rites at death. In addition to the abstentions, his burial cleansing materials of **Uke** and **Agamevu** twigs in addition to the neck of a broken water pot were put under his head in the grave. Whenever suicide, manslaughter or murder was committed in any compound in **Ihe Shikeaguma**, the compound became desecrated and was usually deserted by its residents until the compound was ritually cleansed.

3.5d: Cleansing Rite (Ịlọ Ani)

In **Ihe Shikeaguma**, the chief priest of **Ani Ihe Shikeaguma** prescribed the materials needed for the ritual and he also officiated at the ritual. During the **Nri** civilization, AD 800 – 1700, all cleansing rituals were conducted by **Nri** priests at great cost to the offender's family.

3.5e: The Corpse (Ozu)

In those days in **Ihe Shikeaguma** when there were no hospitals and mortuaries, dead people were buried within one to two days of their death before mid-day or towards sunset inside their compounds, if their deaths were not shameful ones. **Igbo** culture did not see the death of a good adult, especially an aged person, as an evil thing (**Ọnwụ abụghị nsọ**). Such a life was seen as a life well lived, and consequently a home going for the person. Such a life was usually celebrated with a befitting burial ceremony so long as the death was not a shameful one.

3.5f: Preparation of the Corpse for Burial (Idozi Ozu)

Traditionally, when a man was certified dead by two or more elders, nobody was allowed to cry or announce the death. He was laid face up on a bed with his palms on his chest. His mouth was tightly closed, with a strip of cloth or bandage, tied from under the jaw to his head; his legs were stretched, and his two big toes were tied together, all in a bid to keep his body in good shape before burial. **Igbo** culture reminded him that he should carry his unaccomplished good proposals in this life to his next life in reincarnation, by the placing of his two palms on his chest. His body was covered with a sheet of cloth exposing his face which was usually decorated with palm kernel ointment (**Enu**) and white chalk powder (**nzu**) before interment.

A dead woman was also laid face-up on a bed with a strip of cloth or bandage tied from under her jaw to her head. Her legs were closed and stretched. Her two palms, one on top of the other, were used to cover her private part; to remind her that she should carry her fertility to her subsequent life in reincarnation. Her big toes were tied together; to keep her in good shape before interment. The body was then covered with a sheet of cloth exposing her face which was usually rubbed with palm kernel ointment and carmine-wood body-paint (**ufie / edo**) before interment. The strips of cloth or bandage tied on dead bodies were usually removed before interment.

3.5g: Requirements for Burial (Akwukwa Ozu)
Before the preparations of the corpse for burial, messages of the death were sent to close relations before the public announcement. The immediate family members of the dead met to decide on how to provide the requirements for the burial which

included the following; a razor (**agụma**), palm kernel ointment (**enu**), carmine-wood body paint (**ufie / edo**), white chalk-powder (**nzu**), a sheet of cloth, a coffin, a fowl, an egg, fresh water in a palm wine calabash, fetched directly from the stream, thorny twigs of **Uke** and **Agamevu** plants, bottles of gun powder, **Nkwa** or **Opueke** music. After the meeting, one to four-gun shots, depending on the traditional status of the dead were released to announce the death. Mourners and close relatives would start receiving condolences.

If preparations were completed on time, burial took place before midday but if preparations were not completed, the burial took place at sun set or the following morning at sun rise, before midday. **Igbo** culture approved this timing so that the spirit of the dead would go home to spirit land with the rising or setting sun. The burial of a good person was never done at night or at mid-day.

3.5h: Corpse Cleansing Rite (Emume Ozu)

The coffin containing the corpse was brought outside in the open within the compound and raised up above the knee by four members of the family to show continued affection. The palm wine calabash containing the fresh water was smashed on the ground by the eldest man in the compound; to denote the end of physical life and the start of spiritual cleansing. A shaving gesture was made with the razor on the coffin. If the body has not been groomed with palm kernel ointment and carmine-wood body-paint or white chalk powder, these items were rubbed on top of the coffin by an elderly sister or aunt of the dead, as grooming for the journey to spirit land. After killing the fowl, the elderly man held the egg with the left hand and the twigs of **Uke** and **Agamevu** with the right hand. He made a brushing gesture on the coffin and said: "Goodbye. Death is inevitable. We have groomed you for your journey to spirit land and cleansed you of all your Karma and sins in this life so that they will not follow you to your next life in reincarnation. We wish you happiness and success in your subsequent existence". He collected the pieces of the broken calabash, the egg and the twigs, and threw them into an evil spirit grove (**ajọ ọfịa**).

3.5i: Interment (Idọnye Ozu N'ini)

From this spot where cleansing was done, the corpse in the coffin was taken to the grave and was gently and carefully laid into its resting place. The children of the deceased, starting from the eldest, were called upon to put earth into the grave, to indicate the fulfillment of their duty to the dead. The spouse and senior relatives of the dead are not ritually qualified to drop any earth into the grave. As the coffin is being covered with earth, **Nkwa** music for men or **Opueke** music for women was played as a farewell music. At this stage nobody was allowed to dance until the interment was completed because that round of music belonged to the dead. After the interment, rounds of gunshots were released to announce the end of the interment. In addition to the fowl killed, a goat for an ordinary person or a ram for a hero was also killed near the grave. The cooked meat and yams were eaten by the relatives of the dead except the spouse or any person who had a hand in the death of the dead.

3.5j: Burial Ceremony (Ikwa Ozu)

The relatives of the dead usually embarked on the burial ceremony on the second or third day of burial if they could afford it otherwise the ceremony was put off to a later date. When the relatives were ready, a ram or a he-goat for a man or a she-goat for a woman was slaughtered near the grave. Well-to-do relatives of the dead in Igboland killed cows and horses for burial ceremonies. In the evening preceding the first day of the ceremony the interment music (**Nkwa** or **Opueke**) was played to officially open the ceremony (**ọkụ abanị**). Dance troupes presented by relatives and friends of the family displayed their music on the following day to console the mourners and entertain the sympathizers after this official opening. Condolence visitors brought food items, drinks and money gifts to assist the mourners in entertaining their guests. Display of music and entertainment with food and drinks continued till the second or third day.

3.5k: Mourning (Iri Uju/Ikwa Mkpe)

In **Ihe Shikeaguma**, when a person who was above puberty died, if he was the first child, the parents stayed at home for seven native weeks (28 days) without going to work or market and shaved their heads after this period. First children above puberty owed the same period and type of mourning to their parents at their death. If a child above puberty who was not the first child died, the parents stayed at home for three native weeks (12 days) and shaved their heads after the period.

Children who were not first children but above puberty, owed the same period and type of mourning to their parents at their death. If a child was below puberty the only mourning due to him, irrespective of whether he was the first or second child, was a shaving of the head by his parents at the child's death. Both husband and wife owed each other a mourning period of twelve lunar months (one year), divided into two terms of one month and eleven months. The surviving partner shaved his or her head and took a bath after the burial of the spouse. He or she did not leave the compound for any reason, for a period of seven native weeks, except to answer the call of nature.

After this period of twenty-eight days, the mourning spouse shaved his or her head, took a bath and went into a mourning garment for the second mourning period of eleven lunar months.

The mourner did not go to **Eke Ihe** market or attend any public gathering during this period. He or she did not leave the compound at night for any reason and was not ritually qualified to marry another person or look for a child through another person, during this mourning period. After the t w e l v e months mourning period, two or four gunshots were released early in the morning to announce the end of the mourning period. The mourner shaved his or her head and changed into new clothes. He or she collected the hair, the discarded mourning garments and the sleeping mat, and burnt them or threw them into the evil spirit grove (**Ajọ ọfia or Nmụlụ**). A cleansing ritual to free the mourner from the influence of the dead was conducted. Thanksgiving prayers were also said on behalf of the mourner by the elder or priest conducting the cleansing ritual. He or she, in new clothes went to **Eke Ihe** market for an outing ceremony, after which he or she was free to mix with other people and could take another spouse.

3.5l: Feeding the Spirit of the Dead (Ịtụ Nri). Since the **Igbo** believed in the continued existence of the spirit of the dead and in its continued communion with the living, they imagined the spirit as having human attributes. Based on this concept, they interacted with it in practical human ways, such as grooming and cleansing the corpse of the dead; eating and drinking with the spirit of the dead, and channeling prayers and offerings through them to God and the minor deities. Feeding the spirit of the dead (**ịtụ Nri**) was seen by the **Igbo** as a vehicle for communication, with the spirit of the dead after a burial ceremony. This ritual in which the dead person's spirit was believed to invite other spirits was held at any time within the first month after the final burial rites.

In this ritual, a fowl was killed near the grave and was cooked with yam. Some pieces of the yam and meat were cut into small pieces and put in a clay or wooden bowl and mixed with salt and palm oil. The elder conducting the ritual took some of the food and called on the spirit of the dead to come and eat. He scattered some handfuls of the food on the ground near the grave after which a small bowl of the food and a cup of palm wine were left by the side of the grave for the spirits. The remaining food and palm wine were taken by the relatives of the dead. Bunches of unripe oil-palm fruit (**akụ nkọrọ**) were also offered to appease malevolent spirits who were not invited but are believed to come after the good spirits were gone.

3.5m: Spiritual Considerations

Spiritual considerations on behalf of the dead and the living are still the only moving reasons for some traditional burial ceremonies in Igboland today. The traditional **Igbo** still believes that with the completion of these burial rites, he has bid his dead relation farewell to spirit land and has paid the debt due to the dead in spirit land thereby making reincarnation easy for the dead. Some of these burial ceremonies have been escalated in length of time and cost as an honor to the dead or as a show of affluence and material achievement of the dead. Christianity which has taken a firm foothold in Igboland has changed the thinking of Christians about the dead and burial ceremonies. Some of the **Igbo** traditional burial rites have changed places with Christian burial rites. Each Christian denomination has adjusted its teaching on burial rites to accommodate the cultural **Igbo** respect and honor for the good dead person and the spirit.

3.6: SPIRITS

Human Mind
Our earliest ancestors marveled at the performance of the human mind in relation with the power of thought, memory, perception, feeling, the will, and imagination. They could not understand how this mental power functioned. They observed that the human consciousness works ceaselessly through the days and nights of the life of a human person, directing all his brain's master plans into mental and physical actions. This observation led the **Igbo** to believe that the human mind does not sleep or rest, hence the **Igbo** names: **Uch'ezuike** and **Ucheagwu**. During the day the mind contrives all the promptings of the brain into human work and

play. At night while the human body sleeps, the mind goes on to review the actions of the human person during the day, associating them with other life experiences of the sleeping person, thereby building these experiences into various new but often scary images or scenarios which we know as dream. Many of these images or patterns that are painted in sleep by the mind often remain clear to human memory as the sleeper wakes up from sleep, consequently helping to shape his future beliefs, fears and actions.

Igbo ancestors that lived-in South-Eastern Nigeria of West Africa, at least as far back as 100,000 BC. had very strong belief in the existence of spirits. **Igbo** culture through its myths and folk tales suggests that man's first encounter with spirits was probably in his dream. He noticed that he had two personalities or selves at sleep; the one that lay asleep in bed; and the one that went out at the same time, visiting distant places; meeting strange people, and sometimes his dead relatives.

This second person or self, took part in adventures with dangerous animals and unknown phenomena in distant places but came back to unite with the sleeping self in a split second at man's wakefulness. Man was perplexed yet desirous of making more contacts with this second self or personality in order to know him better. He called this his second self; **Mụ ọzọ** (Another me). This name was later shortened by the **Igbo** to; **Mụọ** for spirit. He imagined his second self (**Mụọ**) in his own physical form and capable of using his own mind's power while he sleeps. This thinking led him to believe that at the death of his body, the second self (**Mụọ**) will continue to live with his consciousness, since the action of sleep could not stop his second self from using this consciousness.

With this belief he came to see a spirit abode full of the second selves (**Ndi nmụọ**) of the dead. He also imagined this abode in the form of our world with different sorts of people classified into rich and poor, weak and strong, good and bad, under different principalities and powers. Since his dream encounter, the **Igbo** has continued to make detailed and sustained efforts through prayers, sacrifices, divination and oracles to know the spirits better, in order to relate better with the good ones, and to avoid contacts with the evil ones. He built altars and shrines in his home and in public places where God is worshipped through the spirits. Many **Igbo** names reflect the **Igbo** belief in the existence of spirits. The spirits the **Igbo** has in mind in giving the following names, could be his ancestral spirit, the spirit of a minor deity or the spirit of God. Such names are: **Mụọ dị** (Spirits exist) **Mụọ debelu** (The spirit established him) **Mụọ ma** (The spirit knows) **Mụọ n'eke** (The spirit creates life) etc.

3.7: REINCARNATION

3.7a: Dream Experience

Man's dream experience elicited in him the assurance that even after the body is dead, his spirit would continue to live and continue to interact with the spirit of the dead and the spirit of God. This experience assured him that since the spirit or soul is not controlled or demobilized by the action of sleep, it will not be affected or demobilized by the action of physical death. His conviction of life's imperishable nature further evoked in him the conclusion that the implications of his actions while alive on earth will dwell with his spirit in its subsequent existence after the death of the body. Since the **Igbo** in his culture perceives life in the terms of sowing and reaping, and believes that God is both a just and a merciful father, he maintains that a dead man's spirit must return to a human body on earth to reap the fruit of his labor in his previous life on earth, whether good or bad. Until Christianity came up with the idea of heaven and hell in Igboland recently in the 19th Century, life after death had been reincarnation for the **Igbo**, as far back as 100,000BC.

The original traditional **Igbo** belief was that by living a worthy life during the seven terms (**ụwa esaa**) of repeated existence allowed on earth by God, one's soul achieved the highest status in holiness as a good ancestral (**ichie**) spirit. The good ancestral spirit becomes an intermediary spirit between God and the living on earth. He exists and operates within the realm of deities (**ndi ichie**), below the spirit of God but above hand-made deities because the life span and power of the handmade deity were decided on earth by the ancestors. On the other hand, an ancestral spirit derives its life and power from God. This concept makes it possible for a community in Igboland to come together from time to time to tell their hand-made deity what changes they wish to effect within the powers, life span or jurisdiction of such a deity.

In **Igbo** culture no person has the power to change his ancestors or relocate their spiritual jurisdiction because they were assigned to the ancestors by God. In his mercy, God allowed the ancestors seven terms of reincarnation within which to purify themselves by their good deeds for the status of good ancestral spirits. If within the seven terms of reincarnation a person through sin has not purified his spirit, he attains the status of permanent restriction from the process of reincarnation, spiritual growth or purification (**Iyogholo**). Since the spirit does not die it becomes restless and operates as an evil spirit, causing commotions and inhabiting or haunting people and places. As a ghost or fiend, it terrorizes man on earth.

Igbo culture teaches that nobody on earth knows what term of reincarnation he is serving. Therefore, it enjoins all people on earth to live very meaningful lives, assuming that they are serving their last term. E. N. **Onwu** has this to say on reincarnation:

> *The Igbo belief in the ancestors is a clear expression of the peoples' faith in after life, even though perceived in the context of external return to the earth again in reincarnation. And it is believed that one's status in the afterlife depends entirely on one's status here on earth, since the spirit world is a mirror of the human world with same topography and similar organization. The motion of judgement which everyone is afraid of is clearly spelt out by the Igbo belief in reincarnation.*[24]

The **Igbo** believes that where, when, and how he reincarnates on earth depends largely on the merits or demerits of his actions in his previous life, also on earth.

3.7b: Why Does Reincarnation Occur?

Early in the life of man when his spirit had a more intimate relationship with the spirit of God, the true nature of God was revealed to him. He understood that God was the creator of the universe; a just but a merciful God; who judges everyone according to

---

[24] E. N. **Onwu**, 2002, **Ahiajoku** Lecture, page 16

his work. This knowledge of God and man's other life experiences assured him that there must be a pay-back time in reincarnation for evil doers and good men alike. Our ancestors also knew quite well that life on earth was in the terms of sowing and reaping (**Mkpụrụ onye kụlụ k'ọna aghọta**). They were firm in their belief that life continues after the death of the body, and that life continues to exist in order to reap the fruit of one's actions in one's previous life on earth.

The purification theory in **Igbo** culture instituted the cleansing ritual and backs up the **Igbo** belief that God in his mercy allowed man a seven-term period (**ụwa esaa**) of purification in reincarnation. The **Igbo** believes that this purification period is God's winnowing time for separating good spirits from evil spirits. The theory of destiny (**akara aka**) in **Igbo** culture asserts that when a man is judged by God to undergo a period of vengeance or reward on earth, the man's spirit must certainly come back to earth in reincarnation to complete any remaining part or the totality of his sentence. **Igbo** culture believes that the power of man's spirit makes it possible for him to will certain desires to reality, which is why the **Igbo** say that: "What a man wills is what his spirit wills" (**Onye kwe chi ya ekwe**). Based on this concept the **Igbo** believes that a man who has a worthy life on earth, can will the time and place of his reincarnation, so that he is able to avenge an ill treatment or reward a good gesture.

172

3.7c: Where Does Reincarnation Occur?

Igbo culture in its emphasis on the importance of the immediate and the extended family (**ezi n'ụnọ**), teaches that reincarnation takes place among the children of close relatives and friends of the dead. It is a norm in **Igbo** culture that every **Igbo** person who travels, does come back to Igboland to give account of himself or herself whether successful or not. The **Igbo** believe that on the same vein the spirit of a dead person must also return to his family after death in reincarnation to give account of his previous journey on earth, carrying with himself reward for those who treated him well and vengeance for those who maltreated him in his past life on earth.

It is believed also among the **Igbo** that a gravely maltreated person can reincarnate in the family of his enemy, in order to wreak vengeance on this enemy. The **Igbo** believe in the power of the will, and maintain that man can choose his status (**ibu ọnụ**) or the environment of his next reincarnation, hence some **Igbo** will say: "In my next life, I will or will not reincarnate in my town" etc. The **Igbo** culture makes allowance for the overarching influence of the divine will of God over the will of man in its belief that God can will the place and status of a man in reincarnation as a punishment or reward to him, irrespective of whether God's choice pleases the man's spirit or not. In view of this understanding, the **Igbo**, in their morning prayer

(Ọjị ụtụtụ) call on God to facilitate the quick reincarnation of their good people in the family.

3.7d: When does Reincarnation Occur?

Igbo culture teaches that a good man can make a will to reincarnate as first son in the family of a loved one before his death. If his son's first child behaves like his father, it is usually said that his father made that will when he was alive. Traditionally the **Igbo** believe that every good spirit of the dead stays in spirit land waiting for its turn or God's permission to return to the world of time and space. E. N. **Onwu** (2002) comments on when a person is entitled to reincarnate:

> *The principle of reincarnation is seen as a positive one because it is believed that only people who have lived well and died well are the only persons entitled to reincarnate or re- embody themselves in a beneficent manner.*[25]

During mealtimes, the **Igbo** elder remembers the spirit of his dead relatives and ancestors who have not yet reincarnated and offers food (**itụ aka/ịgọ Nri**) to them. He prays that they reincarnate soonest as successful members of the family. It is common practice in Igboland to consult a diviner to ascertain the name of the person who has reincarnated into a child, if there is no character trait, resemblance,

---

[25] E. N. **Onwu**, 2002, **Ahiajoku** Lecture, page 17

birth mark or self-declaration by the child, to determine the person who has reincarnated.

3.7e: How does Reincarnation Occur?

In **Igbo** culture it is believed that the spirit of the dead takes human flesh (**ịpụta ụwa**) during the early stages of a woman's conception. This new life is delivered as a baby, sometimes retaining the character trait, complexion, resemblance or even birth marks indicating injuries, scars or deformities on the body of the person supposed to be reincarnating. It is believed that the action of the living can also facilitate reincarnation. Where a couple and a dead loved-one had great mutual affection, and the couple has that person always in mind, the dead person is likely to reincarnate quickly in the couple's family. The **Igbo** believes that the action of love crosses the divide between the living and the dead, and thus liberates the spirit of the dead for a quick reincarnation.

Also the traditional **Igbo** believes that the power of the human mind in copying images plays a part in the resemblance aspect of reincarnation hence it is believed that a woman who concentrates her love on any particular person during the earliest days of her pregnancy stands the chance of giving birth to a child that resembles the object of her love. On the other aspect of reincarnation, the **Igbo** believe that the restless spirit of the evil-dead torments the living by its constant reincarnation and death in the **Ọgbanje** phenomenon. In some cases, the (**Ọgbanje**) child retains a certain remarkable feature during its several repeated and short-lived reincarnations in a particular woman's babies, to assure the mother that the repeated coming and going are by one spirit.

3.7f: Reincarnation and Modern Thought

The belief in reincarnation is an age-old ethnic issue that has refused to depart the environs of **Igbo** culture. For thousands of years, it has remained one of the major mysteries in **Igbo** culture. Belief in reincarnation was not particular with Igboland. It was a common belief in most of the ancient cultures of African, Asian and European civilizations.

Recently, towards the end of the 19th Century, the arrival of Christian religious teaching in Igboland, and later developments in genetical and medical research work, changed the mode of modern thought on reincarnation. This new thought has since contested the authenticity of reincarnation and has shown that most of the astounding and remarkable traits and resemblances that repeat themselves in the offspring of so many animals and human beings are purely genetical and not spiritual issues. Medical research also has recently proved that if the blood type of a woman does not agree with her husband's blood type their children may die before adult life, thereby presenting a situation close to the **Ọgbanje** phenomenon. However, in

His redemption work, Jesus Christ through His holy life, death, resurrection and ascension into heaven, has assured humanity of the authenticity of Heaven, for the faithful, and Hell for the wicked, after life on Earth. Since the advent of Christianity, the Church has continued to teach humanity, everywhere, that life after death is not reincarnation on earth but Heaven for the faithful, and Hell for the wicked. This teaching has been substantiated with the lives of saints who lived holy lives on earth and have been raised to Heaven after their lives on Earth.

The lives of saints and their eventual canonization has given proof to humanity that there is really a pay back time in Heaven at the end of live on Earth, and not through reincarnation. As a further assurance that no soul with the stain of sin will enter the Kingdom of Heaven, God in His love for the faithful, created Purgatory for the cleansing of the faithful, of venial sins before their entry into Heaven. From the teaching of the Church and many scientific researches, performed on various animals and human beings, in recent times; it has become evident that reincarnation as believed in by our ancestors is not real. Belief in reincarnation should now be consigned to the storage bin of the ancient beliefs of our forefathers and traditional religion.

Chapter Four

IGBO INSTITUTIONS

4.1 Institutions Component Parts

In dealing with institutions in **Igbo** culture, we shall look at institutions' component parts as made up of important customs, relationships, and behavioral patterns of the **Igbo**, some of which are dedicated by the ancestors to public service in Igboland. Some of those institutions are prehistoric in origin while others are relatively new.

Igbo customs as instituted by **Igbo** ancestors for public guidance are the various practices and rites initiated as norms or common usage (**Ome n'Ani**) in **Igbo** culture. These customs have the force or validity of law and are exhibited in **Igbo** marriage, family life, beliefs, worship, divination, legal system, titles, festivals and burials. **Igbo** customs are not coded in **Igbo** culture, but they are practiced by all and passed on orally by parents to their children, as the foundation on which **Igbo** sociopolitical structure is built

Relationship in **Igbo** culture is made up of: Blood relationship (**Ikwu**) and Social relationship (**Ibe**). Blood relationship is further divided into two parts: Father's relations (**Ikwu nna**) and Mother's relations (**Ikwu nne**). Social relationship (**Ibe**) includes, in-laws (**Ọgọ**), neighbors (**Agbata obi**), and friends (**Enyi**).

Blood and social relationships in Igboland constitute the very strong ties that have held the entire **Igbo** community together for centuries. These relationships nurtured the strong sociopolitical structures that baffled the earliest European visitors during their first contacts with the **Igbo**.

These customs and relationships have been institutionalized in **Igbo** culture for the effective and smooth working of the **Igbo** society without the need for monarchies, a standing army or police force. This social structure has been the bedrock of democracy in Igboland. The Europeans admired the structure but refused to accept it as an original **Igbo** structure. They argued that the structure must have been copied from earlier Hamitic visitors or European nomads. Prior to their contacts with the **Igbo**, those Europeans had the mistaken conclusion that Africans in general lived anarchic and chaotic lives and had no sociopolitical order, no religion and no history.

The behavioral pattern of the **Igbo** from prehistoric times as a democratic people gave rise to the establishment and effective functioning of the admired social order. Also, the resilience of **Igbo** culture which derives from the nature of its cultural institutions enhanced its survival from the buffeting effects of natural disasters, epidemics and wars in the olden days, and the dehumanizing effects of slave trade and European colonialism in recent times.

4.2: MARRIAGE

4.2a: Importance of Marriage

The meticulous preparations and rituals surrounding the institution of marriage in **Igbo** culture highlight the importance attached to the making of new lives in Igboland. Since marriage is the avenue through which life is made and nurtured for the benefit of the community, **Igbo** culture took all the trouble of structuring the marriage institution with all inbuilt precautions and safeguards against marriage breakups, so that the continuity of the community is assured. The marriage institution in **Igbo** culture is made to have a wide and solid base. Contracting a marriage in Igboland takes a long negotiating time and involves many people who are mostly members of both families. In view of this type of structuring, neither a husband nor a wife can come out any day and divorce his or her spouse for any reason without first of all referring the case to the marriage base which is made up of the family of the husband and that of the wife. Children produced in **Igbo** marriages, firstly belong to this base, and secondly to the **Igbo** community (**Oha**) where the man and his wife live. In order to entrench this relationship in the community, **Igbo** culture ensures that some babies are named to indicate community interest in babies, with names like: **Nwadụlụọha, Nwadụlụibe, Adaọha, Obiọha**, etc.

The marriage institution fixes prominently the social status of every individual in the community. A married man with children, especially male children, is a source of joy to his family because through him God has established new lineages for the continuity of his family. His wife through her sons inherits a share in the family's material assets such as the homestead, farmlands and economic trees. On the other hand, a couple without a male child in Igboland are looked upon as laborers working for others because at their death their assets and the harvest of their labor are inherited by other people's sons, since their female children have their own inheritance in their husbands' homes. Unmarried adults are looked upon as having a worse calamity.

V. C. **Uchendu**, (1995), painted this picture of the public image of unmarried **Igbo** adults.

> *Until the Catholic Christian religion introduced celibacy as a virtue, an unmarried Igbo male cut a sad picture of hopeless poverty, and the unmarried female was a social disaster*[26]

---

[26] V. C. **Uchendu**, (1995), **Ahiajoku** Lecture, page 31

The **Igbo** knows that the most valuable gift a person can give is his or her child for the procreation and continuity of another man's family lineage. For this reason, the marriage institution reserves great respect for parents-in-law. Not minding age differences, husbands address the parents of their wives as mothers and fathers-in-law. Wives also address the parents of their husbands in like manner. This family respect is mutually extended to the brothers and sisters of each spouse. The import of this arrangement is that the marriage institution in Igboland expects each spouse to respect and treat his or her parents-in-law as his or her own biological parents. This type of rapport is the oil that lubricates the engine of the marriage institution in **Igbo** culture.

In **Ihe Shikeaguma**, before the advent of Christianity, and its early days, when polygamy was in vogue, girl-child betrothal was practiced. Unmarried girls of the marriage age-bracket of 15 to 20 years were scarce especially those from good parents. Prostitution, abandonment and killing of babies were rare. Women who succeeded in divorcing their husbands got new husbands quickly without waiting for years to engage new husbands. During this era hired farm labor was nonexistent and most men were professional farmers. These farmers who needed strong and reliable work force took to polygamy with its benefit of many family hands as the best resort, irrespective of polygamy's social weaknesses.

When colonialism was forced on the **Igbo**, a lot of things changed, some for better and some for worse. Our culture came under attack by Westernization. Adult male school leavers or dropouts who were usually not properly taught to farm became under employed or jobless. This situation led to adult delinquencies, loss of farm hands and slow decline in the peoples' main source of living.

As if these were not enough, the doctrine of one man one wife became the order of the day. Polygamy gave way to the era of unmarried adult women and its bedmates of prostitution, abortion, and abandonment or killing of unwanted babies. Christianity which came with colonialism encouraged the alternative of celibacy among its male and female adherents as a virtue and preached against these vices associated with this era of unmarried adult men and women.

Fortunately, the wide and solid base of the **Igbo** marriage institution, one of the bedrocks of **Igbo** culture, has facilitated the survival of this institution from the eroding influence of colonialism. Though polygamy is on its way out, the **Igbo** marriage culture is very much alive and strong today. Details of the terms of contracting a marriage in Igboland vary slightly from one community to the other. For a suitor to contract a marriage today in **Ihe Shikeaguma** as in many other **Igbo** communities, the suitor takes the following steps.

4.2b: Finding a Wife (Nchọta Nwanyi)

In the olden days, parents arranged marriage partners for their children. Some underage boys grew up in their homes with their betrothed girl-child wives, but times have changed a lot. Most children finish schooling today as young adults before thinking of marriage which they prefer to arrange by themselves.

Nowadays, a suitor makes enquiries on marriageable girls of his choice in order to know the character of the girls and their parents, and to exclude close blood relatives. When he is satisfied that a particular girl meets his requirements, he consults his parents and introduces the girl to them for their blessing. The parents make their own enquiries about the girl in question and her parents. If the suitor's parents approve of the girl in question and her family, they give approval of his choice.

4.2c: Suitor's First Contact (Ajụjụ Nwanyi)

The suitor's parents or guardians make the first contact with the parents of the chosen girl through a third-party person, man or woman, who knows both families well. About one to two native weeks (4-8 days) before the first visit, the parents of the suitor send a message to the parents of the girl through the third-party person (**Onye ajụjụ nwanyi**). In the message they indicate the purpose of their visit to the family. On the appointed day the parents of the suitor arrive in the company of their son and third-party person with kola nuts and about two gallons of palm wine (**Nmanya ajụjụ nwanyi**) to declare their interest in the girl. The parents of the girl receive the kola nuts and wine with thanks. The father of the girl prays with the kola nuts and palm wine, asking God through the ancestors to bless the intended in-laws in their proposal. The kola and the palm wine are shared with their intended in-laws. The parents of the girl entertain the suitor and his people with food.

After entertaining the intended in-laws with food and drinks, the father of the girl asks the visitors to declare the purpose of bringing the wine, notwithstanding the fact that he had been informed of the purpose by the third-party person. The suitor's father or guardian thanks him and declares their intention. At this stage the parents of the girl do not accept or reject the proposal. If they are traditional worshippers, they ask for time to consult a diviner to ascertain if the marriage has the blessing of the ancestors and the deities. If the parents are Christians, they ask for time to interview their daughter. In fact, most parents use this period to investigate both the suitor and his parents. They also use the time to interview their daughter and perhaps consult a diviner or an oracle, or their church leader, if they are Christians. The girl's father promises to send words at the end of the investigation and consultations.

If no message is sent by the girl's parents after a reasonable period, the suitor and his parents assume that their proposal does not receive the blessing of the girl's parents. If all the investigations and consultations are positive, the parents of the girl send a message through the third-party person for the parents of the suitor to come for the result of their findings. Whenever such a message is sent by the parents of the girl, the parents of the suitor know that their proposal has received the blessing of their intended in-laws. The message is usually returned with a date fixed for the second visit.

4.2d: Suitor's Second Visit (Ibu Nmanya Ụmụnne)

The parents of the suitor in the company of their son, and the third-party person make the second visit, with double the quantity of kola nuts and palm wine used during the first visit. In this second visit the micro family and closer members of their extended family (Ụmụnne) are invited. Also, the food entertainment is increased by the parents of the girl. In the presence of the suitor and the girl the father of the girl announces that his investigation is positive. A cup of wine is presented to the girl by her father to confirm her interest in the marriage proposal, by giving the cup of palm wine to the suitor. She sips the palm wine, kneels beside the suitor, and gives him the wine. If the suitor accepts the wine and drinks it, both families clap for them. After this mutual acceptance rite, the father of the girl asks her, in the presence of everybody: "Now, (the girl's name) if this young man gives me anything on account of this marriage, should I accept it"? The girl will usually say: "Yes Papa, you should accept it". With the above question and answer between the girl and her father, in the presence of the suitor and his own father, the suitor is informed that he is required to pay the bride price.

4.2e: Paying the Bride Price (Ime Enwe Nwanyi)
The parents of the suitor, after consultation with their son, agree with the third-party person on a day to pay the bride price. The third-party person informs the intended in-law of the fixed date, which could be changed if not acceptable to the in-law. On the agreed day the parents of the suitor, the suitor himself and the third-party person visit the parents of the girl, carrying the bride price, kola nuts and palm wine, with them. In **Ihe Shikeaguma**, installment payments of bride price are allowed, and no amount of money is fixed as bride price for any class or age of girls. Land and economic trees are acceptable in lieu of bride price money. Bride price is usually negotiated between the two families in the absence of the girl and sometimes the suitor too. On this day one

person each is selected as the official witness of the marriage by the two families, to handle all the third-party messages in that marriage. It could be the third-party persons who started the marriage contacts, or any other persons chosen by the two families, provided that a first third-party person who started the marriage contacts is compensated for his/her services if he/ she is replaced with another person.

Having settled the issue of witnesses, the payment of the agreed bride price is made. The parents of the suitor give the agreed amount to their own witness, who hands the money to the witness of the girl's family. This second witness counts the money in the presence of everybody, announces the amount and hands it over to the girl's father, after deducting their commission of five per cent of the money. This five percent, (one shilling in a pound or five kobo in one naira) of the total amount is shared into two equal parts by the two witnesses. The suitor's parents and the official witnesses are well entertained after the settlement of the bride price.

4.2f: Suitor's Third Visit (Ibu Nmanya Ụmụnna)
After the payment of the bride price, the next move by the suitor is the presentation of palm wine to the mega family (**ụmụnna**) and the extended family members to inform them of the marriage proposal. The suitor sends his witness to his in-law to ascertain the quantity of the palm wine needed and

when the wine can be presented. In recent times other types of drinks, such as hot drinks, beer and soft drinks are included in what in-laws demand during marriage ceremonies. Traditionally palm wine and kola nuts are mandatory because they are the items used in the various rituals and prayers during marriage ceremonies in Igboland. Having received all the information, he needs for the third visit with **ụmụnna** wine, the suitor consults members of his own mega family in a meeting on this issue. His family makes its contribution of the wine and selects members of the family to accompany him, his parents and his witness to the in-law's place. The suitor having known the number of people to accompany him to his in-law's place provides enough money for the entertainment of members of both families. This money is usually sent to the mother-in-law through the witness while he buys all the wine and kola nuts requested for the occasion.

When the wine is presented to the family, their elders inspect and taste it to ensure that the right type and correct quantity have been presented. If the **ụmụnna** is satisfied with the wine, they now call the girl's father to know whether he has finished with the earlier stages of the marriage rites with the new in-law. If the answer is yes, they now go ahead with the sharing of the wine between the two families. At the end of the sharing of the wine entertainment of guests start. After this ceremony the girl can now visit the suitor. Since some suitors live far away from Igboland, the second and third stages of the marriage rites are held in one ceremony, but this arrangement is made with the approval of the new in-laws and their family.

4.2g: Bride's First Official Visit to Suitor (Ineta Ụnọ)

The girl is now officially allowed to visit the suitor and stay for one or two days, to see what the suitor's home is like. During this first visit, the bride is showered with presents by the suitor, his friends and members of his family. After this visit the suitor and his bride agree on when to visit the bride's maternal grandparents.

4.2h: Suitor's Visit to Bride's Maternal Grandparents (Ọmụlụ be onye?)

Although the kola nuts and palm wine needed for this visit are usually not much, the visit is very important because the suitor is introduced to the maternal root of his bride. This visit gives the suitor a clearer knowledge of his bride's maternal relations and helps to rule out the possibility of any close blood relationship with his bride.

4.2i: Final Marriage Rite (Igba Nkwụ Nwanyi)

In **Igbo** culture, the final marriage rite of presenting wine to the village and all extended family members of a girl, was the last and biggest ceremony in **Igbo** marriages, for several centuries before the colonial masters introduced court and church marriage rites in the 19th Century in Igboland. **Igba nkwụ nwanyi** is usually the celebration of the completion of the marriage act in Igboland. At this time:

* Prayers and sacrifices have been conducted after spiritual consultations by both families.

* The suitor and his bride have agreed to marry in the presence of both families.

* Both parents of the couple have given their blessings to the marriage.

* Members of both families have been informed through the presentation of kola nuts and drinks by the suitor.

* The bride price has been paid, and the two witnesses have taken their commission of 5% of the bride price.

* The girl has officially visited and approved of the suitor's home and people.

Igba nkwụ nwanyi which is a good-bye rite in **Igbo** marriage culture is also a day of eating, drinking and dancing for the two families and their guests. In planning the ceremony, the suitor visits his in-laws about one month earlier and agrees with them on the date and manner of the ceremony.

The cost of the food items needed for the entertainment is estimated and paid to the mother in-law by the suitor. Having settled on food items with his in-laws, the suitor holds another meeting with his own family (**Ụmụnna**) to agree on how to purchase drinks and other requirements for the ceremony. The family members usually show their involvement in the marriage by contributing their time and resources in one form or the other during the ceremony. In a case where the suitor has a financial problem, members of the family give donations or a loan as part of the cost of making the marriage ceremony successful. In the olden days when there were no motor vehicles, large pots of palm wine were carried by head to the in-law's place, by young men for distances of up to five miles. Food gifts at the end of the ceremony by the parents-in-law were also carried back home.

On the appointed day, members of the suitor's family would carry the required items in the company of the suitor, his parents, the witness and a dance troupe to their in-law's place. On their arrival, members of the in-law's family would receive them warmly. Elders of the in-law's family inspect the drinks to ensure that the right type and quantity have been brought by the suitor. After this inspection, if everything is right, the drinks are shared by the two families. Now that the drinks have been shared, all guests get seated and kola nuts are presented by the bride's father to his in-laws.

Prayers are said one after the other by both fathers of the couple, or their representatives. The bridal train made up of the bride's age-grade members welcomes the suitor and members of his family. Food and drinks are served to the guests.

The bride in the company of her age grade members is given a cup of palm wine by her father in the presence of all the guests and asked to give it to her suitor. She guards the cup of palm wine jealously and looks for her man among the guests. On spotting the suitor, she goes to his seat, kneels by his side, sips the wine and hands the cup to him. The suitor receives the cup and drinks the wine. Both are cheered by both families and their guests. From here the couple takes the floor for the bridal dance where money is sprayed on them by all and sundry. At the end of the dance, gifts are presented by friends and relatives. Parents of the bride present food items and household wares for their daughter's use in her new home. The bridegroom thanks the in-laws and guests.

4.2j: Parting Rite (Nsegowe Ite)
One of the empty pots of palm wine with which the groom brought wine is selected by the family elder or the father of the bride. The bride squats beside the old man who may be squatting too. The elder places the pot on the ground in front of himself and the bride with both facing the compound exit gate. He holds a cup of palm wine in his hand and prays

to God and the ancestors to:

* Give the girl and her husband good health and protect them from all evil.

* Give them love and peace in their marriage.

* Give them male and female children.

* Give them wealth with which to look after their children and their parents.

At the end of the prayer, the elder pours the cup of palm wine on the empty pot and places it on the bride's head and bids her goodbye and safe journey. The girl now leaves her parents' home for good in the company of her new husband and his people. As she leaves, she says goodbye to her parents and siblings, sometimes in tears. Young girls of her age see her off singing farewell songs for the couple.

4.2k: Cleansing of Incest (Ọma Ite)

In **Ihe Shikeaguma** during pre-colonial days, it was a sin of incest to marry anybody of a known blood relationship of up to the tenth generation. After the onset of British rule and the resultant availability of job opportunities outside **Igbo** culture area, many **Igbo** children were born outside this culture area. This situation resulted in relatives meeting outside their town and even their culture area, without knowing that they are blood relations. **Ihe Shikeaguma** elders met and made the following traditional declarations.

The first was that marriages cannot be contracted outside **Ihe** community between **Ihe** people without reference to the family base at home, so that the blood relationships can be investigated. Secondly, they conducted a general cleansing rite (**ọma ite**) for all future marriages involving fourth generation relatives. Thirdly, they declared that fourth generation relatives upwards, from two mega families (**ụmụnna**), can marry without committing the sin of incest in the future. Fourthly, the elders insisted that the blood relationship of an intended couple who are third generation relatives still constitute an impediment to the marriage. If this third-generation relationship was not known until after all the marriage rites have been completed; or if a girl is impregnated without knowing the relationship, a ritual cleansing must be carried out to absolve the couple of the sin of incest. Finally, any marriage or sexual relationship between a male and female of the first or second generation is still abomination which is punishable with banishment from **Ihe Shikeaguma**.

4.2l: Divorce (Alụkwaghim)

Igbo ancestors in their wisdom knew that the marriage institution as administered by human beings was bound to have short comings irrespective of all the precautions taken in the execution of its rites of passage. **Igbo** culture in its usual caution created the alternative of divorce for times when unforeseen situations presented themselves, or when the life of any one of the two parties, husband or wife was threatened.

In **Igbo** culture today, whenever there is a threat to the stability of a marriage, that the couple cannot handle, the situation is reported by the aggrieved person, husband or wife, to a parent of either of the couple. If the problem persists after reasonable chance for settlement has been given to the parent involved, parents of the couple meet and try to resolve it. If a solution is still not in sight at this stage, the problem is taken to the joint marriage council of the two mega families (**ụmụnna**), made up of elders. Should the problem persist after this stage, it is taken to the village marriage council constituted by selected elders of both villages of the couple. At this stage, all precautions are taken to give justice where it belongs so that a possible split in the marriage will not affect any future marriage relations between the two villages. If the aggrieved person is still not satisfied with the decision of the two villages, he or she is given the option of divorce.

The aggrieved person holds a meeting with his or her parents on the divorce issue. If they agree on divorce, they send their witness to the other witness and sue for divorce. The other witness on his or her own side holds a meeting with the in-laws of the aggrieved person, and they agree on a date for the checking of the expenses of both families, and the repayment of bride price to the husband. This witness communicates with the aggrieved family on the appointed day for the bride price checking.

4.2 m: Checking and Repayment of Bride Price (Igba Enwe Nwanyi)

During the checking of the bride price, each of the two families can call additional witnesses from either of the two families or villages of the couple. Each side presents its case through its official witness. Two official witnesses of both sides and two elders from each of the two sides constitute the bride price tribunal and their decision is final and binding.

In **Ihe Shikeaguma**, during a bride price checking, all food and drinks given as part of a marriage rite are off-count. Money paid in return for food-gifts (**ụda**) during maternity confinements is not refundable. Only the bride price paid through the witnesses and any other lump-sum given as a loan are refundable. Assistance given at home or in the farm by any of the in-laws is not paid for or received in bride price money terms. Such a type of assistance is acknowledged with gratitude, and good food entertainment. Jewelry and new clothes bought for the former wife, are returnable or paid for in cash to the former husband by the new husband.

At the end of the bride price checking, the tribunal takes 5% of the total amount agreed upon to be refunded, as its commission and the balance is given to the former husband through his own witness. If the agreed balance of the bride price is not ready or complete at this stage it becomes the duty of the wife's family to send the money as quickly as possible through their own witness to the in-law's witness who will ensure that the bride price balance is given to the former husband after he has deducted the tribunal's commission of 5%. After the final settlement of the former husband's bride price, the woman becomes free to take another husband. If she becomes pregnant before this settlement of her bride price, the unborn child belongs to the former husband irrespective of whether the woman has remarried or not. All the children of the annulled marriage belong to the former husband and continue to live with him.

4.3: THE EXTENDED FAMILY SYSTEM

4.3a Role of the Family in the Nation
From prehistoric times, the family has been central in the formulation of most ethnic issues in **Igbo** culture because it is the foundation on which the community is built, and it is the first training ground for its human resources. The family in **Igbo** culture is an empowerment base, an opinion pool, and a political reference point for the adult **Igbo**

engaging in any sociopolitical project in Igboland. In pre-colonial times the extended family supplied the bulk of the human resources needed for the infrastructural developments in the nuclear family in Igboland. Since the family is a focal point of origin for all male kinship units in **Igbo** culture, our ancestors took their time to develop the mega family unit (**ụmụnna**) as the first tier of **Igbo** traditional government.

The importance of the family in the formation and development of the society has received important emphasis by many societies, not only in Igboland but all over the world. The churches in their teaching emphasize the importance of the family as the starting point for education, evangelization and physical empowerment. V. C. **Uchendu** (1985) has this observation on the family.

> *All societies, no matter the level of their technological, industrial, or socio-cultural achievements, have the same genealogical capacity to construct and maintain an extended family. Many do; a few don't; and some of those which developed an extended family network have reversed it because of the hostility of their changing environment.*[27]

The inherent nature of humanity to shy away from responsibilities, in addition to the changing

---

[27] V. C. **Uchendu**, (1995), **Ahiajoku** Lecture, page 40

economic environment and increasing demands on the wealthy for assistance, by the less privileged members of the extended families, have facilitated decreasing interests in the continued patronage of the extended family system, in a world that is becoming more and more selfish and materialistic. Recently in 1989, the United Nations, in view of these developing trends have re-emphasized the importance of the family to the nation.

> *The United Nations General Assembly in its resolution 44/82 of 9th December 1989, had designated 1994 as the international year of the family. This was duly celebrated here at the national, state and local government levels. In these celebrations, attention was drawn to the central role of the family as the most fundamental unit of society which must form the bases for the moral and cultural reconstruction of the state and nation. Only last month the family was also the focus of attention at the fourth world conference of women in Beijing, China.*[28]

4.3b: Concept of the Family System (Ezi N'ụnọ)

In **Igbo** culture the concept of a family is the union in marriage of a man and a woman who become the two pillars upon which the nuclear or immediate family (**Ụnọ**) is built and from where

---

[28] V. C. **Uchendu**, (1995), **Ahiajoku** Lecture, page 7

the extended family (**Ezi**) sprouts for the continued extension of the family system. The roles played by each of the male and female offspring in the formation of the **Igbo** family system (**Ezi n'Ụnọ**) shall be highlighted in this discussion. I shall use the imaginary family of **Okolo Eze** as an example, to facilitate the understanding of the concept of the extended family system in **Igbo** culture.

To remove any confusion that could arise from the meaning of the home-stead (**Ezi** na **Ụnọ**) and the extended family system (**Ezi** n' **Ụnọ**), I refer you to the pie chart (a) on the home-stead (**Ezi na Ụnọ**), and pie chart (b) on the extended family system (**Ezi** n' **Ụnọ**) through the male and female kinship matrices (**Ụmụnna and Ụmụada**).

(**Ezi** n' **Ụnọ**), An extended family unit is a single entity made up of blood relatives of a single nuclear family, separated by distance or marriage, but joined by blood affinity. It has no limit to its growth in number of relatives or distance of habitation. In some Igbo communities, members of this family unit can inter marry after an agreed number of generations, without committing the sin of incest. One extended family unit can grow into a village, town, or even clan as in "**Umuokoloeze or Amaokoloeze.**"

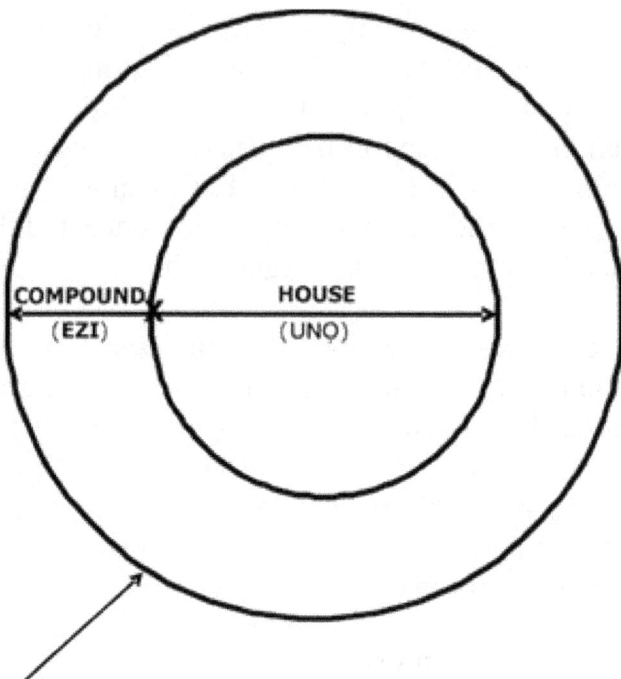

Pie-chart "a" (Home Stead)

Ezi na **Ụnọ** (Homestead) is made up of two separate entities; the compound (**ezi**) and the house (**uno**):

a) **(Ezi)** The compound is a territorial space in which a house or houses that belong to one nuclear family are built. It is sometimes demarcated with a wall or a fence.

b) **(Uno)** The house is a residential structure built inside a compound. It represents a house or several houses in one compound that belong to one nuclear family.

4.3c: Male Kinship Matrix (Ụmụnna)

The male kinship matrix (**Ụmụnna**) of **Okolo Eze** is constituted by all his sons. As these sons of **Okolo Eze**'s nuclear family grow into adults, the eldest continues to live at home in his father's house while the rest build their own houses or move out to their own new homes on their ancestral land, get married and set up their own families, as **Okolo Eze**'s extended family. His grand and great grandsons with their male children also become members of the male kinship matrix, usually called members of the extended family of **Okolo Eze**. In pre-colonial days, all the males of the male kinship matrix, with their nuclear families usually lived in their neighborhood on their ancestral parcels of land as **Ụmụnna**, sharing:

* A common ancestral name, such as **Ụmụ** or **Ama Okoloeze**.

* Inheritance of land and economic trees, Family rights, mutual assistance, protection and responsibilities.

* Ancestral facilities such as, village squares, streams, markets, shrines, farmlands, Moral sanctions and control over one another.

The male kinship matrix has no limit to its number or size but grows with time, from one man's nuclear family to a village, town or clan, bearing one ancestral name in each case. As the population increases beyond the mega family (**Ụmụnna**) level

to the village level, youths of this matrix, intermarry with members of their female kinship matrices and split up into various other nuclear families and villages.

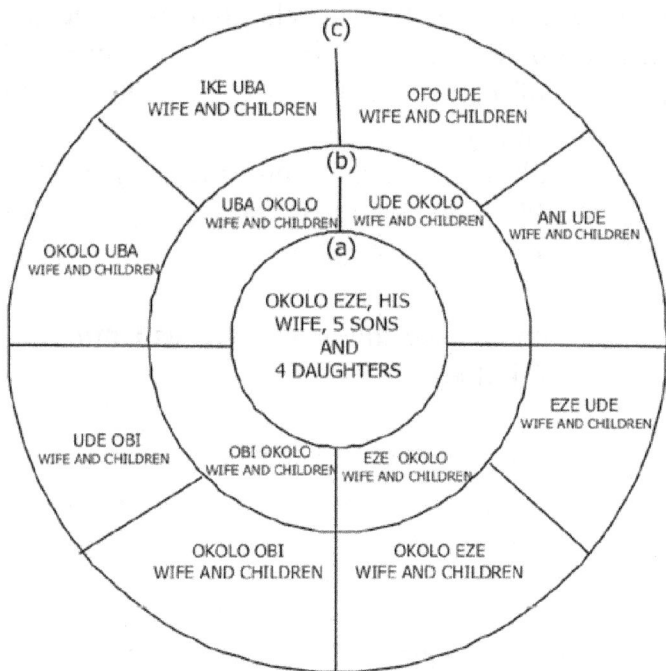

Pie-chart "b" (Male Kinship Matrix in the Extended Family System).

4.3d: THREE STRATA MALE KINSHIP MATRIX (ỤMỤNNA)

(a) Immediate family of **Okolo Eze**, his wife, five young sons and four daughters in the center circle as (**Ụnọ Okolo Eze**) his nuclear family.

(b) The extended family of **Okolo Eze**, made up of his adult sons, their wives and young children in the second circle as **Ezi Okolo Eze**

(c) Grown up grandsons, their wives and children also as (**Ezi Okolo Eze**) **Okolo Eze**'s extended family.

All the members of the three segments of **Okolo Eze**'s family are the constituents of **Umuokoloeze** mega family (**Umunna**). These **Igbo** kinship units are separated by marriage and distance, yet they still loosely maintain blood relationships and common ancestries.

4.3e: Female Kinship Matrix (Ụmụada)

The female kinship matrix (**Ụmụada**) of **Okolo Eze** is made up of his four immediate daughters and all the female offspring of **Ụmụokoloeze**. They grow up into adult women, get married, take their husbands' surnames and set up their own nuclear families. They swell up the ranks of the extended family of **Okolo Eze**, far away from **Ụmụokoloeze**, and help to build other kinship units that bear the ancestral names of their husbands. The tendency of the members of the female kinship matrix to leave the ancestral families of their birth for marriage in distant places is the basis for **Igbo** preference for male offspring, to ensure that there is a caretaker for the ancestral home (**Ụnọukwu**) and ancestral parcels of land. The female kinship matrix (**Ụmụada**) is made up of several clusters of blood relatives.

These relatives are geographically separated by marriage but closely tied to the extended family system by blood affinity. They constitute the powerful female kinship units (**Ụmụada**) in **Igbo** culture that share great mutual respect with their male counterparts in their ancestral families. The children of the female offspring, known as **Ọmụlụbe** and **Ụmụokoloeze** family share mutual respect, assistance, protection and moral sanctions, in addition to the children's rights, obligations and duties in their father's families and ancestral kinship connections. The husbands of **Ụmụada Okolo Eze**, in addition to their own ancestral duties and responsibilities, owe a debt of bride price to their in-laws. In **Igbo** culture the bride price is never complete until the woman is dead. The bride price could be demanded at any time in the form of mutual respect and assistance. The female kinship matrix continues to grow until the fifth generation, when the members of the female and male kinship matrices can intermarry without fear of the sin of incest.

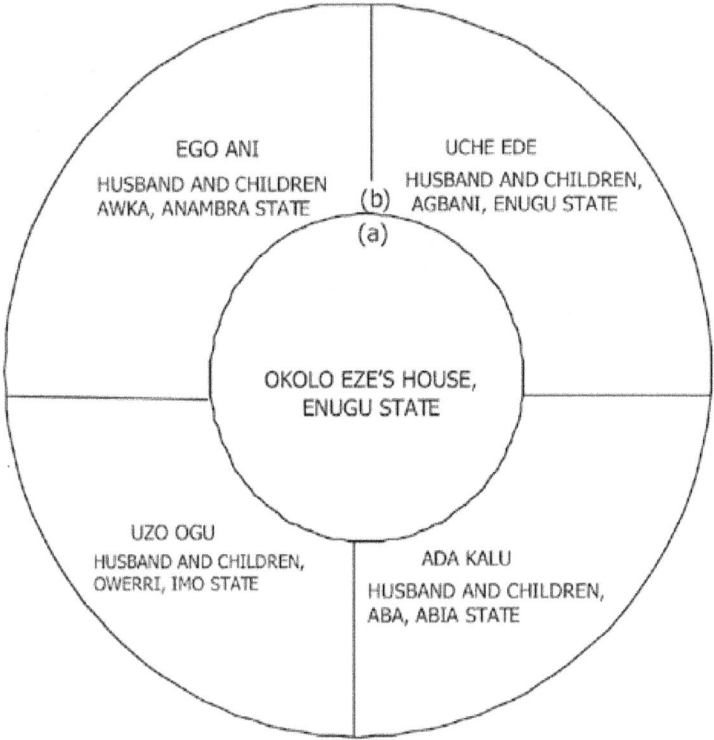

EGO ANI
HUSBAND AND CHILDREN
AWKA, ANAMBRA STATE

(b)

UCHE EDE
HUSBAND AND CHILDREN,
AGBANI, ENUGU STATE

(a)

OKOLO EZE'S HOUSE,
ENUGU STATE

UZO OGU
HUSBAND AND CHILDREN,
OWERRI, IMO STATE

ADA KALU
HUSBAND AND CHILDREN,
ABA, ABIA STATE

4.3f TWO STRATA FEMALE KINSHIP MATRIX UMUADA

(a) **Okolo Eze**'s house at the center circle in **Enugu** State, is the point of origin of the four married daughters of **Okolo Eze**, and all the females born in **Ụmụokoloeze** (**Ụmụada**) by the male members of the male kinship matrix.

(b) The second circle is made up of the four adult daughters of **Okolo Eze**. The **Okolo Eze** daughters have taken their husbands' surnames and are scattered in marriage to four different towns in four States of Nigeria.

4.4: Social Status Structure and Title System

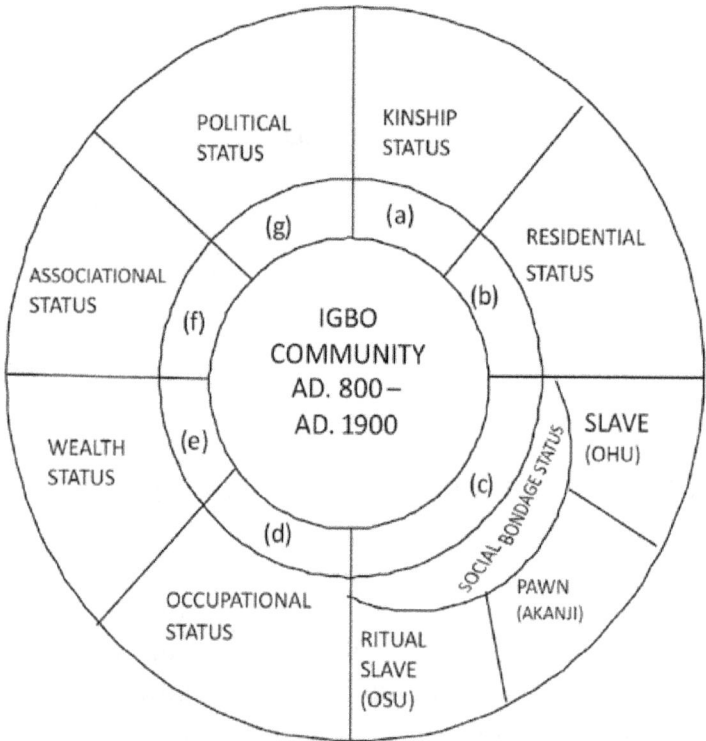

4.4a: Kinship Status

In this topic, I shall use the imaginary name of **Agu Eze** as an example of head of an **Igbo** nuclear family in order to facilitate understanding of the formation and the working of the **Igbo** social status structure and title system. **Agu Eze**, an adult **Igbo** male gets the approval of his parents and moves out of his father's house to a new site on his ancestral land. He builds a homestead and establishes his own nuclear family, made up of **Agu Eze** himself, his two wives and children. In **Igbo** culture, the statuses of the husband, wives and children in the day to day activities of the family are well known for the smooth running of the family. Male precedence and seniority by birth and marriage are emphasized in all responsibility and honor roles in typical **Igbo** families.

4.4b: Residential Status

As the **Agueze** settlement grows from his original nuclear family into a village, other nuclear families pressed by the desire for space, safety, subsistence, economic or religious freedom move into the growing new settlement, now known as **Ụmụagụeze**. Two broad groups, including the **Agu Eze** kinship units in the village, become recognizable, as the aborigines (**Diala** or **Amaala**), and the newcomers or non-indigenes (**Ọbịa or Mbiambia**) of **Ụmụagueze**. The aborigines or indigenes of the settlement are those settlers whose ancestor **Agu Eze**, first settled at

Ụmụagụeze and who have inheritance rights on the land, and economic trees in the new village.

The non-indigenes or newcomers (**Ọbia or Mbiambia**) are those settlers whose parents or ancestors do not have inheritance rights on the ancestral land at **Ụmụagụeze**, notwithstanding the fact that their parents might have been born in the settlement. They depend on the indigenes to officiate on their behalf during prayers and rituals of installation in the few approved titles allowed to the newcomers. The newcomers buy more land in addition to the ones given to them by the aborigines; establish their own shrines, civic and recreational grounds; and grow into a sub village in **Ụmụagụeze**. Where indigenes and non-indigenes are mixed in a social gathering, the indigenes have the duty of enacting or initiating sociopolitical roles that are ritual in nature, such as breaking of the kola nut, officiating as priests in the offering of sacrifice to the land deities, leading in prayers during title taking rituals and during village or town meetings. Indigenes have automatic qualification to most of the titles in the land where they meet up the other economic and moral expectations for the title.

4.4c: Social Bondage Status
The status of non-indigenes or newcomers in **Igbo** culture includes those in social bondage, recognized as, slaves (**Ohu/Oru**), pawns (**Akanji/ Nvunvuego**), and ritual slaves (**Osu**). During

precolonial days, a slave's kinship links were severed forever by the process of being bought by another person. He became the property of his master who had the cultural right to absorb or not absorb him and his nuclear family into the master's own lineage, with some reserved limitations, depending on the behavior and usefulness of the slave to the master and his community. The pawn (**Akanji/ Nvunvuego**) as distinguished from the slave was a person mortgaged as collateral for a debt. The pawn regained his or her freedom whenever the debt was fully paid back to the creditor-master by the pawn, a relative or the debtor-master.

The privilege pawns had over slaves was that they could not be re-pawned or sold as slaves by a creditor-master. A pawn could free himself by surrendering the free days allowed him every week by the creditor-master for several months or years. He could also do that by paying the debt with the proceeds he made from hiring himself out where he practiced his craft, on his work free days.

In **Igbo** culture today, land and economic trees are still pawned to creditors, but human beings are no longer pawned as collateral for debts. The cult slave (**osu**) was not bought with money but freely dedicated as a mark of worship by a parent or relative to the service of the dedicator's deity. The cult slave and his descendants became the property of the deity, and usually lived in a slave (**osu**) settlement, usually located near the grove or shrine of the deity, to facilitate service. In communities where they were dedicated to **Eke/Nkwo** market deities, they lived near the market as **Obu n'eke/ Obu na nkwọ**. In various other communities, the settlements were called different names and dedication rites took different forms. Dedication of one's child or self to the service of a deity as a mark of worship or protection is an age-old practice. It was also practiced several centuries B.C. by the Jews and Arabs in the worship of their deities. In recent times, it is practiced in the Christian faith by priests, monks and nuns for the same worship purposes.

Before the **Nri** civilization which started about A.D. 800, the status of social bondage, made up of slaves, pawns, and cult slaves did not exist in **Igbo** status structure of that period. During the **Nri** civilization that spanned nine centuries (A.D. 800-A.D. 1700), most of the ritualized social statuses in **Igbo** culture were created and have since remained the heritage of **Nri** hegemony. Two distinct status groups consequently emerged in **Igbo** culture during this period: Status of free men and women (**Amadu/Amaala**), and the Status of bondage (**Ohu, Osu/Akanji**). The **Osu** system in **Igbo** culture was legally abolished by the Eastern Nigerian Government in 1956.

4.4d: Occupational Status

The **Igbo** are well known for their commitment to the acquisition of wealth. Different people take to different lucrative occupations. Each person is so dedicated to his occupation that he takes pride in identifying himself with his occupation by taking tradenames like **Dibia** (diviner) **Diji** (yam farmer) **Dinka** (artist) **Dinta** (hunter) **Di ochi** (palm wine tapper) **Diụzụ** (blacksmith) etc.

4.4e: Wealth Status

As some of the settlers of **Umuagueze** engage themselves in various occupational activities, they acquire more wealth than others. Their wealth creates two broad groups; the have-mores (**Ọgaranya**), and the have-littles (**Ogbenye**). As a result of the stratification of the wealth status into these two groups in the society, the have-mores in agreement with the elders and policy makers of the community establish more social status groups and recognize them with achievement status titles like; **Ezeafia, Ezeji, Ezeụzụ, Ogbuu, Ọchịlịọzụa, Ọsụọfia**, etc. These status titles are given to the have-mores in accordance with the commitment of their wealth and know-how to the socio political and infrastructural development of the community.

V. C. Uchendu (1995) made this observation on wealth in **Igbo** culture.

> *It is viewed in Igbo society as a means of achieving prestige; and prestige is the reward which society bestows on those social climbers who use their wealth in ways approved and most esteemed by their neighbors and communities.*[29]

The **Igbo** culture is very well known within the lower Niger area of Nigeria for its recognition of individual effort and individual achievement in the development of the community. The **Igbo** community welcomes the use of wealth for the purpose of status building by both indigenes and non-indigenes in society and gives appropriate recognition to each contributor to society's development; hence there was no formal taxation in Igboland before the advent of colonialism.

4.4f: Associational Status

In this effort of status building with their wealth, irrespective of whether they are indigenes or non-indigenes, the have-mores associate and socialize with other wealthy members of the settlement. In the various sociocultural ceremonies of marriage, title taking, chieftaincy installations, festivals, burials; or sociopolitical functions like launchings, funds-raising, house openings, anniversaries, receptions and sendoffs, organizers of these functions lobby the have-mores with special invitation cards and

---

[29] **V. C. Uchendu**, (1995), **Ahiajoku** Lecture, page 64

various types of invitation gifts in advance of the functions. The have-mores compete among themselves in the use of their wealth in the promotion of these ceremonies to enhance their recognition and eventual elevation to statuses of honor and respect in the community. Based on their promotional abilities, **Igbo** societies award the have-mores chieftaincy titles like, **Akajiakụ, Omeego, Orimmili, Ogbuefi, Otigbuanyinya, Ogbuebini**, etc. Each community sets its own standards for title-awards and the installation ceremonies.

4.4g: Political Status

As the **Ụmụagụeze** settlement grows, it develops its political structure and recognizes political groups and leaders. Some of the have-mores move up from associational recognized statuses because of the leverage they get through their wealth to elevated and socially enhanced political positions of, **Eze, Igwe, Obi**, etc. The have-littles are not completely forgotten in the society. The have-mores after they have been elevated by the society select some up-and-coming have-littles and put them in various community committees, councils, cabinets or use them as errand boys and praise singers. In this way the up-and-coming have-littles are initiated into the lower rungs of the community's associational status. These up-and-coming have-littles eventually grow in substance and popularity and move up to the status of the have-mores.

4.5: FESTIVALS

4.5a: Occasions for Celebration and Thanksgiving

During prehistoric days, **Igbo** ancestors imagined God in human form and interacted with him in practical human ways through created intermediaries. They initiated several festivals during which they created occasions for celebrations to give thanks to God for his bounties and protection through created intermediaries such as the deities and ancestors. The deities and ancestors were looked upon in those days for the protection of social facilities such as homes, markets, civic centers and farms. Shrines of the deities were set up in these facilities. The land deity (**Ani**) was installed in every town; the residential compound deity (**Aniobi**) in every home; the gate deity (**Egbo**) at the entrance of every homestead, market or civic center; the yam deity (**Fiajiọkụ**) in every barn; and the **Ọfọ** stick was placed on farms and valuable possessions as protection against rogues.

The life-in-community concept of the **Igbo** which is reflected in their belief in the extended family units of **Ụmụnna** and **Ụmụnne** demanded that the **Igbo** meet from time to time at home to take care of community's cultural, educational, sociopolitical and infrastructural projects. Throughout **Igbo** major festival periods, mass return of traveled **Igbo** to their various communities take place. Fund raising activities are organized in various forms to build up capital for the execution of the above-mentioned community projects. During the mass returns, the returnees are assessed by the community. The successful members of the community are praised and celebrated as worthy sons and daughters. The praise and endorsements given to the successful returnees encourage school leavers or the jobless to travel out with the returnees in search of greener pastures. The recruitment of the jobless helps in the alleviation of poverty in the community and encourages parents to invest in the education of their children. On the other hand, the honest and hardworking members of the community at home who need help are given both moral and financial assistance by their families and friends.

On the whole, festivals in **Igbo** culture are very important windows that show-case the **Igbo** and their way of life. Their history, relationships, generosity, food, fashion, music and art are highlighted during these colorful cultural celebrations. Also, their religious beliefs are seen in their lives during their festivals. In the **Ani** festival in **Ntuegbe** clan, the valor and combat readiness of the ancestors in addition to the youth activities of the day are also show-cased and celebrated. During the new yam festival, **(Fiajiọkụ)** the gift of the yam through the ancestors is also colorfully celebrated in many communities in Igboland. In these festivals the **Igbo** do not forget to make offerings of thanksgiving to the ancestors, elders, in-laws, relatives and friends who have been God's intermediaries in channeling various blessings to them.

The **Ani** festival in **Ntuegbe** clan, in **Enugu** State of Nigeria, is a celebration in memory of the bravery and the hunting proficiency of **Ntuegbe** ancestors. It takes place in the five **Ntuegbe** towns with emphasis on, hunting expeditions, hunting parades, youth activities, entertainments, and exchange of visits and gifts. In **Ihe Shikeaguma**, of **Ntuegbe** clan for example, the **Ani** festival is a very important festival. It is celebrated once in two years, in December or January of the festival year depending on the lunar calendar of the year. Within the **Ani Ihe** festival are contained minor festivals, such as the **Ani** new moon festival, the hunting festival, the youth games festival, the hunters/hero's day parade, the day of respite, the day of bones, and the dance festival.

4.5b: Ani, a Traditional Core-Igbo Festival

The **Ani** festival is celebrated by most of the core-**Igbo** communities at different times of the year with different traditional ceremonies. **Ani Ihe** festival for example starts late in the fourth lunar month (**Ọnwa ẹnọ**) and ends early in the sixth lunar month (**Ọnwa isi**) It has three major parts. Part one is made up of four mini festivals of; the uprooting of some palm trees for palm wine (**Igwunkwụ Ani**); the Sighting of the new moon (**Igbaọnwa**); the Announcement of the start of the festival (**Ikaani**) and the Hunting festival (**Igbanta Ani**). The second part which is the principal part of the festival starts on the day of leading the cattle home (**Afọ ọchụchụefi**); through the day of slaughter of animals (**Nkwọ Ani Ihe**); to the hunters/ heroes day parade (**Eke Ani Ihe**); the day of respite to animals (**Oye udene**); and ends on the day of bones (**Afọ ntacha ọkpụkpụ**). The third part is the dance festival (**Ite ogeoge**) which starts from the next **Eke** day after **Eke Ani Ihe** and ends on the fifth **Eke** day which is the closing ceremony (**Nvugbe egwu**)

4.5c: Regulations for Ani Ihe Festival

Ani Ihe festival starts towards the end of the fourth lunar month of the year when some palm trees are uprooted to produce palm wine (**Ogwuduani**) for the festival; and continues to the close of the festival at the beginning of the sixth lunar month. During this period the following regulations (**Nsọani**) are strictly observed in order to eliminate other extraneous commitments that could swallow the resources meant for the celebration of **Ani** festival or distract people from observing the solemnity of the festival:

i. No building foundation or any major housework such as walling, or roofing is embarked upon.

ii. No payment of bride price or the undertaking of any major marriage ceremony such as traditional wedding ceremony is undertaken.

iii. The settlement of land disputes is put off till the end of the festival.

iv. All disputes that could result in the exchange of hot words or blows and possibly result in the spilling of human blood on the land are avoided.

v. All **Ihe Shikeaguma** people who killed other **Ihe** natives intentionally in the past are temporally banished from **Ihe Shikeaguma** during the festival.

vi. People who die within the festival period are buried without burial ceremonies

vii. Nobody can be buried or mourned on the day of respite (**Oye udene**) which is the holiest day of the year, until the following day when the corpse is hurriedly and quietly buried without traditional burial ceremonies.

viii. Everybody in **Ihe** is bound to maintain absolute peace during the festival.

As the days of the festival approach, there is joy in every family as traveled relatives arrive from the cities, bringing with them their families and enough supplies for the festival period. Friends and relatives invited from different towns arrive for the festival. This period of mass-return creates lodging problems for some returnees, but everybody is bound to try to accommodate guests, at least for the period of the festival. This period creates fine opportunities for unmarried returnee-youths to find their future spouses. The period provides a boom in the marketing of food items, various types of drinks and clothing for the townsfolks. Parents provide new clothes for their children and some women empty their bank accounts or money boxes to provide the trendiest apparels for the festival. Groups of children provide new uniforms and musical instruments for their dancing activities, in order to give full entertainment to the returnees and guests during the festival.

Most sociocultural associations and village unions in **Ihe Shikeaguma** hold their yearly closing-of-accounts meetings to raise money for development projects. They use this period to collect long-over-due levies and dues of their returnee-members. Although every adult male is bound to clear his union dues, he still strives to provide meat for the kitchen, drinks for the guests, gunpowder for the various gun-shooting outings and his own new clothes for the festival.

4.5d: Sighting of the New Moon for Ani Ihe Festival

Through the year's lunar calendar, the elders know when to expect the new moon for the festival. In **Ihe Shikeaguma** it is an abomination for any other person other than the chief priest of **Ani Ihe** to announce the appearance of the new moon for the festival. A day before the sighting of the new moon, or on those occasions when the moon appears one or two days earlier than expected, children are warned not to look up at the sky. Some rascally children are locked up in the house towards evening.

On the **Nkwọ** market day that the new moon is expected to be ceremoniously greeted by everybody, each village takes its own **Nkwa** dance music and loaded cap guns to **Eke Ihe** market. Each village stays in its own market stall in anticipation of the new moon, exchanging pleasantries around kegs of palm wine. The market is agog with well dressed women and men in battle attire dancing the **Nkwa** music; and children scampering from one stall to the other to catch a glimpse of each dance group. The **Nkwa** music is a war dance and its dancers make gestures of aiming at imaginary targets. They shoot at those targets as if in a real hunting or battle encounter. Elderly women make the **Nkwa** runs with the men, as a memorial of the intertown war years when strong women took water and food to fighting men in the battle field; and the slave raid years when wives had to run with their husbands when attacked in the farm or in their homes.

The merry making lasts till evening when some people start leaving for home to await the gun shot announcement of the sighting of the new moon from the chief priest of **Ani Ihe**. The men reload their cap guns in the market before leaving for home in case the announcement is made while they are on their way home from the market. As the sun sets and the gathering disperses in the market, the chief priest of **Ọgbụlụgbụ** (the goddess wife of **Ani Ihe** deity), who usually comes from **Chime Anioke's** family, in **Ụmụọjị** village goes to the chief priest of **Ani Ihe**, who usually comes from **Nwankwọ Okeleke's** family of **Awkụnanọ** village and asks him whether he has looked up at the sky.

The chief priest of **Ani Ihe** takes his cap gun; goes outside; looks at the sky; mutters prayers of thanksgiving to **Ani Ihe**; and announces the appearance of the new moon with a gunshot (**Igba Ọnwa**). The shooting of cap guns from all directions follow the chief priest's gunshot. Within minutes, gunshot sounds fill up the air in **Ihe** town, for as long as two to three hours into the night, as if in a war zone. As the gunshots subside, one could hear shouts of joy from all and sundry. Prayers of thanksgiving to **Ani Ihe** could be heard from the elders, for bringing them safely into another festival year. They also pray for the safe arrival of their children from the cities and the provision of their needs for the celebration of the festival.

4.5e: Announcing the start of Ani Ihe Festival
On the following **Eke** day after the sighting of the **Ani** festival new moon, the chief priest announces the start of the principal part of the festival. On that day, **Eke** market is full of well-dressed spectators from the villages of **Ihe** and the neighboring towns, who have come to witness the announcement of the start of the festival. The village market-stalls are full of groups of people around kegs of palm wine, waiting for the arrival of the chief priest of **Ani Ihe**.

At last the chief priest arrives in his full battle regalia with his staff of office in his left hand and an iron scepter (**Ojji**) in his right hand. He is accompanied by his wife who is dressed in full traditional festival attire. His armor bearer carries a loaded cap gun and trails behind his wife. The chief priest strikes the pointed end of the scepter on the ground, from time to time, thereby producing a jingling sound that scares away anybody on his way. He walks majestically like a warrior along the traditional route in full view of the spectators. While he walks along the route, four times incommunicado, spectators stand clear of this route to avoid the ancestors' wrath that would come on anybody that talks to or touches him during this journey to the proclamation spot.

As the chief priest arrives at the proclamation spot, at the center of the market; he stops, mutters some prayers, and receives his loaded cap gun from his armor bearer. He announces the starting day of the festival proper and fires a gunshot into the air. The start of the festival is usually the fifth **Nkwọ** day (**Izu ise**) from the day of sighting the new moon. After the gunshot, the spectators shout for joy, praising God for the successful announcement of the start of the festival. The wife of the chief priest, her relatives and friends rejoice for the successful announcement because it was believed that if the chief priest stumbled on any object and fell before the announcement, he would die, and the festival would not hold in that year.

4.5f: The Hunting Festival

In the olden days when hunting was the main occupation of **Ihe Shikeaguma**, most of the meat needed for **Ani** festival was got from hunting on **Nkwo** market days during the festival month. Any surplus game killed by a hunter was sold on the following **Eke** market day by exchanging it by barter for some other food stuff for the festival. In this way hunters had meat and some food stuff while farmers had food stuff and some meat.

When the population of **Ihe** community grew and food production technics improved, the desire for better celebrations of the hunting festival increased. The villages of **Ihe** community were grouped according to cultural ties into four units for the purposes of rotating the hunting festival and facilitating the exchange of visits and gifts during the festival. The cultural units according to age are: **Ụmụọgbee, EnugwuOke, Ẹnugwuẹgụ/ Awkụnanọ, and Enugwuechi. Ụmụọgbee** as the eldest unit usually took the first turn on the first **Eke** market day after the announcement of the start of the festival. On the three subsequent **Eke** market days, the other three groups of villages took their turns according to their ages. Members of each group invited friends and relatives from the other groups of villages and entertained them in their homes before taking them to **Eke** market. In the market, hunters presented their arms in a single file to show their preparedness for the festival, their combat readiness for battle and proficiency in hunting. The hunters dressed like warriors, carrying loaded cap guns on their shoulders and swords on their right sides. On their left sides were bags containing bottles of gun powder and tins of gun caps. Some hunters carried skulls and skins of animals killed during the hunting season.

After the hunting parade and display of arms the men retired to their market stalls to entertain their friends with palm wine. On the fifth **Eke** day after the announcement of the day of the festival, all the four cultural groups of villages celebrated together the closing part of the hunting festival (**Mgbagba nta**). This celebration was a rehearsal of the **Shikeaguma** hunters/hero's day parade which was yet to take place in four days' time.

4.5g: Day of Taking the Cattle Home

In the olden days when young cows dedicated to **Ani Ihe** deity were allowed free range in the town, their mature males were caught, tied up and taken home on **Afọ ọchụchụefi** for slaughter at **Ani Ihe** shrine on the following day. Also, other dedicated mature male animals such as lambs and he-goats were all caught and tied up on this day for slaughter.

As the population of the people grew and dependence on farming increased, giving free range to all animals was prohibited in **Ihe Shikeaguma**. Dedicated animals were put under the care of those who offered the animals. On this day of leading the cattle home, the keepers of these animals catch the mature males and tie them up for slaughter at **Ani Ihe** shrine the following day (**Nkwọ Ani Ihe**). Pledged animals are also tied up for slaughter on this day by the traditional worshippers who pledged to sacrifice the animals. Bulls, lambs, he-goats and cocks bought for sacrifice at **Ani** deity during the festival are also tied up for slaughter. Final arrangements are made on this day for the slaughter and sharing of the meat of all these animals for the festival. Exchange of gifts like palm wine, yams, animals, dressing apparels and money starts on this day between in-laws, relatives and friends.

4.5h: Day of Slaughter of Animals

Early in the morning on this day, various animals are slaughtered in every home for the festival. The meat is cut into various traditional parts for gifts to kinsfolk, in-laws and friends while some of the meat is reserved for the family kitchen. Keepers of cattle and other livestock for **Ani Ihe** deity take the mature males that were caught and tied up the day before, to **Ani Ihe** shrine where they are slaughtered and shared according to **Ihe Shikeaguma** tradition. Traditional worshippers who made pledges to sacrifice animals to **Ani** deity for keeping them alive till the current year's festival, for protecting them through a period of illness, for giving them a favor, or for averting some danger or illness in their lives converge at **Ani Ihe** shrine with the pledged animals. Some of them wait for hours on end because the priests have hundreds of pledged animals to sacrifice to the deity. The worshippers take the waiting in good faith as part of the sacrifice.

Sociocultural organizations such as clubs, age grades, unions and other groups of people that jointly bought animals for the festival come together early in the morning to slaughter and share the meat of the animals. In the market one finds it difficult to move about because of all sorts of food items displayed for sale, especially live animals, bush meat, and various types of drinks, brought in from the neighboring towns. Palm wine tappers and traders do a lot of brisk business on this day as they hawk their goods from one place to the other. Housewives struggle in the kitchen to get various types of food ready before noon when festivities are at the peak. Dishes of tapioca, rice, **yam-foofoo**, etc. are prepared for the family and the guests.

After mid-day meals, small dance groups of children in all sorts of colors and uniforms go around from house to house to entertain guests. Sporadic gunshots are released in the villages by men warming up for the hunters/heroes day parade. Along the **Enugu – Awgu** old road that passes through the community, daintily dressed ladies and young men are seen visiting friends or going from one shop to the other. On this day, most people stay in their homes entertaining guests from other towns.

4.5i: Shikeaguma Hunters / Heroes Day Parade
On this day (**Eke Ani Ihe**), we have the climax of events in the festival. The people celebrate the memorial of bravery and combat readiness of their ancestors and those inter town struggle days when this exhibition and memorial sent warning signals to neighboring towns that were nursing the thought of going to war with **Ihe Shikeaguma**.

Early in the morning the **Ikpa** war dance usually wakes people up with its calling tunes. Hunters and inter town war heroes are heard in different villages answering the calling tunes of the war dance. Also praise singers are heard extolling war veterans and popular hunters in their poetic tunes, reminding them of the importance of the day's outing. As these warrior leaders move out with swords (**nmaọbọ**) in their side-scabbards and loaded cap guns in their hands, they run to the early morning **Ikpa** war dance to shake off the previous day's alcohol hang over, in preparation for the hunters parade later at **Eke** market. On arrival at the war dance arena, the hunter's horn calls the heroes one after the other, reminding them of their past exploits. The heroes acknowledge the horn's praises with loud frightening battle-cries, followed by their gunshots into the air, before going down on the war dance twists and jumps. Sporadic gunshots warm up the already hilarious festival air.

The early morning **Ikpa** war dance goes on while some people are busy slaughtering animals to provide meat to be used as gifts or for the preparation of food for expected guests. Part of the meat is reserved for the next day which is the day of respite to all animals. Guests arrive by noon carrying kegs of palm wine and other gift items. Women are seen in every home serving entertainment hurriedly to the guests to ensure that they are not late for the hunters parade at **Eke** market.

Some guests arrive **Ihe** on the day before and sleep over, to be able to arrive at the market early enough to occupy vantage positions from where to witness the beginning and end of the hunters parade. As the men are busy dressing up at home in their battle attire, well dressed guests move fast to **Eke** market to take vantage positions before the hunters arrive.

Heroes and hunters in the parade look fearsome in their loin clothes, belly armor-belts, multicolored hats, and painted faces. Some of t h e m carry the skulls or skins of some animals like tigers, leopards, deer, antelopes, and monkeys as proof of their hunting skill. Most of the hunters carry cap guns on their shoulders, sheathed swords by their right sides and bottles or boxes of gun powder in the bags hanging by their other side. Few of the hunters who have no guns carry spears, clubs or only swords decorated in multi colors.

Hunters of each village come together in their village square or an agreed place from where they take off in a single file, singing war songs as they match to **Eke** market. The villages that arrive earlier do not go into the market. They wait at their **Eke** market entrances for other villages to arrive. Various war songs and battle cries are heard from these village groups while waiting for other hunters to arrive. No hunter releases any shot while waiting for others. When majority of the villages arrive at the market entrances, the parade leaders signal to the villages to match through the traditional route round the market before entering the center of the market square. As the hunters are encircling the market with deafening war songs, each village group tries to be louder than the others. Currently the market stalls are full of excited children, women and guests.

When the parade completely encircles the market, the parade leaders blow their horns as a signal to those hunters with guns to come to the center of the market square, with their guns pointed to the sky. When the leading warrior or hunter, at the center of the market square fires a shot into the air, every hunter in the square fires his gun into the air. A deafening sound of gunfire fills the air for some time, followed by a blanket of choking gun-powder smoke that initially covers the sky but descends later, on the spectators and hunters on the ground.

Some women and children stop their ears with their fingers while the shooting is going on, but later cover their nostrils and eyes with their palms from choking smoke. The deafening sound of gunshots are heard several miles away from **Ihe**. After the first round of gunshots, some hunters reload and fire more rounds into the air till they are done with firing. They retire to their stalls to join their friends and relatives in their merriments. As the parade splits after the main shooting of cap guns, groups of age grades, singing war songs are seen in front of village stalls with their guns dancing to the tunes of **Ikpa** war dance and making various hunting and battle movements that culminate in gunshots into the air. At this stage of the parade, guests from distant places leave the arena for home. Some women and children reluctantly leave with the guests while the men continue with merriments and firing out their remaining gunpowder until they are left with one or two shots with which to announce their return home from the hunters' parade.

When the sun sinks into the western horizon, the next day which is the day of respite to all animals (**Oye udene**) is expected. Elders ask all the people in the market to quietly leave the market and go home in peace, to avert any injuries or the spilling of any human blood on the land. Finally, the parade ends, and the hunters walk home in small groups; some singing; some mute with tiredness and some swagger silently on their way home after being soaked with palm wine. As darkness falls, sporadic gunshots in the villages announce the safe return of the heroes and hunters to their respective homes.

4.5j: Day of Respite to Animals
In precolonial days, the entire fifth lunar month of **Ani Ihe** festival was a solemn period when our ancestors who were traditional worshippers dedicated the lives and property of every **Ihe Shikeaguma** person to **Ani Ihe** deity for protection. It was a period of peace and was an abomination to steal or destroy the property of any **Ihe** person. All land disputes were put off. No human blood was spilled on the land. Natives of **Ihe Shikeaguma** did not go to war unless they

were attacked first, by the enemy. During the slave trade, no **Ihe** native could sell another **Ihe** person. No one could sue his neighbor to any court of traditional law, for an offence committed during this solemnity.

In the wisdom of our ancestors, and in the spirit of the festival, they extended one day of peace to all the surviving animals whose kin were hunted down and killed during the period of the festival. They allowed them a day of respite on **Oye udene** day. On this day no animal was killed either at home or by hunting in the bush. **Igbo** tradition sees the vulture as a ritual messenger of the gods during **Igbo** worship ceremonies. Based on the above reason, the name of the vulture (**Udene**) was used for this solemn day of respite as **Oye udene**. Secondly there was usually plenty of meat on this day after two days of slaughtering animals in every home; and scraps of meat were available for vultures that swarmed the villages during this period. Up till today, the **Ẹdẹ** activities which included; the runs, the jumps, the assessment of youth population, and the leaf-plucking exercise take place in **Ihe Shikeaguma** in four centers at the same time on **Oye udene** day. These centers include:

* **Obodo Ụmụọha** for **Ụmụọgbẹẹ** village.
* **Ọkpa-atụ** grounds for **Enugwuoke** kindred.
* **Ọzala** grounds for **Ẹnugwuẹgụ** kindred.
* **Obodo Ukwu** for **Enugwuechi** kindred.

Since the activities performed in these centers are about the same, I shall concentrate on the activities at **Ọkpa-atụ** grounds. On this day of respite, the tender palm frond (**Ọmụ**) which is a symbol of peace is carried by every youth on his way to the **Ẹdẹ** games arena. If any youth is seen on the way to the games without this symbol of peace, other youths approach him in a friendly joking way, to remind him of the symbol, after which they give him one frond or part of it. These fronds are carried for the whole day until everybody throws his frond and **Ẹdẹ** leaves around the base of the **Ẹdẹ** tree, as a mark of the end of the youth activities of the day of respite. The tree rests for two years, after which the leaves are plucked again during the next day of respite.

Early in the morning on the day of respite, the xylophone music (**Oge**) reminds the youth that the day is for youth games. All able-bodied young men run to the **Ẹdẹ** grounds to dance the xylophone music and to play other games, till mid-morning when they go home to prepare for the remaining **Ẹdẹ** activities later in the day. When the youths return to the **Ẹdẹ** grounds in the afternoon with their palm fronds, they stand in a single line, with their backs on the **Ẹdẹ** wall. Strangers, women and girls stand or sit under the shades at the northern, western and eastern fringes of the arena as spectators.

While the **Ẹdẹ** games-leaders are being awaited, and the arena is being filled with surging youths and spectators, some jesters entertain the spectators. **Udene fenegbo ọda** "diviner" and his assistant who carries his divination basket (**Abọ**) round the arena reminding those traveled members of **Ihe Shikeaguma** community who could not return for the festival that one day something will force them to return. As the acting diviner talks, he shakes his iron scepter (**Ojji**) and strikes it on the ground with the force of certainty. **Udene fenegbo ọda** is an **Ihe Shikeaguma** saying which means that, "no matter how high a vulture flies, it must one day come down to the ground". Some young boys act girls. They dress like girls, talk like girls and behave like girls. While the jesters are busy entertaining the spectators, some **Ẹdẹ** veterans with palm fronds in both hands and belly armor belts run along the **Ẹdẹ** inner wall to greet the youths who have come for the youths' day activities. As they run along the wall in front of the youths, they sing the **Ẹdẹ** anthem, **Ụmụ Ẹdẹ nmili eyine ọba** and the youths reply with a loud and drawn, **Nmili, nmili eyine ọba.**

The **Ẹdẹ** walls which are centuries old were made to protect early farms from domestic animals, when cattle, sheep and goat rearing was the major profession of some members of **Ihe Shikeaguma** community. During that time those animals were allowed to wander about free range in the villages. The four feet inner wall which started from **Ọgbụlụgbụ** grove and made a westward "c" curve ended at **Ụmụẹbẹkẹ** road. It included an area of land equal to about four football fields, which is the **Ẹdẹ** arena. It usually accommodates hundreds of youths standing side by side on the wall. Behind this inner wall is three feet footpath which runs from **Uhueze** through the **Ọgbụlụgbụ** grove to **Ngene Ọgba** stream in **Ụmụsike** village. On the other side of the footpath is another four feet mud-wall enclosing another area of farmland which extends to **Ụmụsike**. Both parcels of land are usually tilled and cleared, ready for the **Ẹdẹ** games, and for the planting of early yams, which takes place after the festival.

As the **Ẹdẹ** veterans make the **Ẹdẹ** runs to greet the youths with the **Ẹdẹ** anthem, another group of two or three veterans who had jumped the walls in the past arrive with palm fronds in both hands and belly armor-belts around their trunks. They also sing the **Ẹdẹ** anthem while the youths reply with even louder refrain: **Nmili nmili eyine ọba**. As they run in front of jubilant youths waving palm fronds along the length of the inner wall, they signal for wall-jumpers to come out. The youths who volunteer to jump do so at their own risk because any jumper who does not clear the two walls gets bruises from the centuries-old dry mud-walls and is booed by the spectators. Those who jump the walls without bruises are hailed and feted as youths of the year. They are cheered by thousands of on lookers who watch from the fringes of the arena. Symbolically, the two walls represent features such as, trenches, gullies and brooks that men jump in war fronts or hunting expeditions while chasing the enemy or animals. In this jump, youths demonstrate their maturity to take part in warfare or in hunting expeditions while the elders look on to take note of prospective hunting and battle materials.

While the **Ẹdẹ** jumps are going on, the leader of the **Ẹdẹ** games arrives with a loaded cap gun in the company of two men; and the youths return to the inner wall. He starts running from the western end of the **Ẹdẹ** wall to the eastern end inspecting the youths' line-up on the wall. As he runs, he takes note of the youth population and compares it with past years' population limits. This youth-population assessment helped the community during the inter-town war years, to take strategic decisions within the next two years.

As he runs past hundreds of jubilant youths waving palm fronds, he sings the anthem; **Ụmụ ẹdẹ nmili ẹyine ọba**, and the youths respond with a long-drawn refrain; **Nmili nmili ẹyine ọba**. This prehistoric anthem is a prayer by the leader, that the youth games (the floating calabash) may never sink. On coming to the end of the wall, he makes straight to the center of the arena with his entourage. At the center of the arena he mutters prayers of thanksgiving to God, the minor deities and the ancestors for the well- being of the youths.

He fires a gunshot into the air, and the **Ede** run, from all corners of the arena starts; hundreds of youths moving to a point; and the **Ẹdẹ** tree is the target. Now the youths reach the **Ẹdẹ** tree (**an ọgilisi** tree surrounded by shrubs) and the struggle to protect the topmost branch from being torn to shreds by the surging youths starts. Each person struggles to pluck at least a leaf from the tree. Plucking a leaf from the **Ẹdẹ** tree is like winning a medal.

The scene of the struggle is unforgettable to those who watch, as the sweating, grunting, dust- haired young men at the bottom, with their arms raised or linked in an effort to climb, support a human pyramid surging to the top of the tree. The tree sways to and from with the weight of climbers, but one of the youths invariably makes it to the top, whether it takes him a few minutes or half an hour. For the fastest youth who reaches the top first, to protect the tree-top main branch, the memory of scaling the tree and the week of glory that follows, as he is feted like a war leader, remain strong. He holds on tightly to the treetop protecting the tallest branch; and sways from one side to the other, as the youths tear-down the remaining branches to pieces. Late arrivals to the tree snatch some leaves from those who got many leaves.

The **Ẹdẹ** tree-climb helps to build team spirit in a struggle among the youth. After the climb and the eventual tearing down of the lower branches of the tree, the youths raise their leaves or branches above their heads as they run around the **Ẹdẹ** arena chanting the anthem. Elders watch from the fringes of the arena, to assess the community's prospective fighting force and its team spirit. The **Ẹdẹ** climb has occupied a hallowed place in **Ani Ihe** festival tradition for centuries. For the **Ihe Shikeaguma** youth, the climb represents a true test of survival of the fittest. At the end of the jubilation some of the spectators and some youths leave for home while some other youths go to dance the **Ukpoko** dance till sundown, when everybody leaves for home.

Youth games festivals are held all over Igboland, especially during annual festival periods, in different forms, in line with the tradition and physical environment of each community. Many **Igbo** communities have several village squares, water fronts, pools and games-grounds in addition to their compounds, where different games are played by both young and old, for amusement and for competition. In the riverine areas, apart from indoor games, swimming, paddling and fishing contests are held. In upland areas, indoor games include different forms of seed games (**Okwe**), and other games like, hide-and-seek, folk tales and guessing games. Out-door games include running, jumping, climbing, hunting, wrestling, shooting, boxing, dancing, masquerading and swinging with vine-stems in sacred groves reserved for traditional religious purposes.

Games in **Igbo** culture play an important role in informal teaching and learning and prepare the **Igbo** youth for the life of competition which marks out the **Igbo** as a courageous and aggressively enterprising individual.

4.5k: Day of Bones

The four days of festivities that constitute the second and main part of **Ani Ihe** festival, start with the day of leading the cattle home (**Afọ ọchuchuefi**), and goes through the day of slaughtering animals (**Nkwọ Ani Ihe**), the hunters/heroes day parade (**Eke Ani Ihe**), the day of respite to animals (**Oye-udene**), to the day of eating bones (**Afọ ntacha ọkpụkpụ**). Early in the morning on the day of bones, the flute wakes the youths up reminding them that the day is the day of wrestling at the **Ẹdẹ** arena. The flute is blown from village to village showering praises on wrestling veterans who organize the age grade wrestling competition and reminding them of the second part of the **Ẹdẹ** youth activities which usually starts before sunrise.

The **Ẹdẹ** youth wrestling match is organized on age grade basis, unlike those of the annual wrestling festival (**Mgba Ajaeke** and **mgba Ajanwaafia**)

241

that were organized on village bases. Only young men between the ages of about 20 and 35 take part in the competition. At the **Ọkpa atụ** grounds, competitors come from the villages of **Enugwuoke**. The youngest age grade is made up of youths who are between 20 and 25 years of age. The second age grade is made up of those between 25 and 30 years while the third age grade members are those whose ages range between 30 and 35 years. This arrangement is aimed at fostering the spirit of peace in the youth wrestling activities and in the solemnity of **Ani** festival. It also forestalls inter-village bickerings arising from usual competition differences in judgement.

Each of these three age grades has its own group-leader. Each group stays together and acts together as if they were from one village. A person can wrestle with his own brother or anybody from any of the other two age-grades. When a member of an age grade wins a wrestling match, his age grade rejoices together and when a member loses in a combat, all the members of his age grade nurse their loss together. The winning of wrestling combats is important to each of the age grades but the main lesson of the age grade wrestling competition is that members of the senior age grade use this occasion to teach members of the junior age grades some wrestling tactics while members of the junior age grades exhibit their youthful exuberance and energy during the wrestling combats. The wrestling competition was designed by our ancestors to develop team spirit and comradeship in all struggles among the youths.

As noon approaches, the **Ẹdẹ** youths' wrestling match is concluded with the dancing of the xylophone (**Oge**) dance music by the wrestlers including those who lost and those who won in the competition. As the music plays the champions' tune; **Onye akpana nwagu aka n'ọdụ**, the youths sing the wordings. At this stage the wrestling veterans show their stuff; as they appear in their heroes' attire, wearing belly armor-belts which are champions' belts in **Ihe Shikeaguma** tradition.

The music stops briefly as a mark of honor to the heroes for their bravery; and starts again, calling the heroes by their praise-names. The heroes dance the heroes' tune which brings the competition to an end at mid-day. New friendships develop between wrestling combatants, and sometimes continue till later in their lives, to the extent that some of the youths organize return matches during future age grade wrestling competitions. As the day advances, festivities continue as usual and guests arrive from all directions.

The day of bones is not necessarily the day that only bones are eaten but it is the day when most of the meat from the slaughtered animals is used up; and most families have more bones than meat.

Families use this day to take stock of their leftovers of food. They use the day to entertain members of their families with whatever food left in their homes. On this day parents-in-law are entertained especially by newly married couples who have not yet got many children to care for. Some couples who cannot invite their parents-in-law for one reason or the other use the day to take presents of palm wine, yams and other foodstuff to them.

From this day some of the guests from distant places who arrived in **Ihe Shikeaguma** at the beginning of the festival start leaving for home. Some of them carry some leftovers of raw food items, meat and cooked food for the members of their families who could not attend the festival. With the major part of the festival over, some returnees from distant places, while waiting for the dance festival outings, organize political assemblies and fund-raising activities for community development projects. Some use the period to recruit school leavers for work outside **Ihe** community while others use the period to complete marriage arrangements for new wives. These arrangements are implemented after the final closing ceremonies of the festival.

4.5 l: The Dance Festival
The dance festival starts on the **Eke** market day after the day of bones. It is a rotatory event hence

the name, **Ogeoge** (turn by turn). Like the hunting festival the event rotates from **Ụmụọgbẹẹ** village on first **Eke** market day after the hunters/hero's parade and goes to **Enugwuoke** on the second **Eke** market day. On the third **Eke** market day, it is the turn of **Enugwuegu** and **Awkụnanọ** villages. On the fourth **Eke** market day, it is the turn of **Enugwuechi**. The final ceremony, **Nvugbe egwu** comes off on the fifth **Eke** market day.

During the period of the dance festival, members of the kindred whose turn it is to host the festival invite their relatives, in-laws and friends from other villages. It is a one-day affair. Guests start arriving early in the noon, to be able to finish their food and drinks before going to the market square for the dancing entertainment. This arrangement is considered hasty by some people who prefer to entertain their guests with food and drinks at **Eke** market where the dancing takes place, to avoid unnecessary haste on both sides.

In this case the market stalls of the kindred hosting the festival are turned into eatery houses on that day, with women scrambling for space. All sorts of food and drinks are available in surplus quantities. The villages hosting the dance festival take all their danceable music to the market. Any dance music that does not feature is packed up until the next two years when the festival holds again. Each dance troupe prepares for the day in a special way. Some of the troupes buy new musical instruments while some concentrate on new dance uniforms. The days of belly amour-belts, skulls and skins give way to days of colorful uniforms, except for a few ceremonial dancers of the **Ikpa** and **Nkwa** war dances that also feature on this day. Some men dress in their wrestling attire to dance the **Oge** and **Ukpoko** xylophone music. Some dress up in dance uniforms for the **Ọdabala and Ụbọ ọgazi** dance music.

Some elderly men and women dress up for the unisex **Opueke** dance. Middle aged women dress up gorgeously in the multicolored **Udu** dance uniform with wrist bangles, anklets, and rattling chimes. They wear uniform headgears or hairdos to match. Their faces, hands and legs are decorated with **Uli** tattoo designs on top of which skin creams are lavishly applied. Spectators fall upon themselves; some pushing and some pulling other spectators; to get a glimpse of these women dancers; who dance as if there is no other day to dance in their lives. The girls are not left out. Like their mothers they are well groomed and well dressed in their own dance uniforms.

They are the center of attraction in the market; the girls know that and add more grace to their movements and dance steps. Young men looking for wives do not go away from their dancing area till the dance is over.

All the villages of the kindred hosting a round of the dance festival bring all their dance troupes; and these dance troupes play their music at the same time. Spectators have a great variety from where to make a choice of what to watch and where to go. Some people spend the whole dancing time with one dance group while others scamper from troupe to troupe and from one village stall to the other to feast their eyes on different dance groups. After watching one or two dances some people spend the rest of the day eating and drinking in the market stalls. The stalls are busy throughout the day as dancers retire to the stalls whenever they become tired of dancing, in order to refresh themselves with eating and drinking. As the night approaches after sun set, dancers, spectators and guests walk home from the market in small groups. The music makers are seen carrying their musical instruments home, some on their heads and others on their shoulders.

4.5m: Finale of the Dance Festival

The final ceremony of the dance festival (**Nvugbe egwu**) comes up on the fifth **Eke** market day after the hunters' parade. Each of the eleven villages of **Ihe Shikeaguma** goes to **Eke** market with two dance groups; one group for men and the other for women. On this last day of the festival, each family head entertains himself and members of his family with food and drinks. After one month of sumptuous festivities, some people still reserve some extra food-items with which to entertain a few guests from other towns who could not attend the festival proper for one reason or the other. All the guests arrive early and converge at **Eke** market in the afternoon. Since this occasion is the formal closing ceremony of **Ani Ihe** festival, entertainments with food and drinks are generally light and guests are fewer; but the feeling of satisfaction is visible on everybody's face.

As the guests arrive in the afternoon, they are entertained in the market stalls before they come out into the market square to entertain themselves with watching various dance groups. Eating and drinking go on in the market stalls while dancing continues outside in the market square and in front of the village market stalls. Lovers of dance music who know that the closing ceremony provides their last dancing opportunity for the season dance their heads out, sweating profusely until they are tired of dancing.

The respected **Opueke** dance music which is the oldest unisex dance music in **Ihe Shikeaguma** is usually danced by titled men and women. Each pair dances four tunes before giving way to another pair of titled man and woman. After other dance groups have stopped dancing in the market at sunset, the **Opueke** dance music continues with its trumpets initiating song tunes while the dancing men and women sing the words. Spectators from other dance groups that had stopped dancing join in the songs. All the songs refer to suggestions that as festivities are over everybody should be ready to go to the farm. One of the tunes played is the **Otegbulu welu ẹjụ** which means that after that final dance everybody should pick up the pad. The pad is a small circular pillow placed on the head or shoulder before placing a load of farm tools, planting materials or yam-stakes for the farm. At the end of the **Opueke** dance the men hug the women and everybody leaves the market for home in a very happy mood. Some elderly men and women continue singing on their way home. Some are full of prayers of thanksgiving to God and **Ani Ihe** deity, for keeping them safe through the period of the festival, while others discuss the entire festival or the closing ceremony.

4.5n: Igbo Festivals

From prehistoric times the **Igbo** community was not organized as one political entity under one legal or administrative head. Each of the **Igbo** clans existed and functioned as an autonomous entity in no way subject to any other political authority from outside the clan. Consequently, **Igbo** traditional festivals did not take place on the same days or in the same form throughout this culture area. Each community or clan had its own timing; held its own version of the festivals and determined the activities in each festival in line with its local sociocultural convenience. Apart from the **Ani** and **Fiajioku** festivals, there are other festivals in Igboland, during which time the **Igbo** relive their past; honor their ancestors and deities; or initiate some youths into one cult or the other. These cult festivals include child presentation to the goddess of fertility festival (**Aja ọmụmụ or Ofili**), youth clothing festival (**Iwa akwa**), masquerade festival (**Oku mmanwụ**), etc.

All these festivals had been handed down to the present generation from the ancestors who started the festivals thousands of years ago. Surprisingly there has not been major changes in the festival timing, program, and spirit of most of the festivals except that recently some modernity has been shown in the mode of dressing, entertainment and religious beliefs in the festivals. Some Christians take part in those areas of the festivals that do not involve idol worship rituals while some prefer to stay away completely from the public outings of the festivals because most of these Christians spent the greater part of their lives in towns outside their culture area, and were not properly taught at home in their childhood on how to take part in these activities. The returnees concentrate their efforts and funds on socio-political meetings, conferences, annual assemblies and fund-raising activities for community development purposes, as innovations to **Igbo** festival activities.

4.6: INFORMAL EDUCATION

Education in a traditional **Igbo** setting started from prehistoric times and has been informal. The System has always aimed at giving a functional education to every **Igbo** child to prepare him for a meaningful adult life. In doing this, it set out to bring every child to the knowledge and worship of God, and to recognize the existence and functioning of **Igbo** tradition and its social status structure. This teaching though informal started at birth and continued through adult life. **R. O. Ohuche** made this observation.

> *In its original form, traditional education among the Igbo people was in the main out-of-school education. There were no formal schools, but the homes served as congenial "schools" where children did not have to travel to be educated. Teaching was informal, practical, utilitarian and geared to the needs of society. The curriculum was undocumented and unwritten, but it had to do with the welfare of the individual, the overall needs of the society and the roles which young persons were to be trained to fulfil.*[30]

When a baby is born, the close mother-and-child bonding that started during pregnancy continues during the maternity confinement period of seven

---

[30] **Ohuche** (1991), **Ahiajoku** Lecture, page 24

native weeks (28 days). The baby is in close body contact with the mother and is fed with her breast milk throughout the confinement. In this way the mother becomes the first human acquaintance and teacher of the baby. Naturally the baby's first lesson is to recognize the mother's body scent, her voice, and appearance as against those of other people, hence some babies cry when carried by other people. Soon the baby is able to communicate with the mother by reacting to smiles, frowning of the face, hugs, sounds, taste, light etc. At this stage the mother starts with teaching the baby how to cope with the basic issues of life such as, drinking, eating, stooling, bathing, playing, sleeping etc. She introduces other members of the family such as the father, the brothers and sisters to the baby by handing the baby to them with smiles that communicate mother's approval to the baby.

As the baby grows into childhood, the number of its teachers and role models increase. Apart from the early lessons imparted by parents, and other family members, the child through observation and imitation learns how to talk, walk, tell stories, worship, run messages, cook and keep the house. Through his association with his peer group and friends in his community, he learns how to play games, sing songs, dance and socialize with other members of his community. In his effort to learn a trade as a life pursuit, the **Igbo** child goes into apprenticeship with a relative or a friend of the family, where he learns the occupational skills of that trade. Among those trades from where he chooses are farming, smiting, carving, trading, building, fishing, hunting, divination etc. In some areas of Igboland, certain trades are learned by children through their parents' professions as basic education. In the riverine areas for instance every child learns to swim, paddle and fish while in the upland areas where farming is the main occupation of the people, every child learns to hunt and farm. In those other areas where land is either not good enough or unavailable for farming, some parents take to trading, smiting, carving, pot making, or building as their occupation, and their children learn these occupations by imitation. In this way education continues at home and at work within the community, during job orientations and training, sociopolitical participations, and inductions into certain cultural organizations.

The **Igbo** social status structure is the main pillar of **Igbo** social life and is taught to every child before he/she grows into a full adult. The **Igbo** kinship statuses of father, mother, husband, wife, brother and sister become important lessons to every child. In the day to day activities of the family, the emphasis of male precedence and seniority by birth or marriage in all responsibility and honor roles are taught to the children from their earliest childhood. As they grow up into adults, they are made aware of **Igbo** emphasis on kinship, residential, occupational, associational, wealth and political statuses that have regulated **Igbo** community life from prehistoric times. Each child is taught where he/she belongs and how he/she should relate with others in the community

Inductions into certain traditional cults start from birth and continue to adult age. A baby's first induction is the initiation into the family during the baby's naming ceremony after the appearance of the first tooth; then the initiation into adult hood during the clothing (**Iwa akwa**) ceremony; up to the initiation into parenthood through marriage ceremonies. Initiations into other organizations like dance groups, masquerade cults, religious dedications, and socio-occupational guilds take place at any time between childhood and adult age.

Since the early part of the nineteenth century when Europeans colonized African communities and introduced formal education in primary, secondary and tertiary institutions, the teaching of children by their parents at home has lost some emphasis. Nevertheless, the **Igbo** traditional system has continued at home with those aspects of cultural education that do not receive full integration into the colonial education system. In early formal school days, for example, greetings, songs, stories, games, and counting, that are learned at home in early childhood in the vernacular help the children to start off well at school by providing them with ideas which are associated with their early primary education. The benefit of good home upbringing of children is realized in school during the early days of primary school. This emphasizes the importance of proper parental influence and upbringing at home which **Igbo** traditional education insists in giving to every child right from birth.

In all formal school systems, an important home influence exhibited by each **Igbo** child is that of discipline which traditional education cultivates at home in line with **Igbo** concepts of community life. The **Igbo** concept of work as an honorable and traditional means of meaningful existence prepares the **Igbo** child to easily adapt with manual and mental work assigned to him in school or in the community in later life. In early adult life, these **Igbo** orientations start to manifest in the youth. He starts to exhibit the usual **Igbo** love and ambition for learning and embarking on profitable ventures that facilitate his acquisition of wealth and the exulted status one gets through its leverage.

In addition to all the above the **Igbo** child is taught at home to be self-reliant, honest and hardworking. This home acquired training rather than the effect of formal school education produced those good qualities of the **Igbo** that impressed the earliest Europeans who enlisted the services of **Igbo** youths in colonial and mission work in every nook and cranny of Nigeria.

Reuben K. Eneze

Irrespective of the practical job training and inductions of children into various traditional cults and occupational guilds for worthwhile behavior in adult life, this traditional system of education had its short comings that slowed down the emergence of an earlier **Igbo** civilization. Lack of a developed form of writing in **Igbo** culture for the purposes of recording and preserving innovations and findings, prior to the advent of Europeans, hampered an earlier growth and spread of **Igbo** craftsmanship or what one will call "**Igbo** technology" in today's terminology. Consequently, the traditional **Igbo** system of education lacked sufficient innovative expositions and transformations needed for an earlier fast development of an **Igbo** civilization. However, some skills and technical innovations were cultically preserved and protected orally by families and individuals as the only way of preserving those findings, with the result that such knowledge or parts of it was lost to posterity at the death of such families or individuals.

Luckily some of the innovations and findings of those yester years have survived the long period of oral preservation and are found in available human work of the **Igbo**. In agriculture, **Igbo** ancestors who inhabited the Scarp lands of south eastern Nigeria as far back as 100,000 BC, through empirical innovations developed metal diggers and small hoes for making contoured ridges where they planted yams and vegetables on the stony hillsides while large hoes were developed for making large hemispheric mounds for the planting of yams at the water-logged flood basins. Through careful breeding they developed many species of yams, vegetables and animals.

In medicine various types of herbal medicine in balls, powder, paste or liquid for the treatment of different types of ill-health and for use as cosmetics were developed. Some of these herbal medicines are still used today in Nigeria as alternative medicine.

In building, specially prepared soils were used in building compound and house walls that survived many decades of heavy weathering. Conical roof frameworks were made of bush poles and vine ropes; and covered with dry grass or palm frond matting. The roofs were protected from insect attack and decay with wood fire smoke fumes from inside the buildings. Some of the roofs lasted for decades before renovation.

Building walls and floors were usually finished with red earth and decorated with murals and mosaic designs using plant stones (**okwe**), silica pebbles (**aja iyi**), etc. In art and craft, the recent archeological investigations that located heaps upon heaps of stone tools and weapons at **Ugwuele** in Igboland, dating back to about 500,000 years ago has shown the extent of the artistic experimentation and innovations undertaken by **Igbo** ancestors.

In weaving, the raffia and oil palm trees that are indigenous to Igboland supplied various types of fibers from their leaves and roots for weaving various domestic articles and utensils. The stem of the cane plant was used for weaving various items of furniture and domestic utensils. Sleeping mats were woven with dry strips of the leaves of the **Abụba** plant and other reeds while their fibrous stems were split into fine strings for making ropes. The waist brace (**aji**) which was made from the tough fibers of the fig tree (**ọgbụ**) was reinforced by drying and has been used as belly armor belt in tribal war combat operations from prehistoric times till the eighteenth century.

Igbo ancestors developed clothing materials from animal skins and the raffia palm leaf fiber (**ẹgwọ**) which was woven into raffia cloth (**avụlụma**) used as loin cloth and for bag making. They later discovered cotton from the cotton tree (**akpụ**), another indigenous forest plant and wove narrow strips of cloth (**ịgba or ọgọdọ**) used as men's loin cloth. Some strips of the cloth were sewn together with thread into wider cloth (**obolo**) for women. Although this wild cotton was difficult to spin, still it provided the best weaving material for the time. When other types of cotton that were easier to spin into yarn were introduced through barter trade with **Igala** traders during the **Nri** civilization, **Igbo** traditional weaving continued with some improvements till the eighteenth century when European traders visited the west African coast with better spinning devices and wider looms for weaving wider and better cloth.

Smiting, iron smelting and bronze casting which were developed in Igboland before AD 900 were among the many innovations that could have projected **Igbo** craftsmanship into world repute before the advent of Europeans, were it not for the absence of a developed form of writing and lack of good communication network within the West African zone. In government, the **Igbo** practiced traditional democratic governance which had the ancestor as a focal point of origin and source of titular leadership many centuries BC as explained in chapter 2.3e of this book.

Formal education is now a primary project of every family and government in Igboland. Many primary, secondary, and tertiary institutions are available to **Igbo** youths who have fully embraced education because of the exposure to economic and political power it bestows on the educated. The **Igbo** concept of competition as a task where his motto is: (I.G.B.O.) "I go before others", has propelled him to greater heights in education with the result that he can now favorably compete with those of other tribes in Africa who embraced formal education half a century before him.

In his observation on **Igbo** pioneer education, Professor R. O. **Ohuche** (1991) has this to say:

> *The Igbo considered education a most fruitful and useful investment. No sacrifice was too much for an Igbo to make to secure education, not only for his own children and immediate relatives but also for other intelligent children in the community.*[31]

4.7: TRADITIONAL LAW

Igbo tradition (Omenani), which is the established **Igbo** way of living was enacted by the ancestors and handed down orally from one generation to the other in order to enhance compliance with societal peace and harmony. **Igbo** ancestors stipulated the way things are done as tradition (**omenani**) and what must not be done in a typical **Igbo** community as abomination **(Nsọani)**, with regards to the protection of the fundamental rights of a person in relation to his life, birth, marriage, worship, work, inheritance, property, residence, death and burial.

---

[31] **Ohuche** (1991), **Ahiajoku** Lecture, page 31

The violations of these fundamental rights of an individual or community as in abortion, murder, manslaughter, incest, arson, stealing, destruction of private or public property, are considered abomination in **Igbo** tradition.

In precolonial days these violations attracted heavy punishments like hanging, banishments and heavy fines in addition to ritual cleansing. Minor or partial violations such as abandonment of parental care of a child, fighting, damage or misuse of another person's property, minor theft, encroachment on private or public property, etc., attracted reprimands, fines, payment of compensation and isolation from the community, where necessary, until redress was made. Through these laws of the land, redress for grievances was obtained as an expression of fair play and justice in the community.

In **Igbo** culture, from prehistoric times, the ancestors are regarded as intermediaries between God and man. It is believed that the jurisdiction of ancestors as family heads was assigned to them by God, and that no one has the power to change his ancestor or relocate his spiritual and secular jurisdictions over his descendants. This belief explains why many **Igbo** villages and towns are named after the ancestors as in, **Ụmụeze**, **Ụmụagụ**, etc. Based on this belief, the **Igbo** do not toy with their traditional laws that were handed down orally to them by the ancestors through **Igbo** elders, who are regarded as titular heads and **Ọfọ** holders of the community. In **Igbo** culture, **Ọfọ** stick which is a staff of office and a symbol of fair play is believed to bestow on the elders the custody of justice, truth and fair play as representatives of the ancestors.

The elders in the discharge of their titular duties to the community either as lawgivers or judges believe that they are accountable to God, the minor deities and the ancestors, but not to any temporal ruler or force. **Igbo** traditional concept of life and property is that they come from God **(Chinenye ndụ/akụ)**, and **Igbo** traditional law insists that both must be protected from violation at all costs in order not to incur the anger of God. It was this violation issue that often led to inter-community wars in the past.

The **Igbo** has freedom of worship, of thought, of speech, of pursuit and of movement but no one has the freedom over his own life or that of another person because the **Igbo** believes that all life belong to God **(Chi nwe ndụ)**. This is why the body of any person who takes his or her own life in **Ihe Shikeaguma** for instance is treated like the body of a condemned criminal. The body is hurriedly buried in the bush without any burial rites or ceremonies. The **Igbo** holds human blood as sacred and whoever spills human blood even in self-defense commits a serious crime against God and the ancestors. Such a person must undergo ritual cleansing and show some form of repentance. In **Ihe Shikeaguma** for example, people who killed the enemy in fighting during the intertown wars were hailed as heroes, yet they were taken straight from the war front to the shrine for ritual cleansing (**Igwa aka**), before joining their families at home

Since the **Igbo** see their community as one extended family, various laws were made by the ancestors to protect the interest and welfare of every member of the community. Culturally the **Igbo** treat every homestead as sacred because of the number of shrines of deities established in it and the bodies of ancestors buried in it as in **Ihe Shikeaguma**; consequently, various traditional laws were made to protect the homestead from being violated by strangers and residents alike. Many community facilities such as land, streams, markets, civic centers, farms and homesteads were protected with the establishment of shrines; and rules that regulated ownership, usage and upkeep of such facilities. Any violation of any of the above facilities needed one form or the other of cleansing, plus the appeasement of the deities, the ancestors or the community. Each community or clan in Igboland has its own version of the **Igbo** traditional law and has its own forms of redress and appeasements for various grievances and offences.

In the olden days in Igboland, punishments for offences against traditional law were humane but strictly enforced. The elders who were judges were firm and fearless but fair in their judgments of others because they believed that they were accountable to God and the ancestors; and were bound by the same traditional law to be fair in their judgements. In making the traditional laws our ancestors who believed that God was a merciful God (**Chukwu onye ebele**) had humane options for all punishments especially the most serious ones.

In **Ihe Shikeaguma** for example, when a murderer was to take his life by hanging, usually there was an option of banishment for life from **Ihe** community and **Ntuegbe** clan. He was also allowed to choose the time and place of his hanging or town of his exile. However, he was not allowed to hang in any home including his own home because homesteads in **Igbo** culture are sacred and belong to the ancestors. Also, he was not allowed to hang in any public facility or shrine. If he refused to hang himself or go into exile within the time frame allowed to him, he was then forced to comply with the community's choice of time and place for any of the two options of punishment deemed appropriate by the community elders.

In view of the seriousness of punishments attached to abominations, several other laws were made to forestall the occurrence of those situations that resulted in the occasion of those crimes. In those days minor violations of the law were visited with punishments varying from cutting off one ear or one finger for notorious criminals and cautions, whippings, and fines for first offenders; if sufficient remorse was shown for the violations. In recent times in Igboland, there are many forms of redress for grievances or damages. They include cautions, public apology, replacement of damages, loss of some freedom, or complete excommunication from the family or community, until enough repentance is shown, and appropriate fines are paid. These measures are in addition to police and court actions taken on criminal violations that cannot now be handled by the community.

4.8: COMMUNITY SERVICE

Community service in **Igbo** culture which aimed at the welfare of the extended family and the community started in prehistoric times in **Igbo** settlements and has survived hundreds of centuries of oral handing down from generation to generation. It was a product of the extended family system and has since provided social security, social mobilization and social harmony among the **Igbo** without the need for a monarchy, a formal police force or army. The **Igbo** social structure encouraged the idea of living together for a culture of mutual protection and communal participation of every member of the **Igbo** community in all projects that enhanced the well-being of the community.

During their morning prayer (**Ọjị ụtụtụ**), and sacrifices, elders who were respected in **Igbo** culture as representatives of the ancestors prayed for their children, their extended family and their community. They ensured strict adherence of the people to **Igbo** tradition by acting as consultants and judges on such issues that related to worship rituals, inheritances, marriage, and traditional law. Every **Igbo** elder treated every child in the community as his own child and called each child by the pet-name, my child (**Nwam**). The elders believed that they were accountable to the ancestors on how they looked after the children of the community in relation to their adherence to **Igbo** tradition.

The running of errands by children for elders of the community was mandatory as a starting point for community service in **Igbo** culture. All children owed a debt of respect and appropriate greetings to elders and leaders. As the children grew up into young adults, they got more involved in community service by joining age grades and handling such community services as the sweeping of village squares, shrines, access roads, marketplaces, water fronts, etc. The age-grade and trade-guild systems were some of the social organizations crafted by the ancestors to enhance the mobilization of the society for the execution of community service. Each age grade struggled to creditably complete any community project assigned to it.

Also, each trade guild ensured that its own contributions were registered in the execution of community projects. Every individual **Igbo** tried in one way or the other to give free service to other members of the community by receiving only token compensations in those services where he/she worked as, a farm hand, craft person, health practitioner, diviner, priest, musician, baby-sitter, house help, etc. Individuals who lived outside their ancestral areas provided funds and material assistance for the upkeep of elders at home and for the implementation of their community development projects. Services rendered by every **Igbo** to the community were not measured or paid for by the community in money terms but received with great appreciation, recognition and eventual elevation of the giver to a status of honor in the community.

Community service took priority position in the day to day life of the **Igbo**. Community projects such as defense, firefighting, public works, delegations, communal religious worship, burial ceremonies, and political assemblies were considered as more important than personal projects or commitments. Every **Igbo** traditionally abandoned personal commitment to attend to community issues whenever they arose. Women were not left out in community service. They were always vigilant as informants (**Ẹgẹbẹ**) and collected security information that was strategic to the community's security needs. Whenever the security of the life or property of any member of the community was threatened, as in a fire outbreak, robbery, animal or enemy attack, any woman in the vicinity raised an alarm and continued a distress call, sometimes at the risk of her life. This distress call went from woman to woman and reached the ends of the community in minutes.

On receiving this distress call, hunters blew their horns asking all men to be armed in the case of a robbery, animal or enemy attack. Some of the hunters hastened to the community's exit roads where they laid ambush. All able-bodied men who heard the call for assistance abandoned whatever personal commitment on hand; took whatever weapon available and ran to the part of the community in distress. Even old men who could not run raised threatening shouts to whatever was causing the distress and encouraged the able-bodied men to deal ruthlessly with whatever was causing the distress. In a matter of minutes, the place in distress was full of armed men surging from all the corners of the community. On arrival everybody joined in the effort to remove the distress without minding the cost of the exercise or asking for any remuneration from the person or persons involved in the distress.

From the fore-going one can see that the **Igbo** community's social security, social mobilization, social harmony, political and economic power were in the hands of the people and not in the hands of any monarch, hence the saying; **Igbo** are not ruled by kings **(Igbo enwe Eze).** The **Igbo** were not ruled by kings, but they had good, selfless and democratic leaders that ensured the effectiveness of community service and the survival of the **Igbo** nation for centuries.

When the British took over political administration in Nigeria, they admired the effectiveness of the **Igbo** traditional system of community service and recognized or appointed some local leaders as warrant chiefs for the purpose of mobilizing the people for colonial service rather than the political administration of the people. Expectedly most of the chiefs remained essentially mobilization and ceremonial instruments of the British government.

4.9: RELIGION

4.9a: Spirits
For the purposes of clarity and emphasis, let us revisit Chapter 3.6 of this book on the issue of **Igbo** belief in the existence of spirits.

> *Igbo ancestors that lived in south-eastern Nigeria of West Africa, at least as far back as 100,000 BC had very strong belief in the*

existence of spirits. Igbo culture through its myths and folk tales suggests that man's first encounter with spirits was probably in his dream. He noticed that he had two personalities or selves at sleep; the one that lay asleep in bed; and the one that went out at the same time visiting distant places, meeting strange people, and sometimes his dead relatives and friends. This second personality or self, took part in adventures with dangerous animals and unknown phenomena in distant places but came back to unite with the sleeping self in a split second at man's wakefulness. Man was perplexed yet desirous of making more contacts with this second self or personality in order to know him better. He called this his second self, mụ ọzọ; a name the Igbo later shortened to, mụọ' for spirit.

The more the **Igbo** ancestor tried to know the ways and true nature of his second self (**mụọ**), the more he met deeper mysteries about him. This effort in his thought propelled him to conjecture that there must be a third personality or guide that made the smooth working relationship at sleep between his two personalities or selves possible. He called this third personality, **mụ ọma**, (my welfare) for guardian spirit. His spiritual journey to the unknown, in search of the origin of the guardian spirit probably led him to the revelation of the existence of the spirit world that originated through the wisdom of an original, powerful and skillful spirit-designer of his two personalities, the guardian spirit and man's physical environment. He called the spirit-designer, **Chiukwu okike,** (Supreme spirit-creator), and his guardian spirit, **chi** (minor spirit of God). The revelation established in him the concept of a spirit-king that controls both the spiritual and the physical worlds.

4.9b: God as Spirit King

Our ancestors imagined this spirit king in human form, and since then have tried to relate with him and other spirits in practical human ways through animate and inanimate intermediaries. This desire to relate with the spirit-king (**Chiukwu okike**) and other spirits (**Ndị mụọ**) was the beginning of **Igbo** traditional religion. The **Igbo** from prehistoric times have given reverence to God as a supernatural king, accepted as creator and governor of the universe. These concepts of God are enshrined in **Igbo** names like, **Chukwudi** (God exists), **Chibụeze** (God is king), **Chika** (God is supreme) etc. Also, the **Igbo** reverence to God can be seen in other names like, **Chukwuebuka** (God is great), **Chiamaka** (God is good), **Kelechi, To-ochi**, or **Ja-Achi** (Praise God) etc.

4.9c: Human Interactions with Spirits

The **Igbo** spiritual awareness led them to a number of human interactions with spirits through the instrumentality of dreams, trances, prayers, prophecies, divination and sacrifices that resulted in their making of physical images of some of these spirits which the **Igbo** worshipped as idols many centuries before Christ. The **Igbo** belief that the happenings in his world are controlled by God is seen in **Igbo** names like, **Mụọneme** (It is the work of the spirit), **Mụọneke,** (The spirit creates life). Traditionally this spirit is the spirit of God. In view of this awareness the **Igbo** is traditionally a prayerful individual. He makes one form of petition or the other to God or the ancestral spirits before important projects in his life.

Before the advent of Christianity in Igboland, it was mandatory on every male family elder, usually recognized by **Igbo** culture as head of the family, to say the morning prayers (**Ọjị ụtụtụ),** in order to reaffirm his belief in God and the ancestors, and to ask for the realization of the traditional **Igbo** aspirations of life (good health), love, peace, wealth and children, on behalf of his family and his community. It was also mandatory on him to perform the meal rite of offering food **(Itụ aka/Igọ Nri)** to God and the ancestral spirits who were believed to be watching the family at meals. On the part of women, it was mandatory on every married adult woman to perform the early morning oblation of washing the face (**Isa ihu / iru),** outside the compound gate.

During this exercise, the woman woke up early in the morning before greeting anybody; took a bowl of water to the outside of the compound gate; washed her hands and face; thanked God, the minor deities and the ancestral spirits for preserving the lives of all members of the family during the night. She then prayed for the protection of the family during the day. After this oblation she went back to her house, prepared a pepper paste (**Ose ọjị**) for eating kola nuts, and joined her husband in the morning prayers (**Ọjị ụtụtụ**).

In **Ihe Shikeaguma**, women performed the annual cleansing rite (**Ichụ afọ**), to cleanse the community of evil spirits who were believed to cause misfortunes, illness and death. This exercise took place early in the morning on last **Nkwọ** market day of the first lunar month of the year (August), before the appearance of the new moon for **Ọgbụlụgbụ** festival. Before the day of the cleansing exercise, elderly women of the town organized themselves in a small representative group and sacrificed a hen to **Ọgbụlụgbụ** deity on behalf of their villages for the protection of all the women who took part in the exercise.

Every woman who was going to take part in the cleansing exercise went to the shrine of her guardian spirit (Chi), with a bowl of water and prayed for her protection during the exercise. On the day of the cleansing exercise, each adult woman woke up at first cock's crow, as early as 4:00 AM or 5:00 AM with an already provided palm frond stump in her hand and her loincloth firmly tied around her waist. She knocked the stump on the ground, and this produced a loud explosive sound. In a loud voice she commanded all evil spirits in the compound to leave. She continued knocking the stump on the ground as she shouted the command loudly as in a chase. She continued the chase with the words of cleansing, **Gbuo! Gbuo! Gbuo-o-o**! (Kill the evil spirits), until she came to the village square where all the women converged, with their stumps in hand. The village women continued the chase singing the cleansing words loudly and knocking the stumps on the ground as they moved until they reached another meeting place of all the women of the kindred. From this meeting point of each kindred the women took the chase to **Ekwunatọ** lake where they believed that all the evil spirits got drowned. The women took the cleansing bath and left for home quietly.

During the cleansing exercise, there was observance of complete lights out in the town. All males and children stayed in their homes until the women returned home. It was believed that by staying in the way of the women, one incurred the anger of the deities and could also encounter escaping evil spirits. Also, all women were warned to be careful in their chase of the evil spirits because it was believed that any woman who fell during the chase died within the year and did not live to take another chase. This chase was based on the images of spirits painted in the minds of **Igbo** earliest ancestors during their encounters with spirits in dreams and trances. The ancestors originated the cleansing of evil spirits as a means of protecting the community from the uncertainties of life. The imperfection of the human mind and the hazy nature of images painted in dreams and trances made the interpretation of these mental experiences difficult for the ordinary man, and thus created a need for talented people to interpret these mental images for the common man.

4.9d: Interpretation of Mental Images

As interpreters of mental images; dreamers, seers, diviners, and oracles emerged, and have since played very important roles in the establishment and maintenance of **Igbo** traditional religion. They interpreted their own spiritual encounters; and other peoples' experiences, when consulted. They usually contacted or assembled the affected people whenever they had a need to deliver a spiritual message. Some of these meetings resulted in the establishment of avenues for group interactions with the spirits, such as prayers, sacrifices, appeasements, pledges or the establishment of new deities, for the protection, direction or guidance of the people, especially during uncertain times like the period of famine, wars, epidemics, disasters and other emergencies.

4.9e: Dispensation of Health Care Services

The dispensation of health care services in **Igbo** culture was our ancestors' primary preoccupation aimed at solving their health problems. Their spiritual awareness led them to believe that some of their health problems needed supernatural interventions; and that God in his wisdom endowed some people with special mental, spiritual and physical talents for the enhancement of man's continued existence on earth. Their various spiritual and physical efforts resulted in the discovery of treatments for some of their health problems.

In their sustained effort and training to discover effective ways of handling their health and social problems, they developed their talents further and had schools of thought on various issues of mental and physical health. In those days, the **Igbo** practitioners of these schools of thought on health care were respected in **Igbo** communities and called, **Dibia** (person trained in the healing art). These practitioners on their own part recognized their healing services as rendered in the service of God who endowed them with their talents hence, they accepted token rewards for their services.

By AD 800, **Eri**, the ancestor of **Nri** clan arrived in Igboland by sailing down the **Anambra** River, according to **Nri** myth of their origin. He settled at **Aguleri** and from there he introduced a new version of God worship which merged with the existing **Igbo** traditional religion. He strengthened **Igbo** traditional precepts with new concepts and moral values. The **Nri** spread a ritualized kingship system on both sides of the lower Niger; developed a more unified worship system in **Igbo** traditional religion; and introduced new ways of treating ill health in Igboland.

They established moral codes and punishments for the violations of these codes. They perfected the business of divination and established several oracles with ubiquitous agents that were used as **Nri** scouts for the enforcement of their moral codes and value systems that left indelible stripes on **Igbo** traditional religion and **Igbo** culture in general. Through the enforcement of these moral codes, **Nri** agents, **Nri** migrant traditional priests, and **Nri** diplomats stabilized **Igbo** economy and sustained **Nri** civilization for nine centuries, AD 800 to AD 1700. Two important legacies of **Nri** civilization are the improvement of the healing art, through the introduction of new herbal treatments for both mental and physical health, and the development of **Igbo** culture into a highly ritualized and symbolic culture.

4.9f: Health Care Practitioners
Among the practitioners in the traditional healing schools in **Igbo** culture today are:

* Diviner or fortuneteller (**Dibia afa/dibia agwụ**): He predicts future events or recalls past events for a reward. He is usually consulted in his home or invited to other people's homes. Itinerant diviners and fortunetellers are common features in traditional **Igbo** spiritual and social systems. The **Igbo** diviner or fortuneteller uses one of such media as: Seed-stones of a plant (**Mkpụlụ afa**), seashells (**Eze azụ**) kernel of **ụkpụkpa** fruits (**ụkpụkpa**). In using any of the above media, he recites an incantation and juggles the medium for signs which he interprets to his client as his predictions. He also uses other media for divination.

He recites an incantation; draws lines or curves on the floor with white chalk (**nzu**) and interprets the drawing as his predictions.

He recites an incantation, looks into a bowl of water and makes his predictions to the client.

He recites an incantation while looking at a mirror and makes his predictions.

There could be other media in other areas of Igboland but one common feature of divination in **Igbo** culture is that there is usually a recitation of an incantation before any prediction. The recitation among other things includes a plea or exhortation for assistance to **Agwụ** deity believed to be responsible for spiritual consultations and predictions. Another common feature is that most predictions are accompanied with prescriptions for thanksgiving, sacrifices, appeasements, reparations, restorations or pledges to show gratitude for good times or to pacify the deities or malevolent spirits for past misdeeds.

* Oracle priest (**Dibia mmụọ/dibia agbala**): He serves as a soothsayer in the shrine of an oracle. Unlike the itinerant diviner, all his predictions are made within the shrine of an oracle where the media for predictions are installed or stored. In some oracles a group of diviners constitute a predictions council that handles difficult spiritual and social issues. During the **Aro** civilization, for example, the **Ibunu Ukpabi** oracle predicted future events; recalled past events; and judged inter persons and inter community cases. It passed stiff sentences that ranged from heavy fines to death penalties on those found guilty. Other **Igbo** oracles that had identical powers were: **Igweka ala** of

Ụmụnneọha, **Agbara** of **Awka**, **Amadiọha** of **Ozuzu**, etc.

* Worship priest or administrator of sacrifices (**Dibia aja**): He executes the prescriptions of diviners and fortune tellers by offering prayers during traditional sacrifices (**Igb'aja**) to ancestral spirits or deities on behalf of other people. In **Igbo** culture, he is usually an itinerant priest and a powerful prayer warrior.

* Juju priest (**Dibia nsi**): He offers occult, magic and fetish services to those who consult him for assistance. He also prepares amulets and charms as a talisman against evil or injury, and for the spiritual control or harm of another person.

* Herbalist (**Dibia ọgwụ/dibia mgbọlọgwụ**): He collects, prepares, and administers herbs for the treatment of ill health. In **Igbo** culture, there are other herbalists who specialize in other areas of herbal medicine such as, collectors and manufacturers. Collectors plant or collect herbs for sale to other herbalists who use them directly or manufacture drugs with them for the treatment of ill health. They usually have shops or market stalls where they sell their herbs. Manufacturers collect or buy herbs and process them into herbal powder, balls, pills, balms, pastes, or liquids as drugs for the treatment of ill health.

Since there were no clear-cut controls or licenses for the various providers of health care services in those days, there were abuses and false claims by some health practitioners who worked as diviners, administrators of sacrifices, providers of occult services and herbalists, all at the same time. Consequently, health practitioners in Igboland were judged and rewarded by each client in accordance with the quality and efficacy of the practitioners' services rendered to the client. On the other hand, there were devoted practitioners who specialized in the treatment of only one type of ill health such as, mental illness, broken bones, bad sight, etc. There were well known and respected magneto paths (witch "doctors") who cured snake bites and scorpion stings by rubbing the area of the bite or sting while reciting an incantation. In this category of traditional health specialists were the traditional nurse practitioners **(Di ime)** who delivered women in labor; **(Di ugwu)** who circumcised babies and those that attended to the prenatal and post-natal needs of mothers. These traditional health specialists were well rewarded and patronized in **Igbo** communities.

From the foregoing one can see that religion and health care are interwoven in **Igbo** culture because religion for the **Igbo** is meant to ensure the spiritual and physical wellbeing of the individual. However, the inconsistencies in the availability and dosage of herbal medicine, and the use of ritual practices in the administration of herbal treatment by some practitioners have reduced patronage of traditional medicine in recent times. Also, the advent of Christianity and modern medicine since the beginning of the 19th Century have reduced emphasis in the use of herbal medicine for the treatment of ill health in Igboland. Fortunately, the Nigerian Federal Ministry of health has set up licensing authorities for assistance and quality control, in the manufacture and dispensation of herbal medicine, now widely known as alternative medicine in Nigeria. Currently, some Christian church leaders in Igboland encourage its adherents to use or administer herbal medicine as gift of God, where necessary, if the usage or administration is not accompanied or associated with any traditional religious rituals or incantations.

Since the Nigerian Federal Ministry of Health set up licensing authority for quality control of alternative medicine, many enterprising Nigerians have invested large sums of money in the manufacture and marketing of alternative medicine in pills, powder and liquids.

The ventures have provided work for many unemployed youths and has by so doing helped to strengthen the economy of the people; and in the treatment of various types of ill health in Nigeria.

Chapter Five

SYMBOLISM IN **IGBO** CULTURE

5.a: OBJECTS AND EXPRESSIONS

Objects and verbal expressions in **Igbo** culture have socio-cultural or religious symbolisms. These objects and spoken words are also used as symbols or instruments of **Igbo** philosophical expressions and concepts. Since many **Igbo** communities have different dialects, they also have variants of symbolic significances of the same objects and expressions. The symbolism of most of these objects and expressions are as old as **Igbo** language and culture while some of them were introduced and ritualized by **Nri** civilization which lasted for about nine centuries, AD 800 – AD1700.

These symbolic objects in their natural state should not be seen as items of idol worship; unless, or until they are ritualized by a priest in **Igbo** traditional worship with an invocation or incantation; and with the blood of a sacrificed animal; or placed in the shrine or altar of a deity; otherwise the object or the expression relating to it symbolizes ordinary philosophical expression in **Igbo** culture. A young palm frond (**ọmụ**), for instance can be ritualized by an **Igbo** traditional priest during idol worship.

Equally it can be ritualized by a Christian priest during Palm Sunday or Ash Wednesday ceremonies. Ordinarily a young palm frond (**ọmụ**) can be used for tying wood or other household items. In an ordinary and natural sense also, the **Ọfọ** stick (**Osisi ọfọ**) for example is wood and can be used as such in the house and in the farm. The expression: **Ejim ọfọ** (I hold **Ọfọ** stick, while claiming my innocence) without holding the **Ọfọ** stick in hand is an ordinary **Igbo** philosophical expression and not a ritual statement. When a ritualized object is held in one's hand and is invoked or physically placed on a public property or a personal belonging as a protection for that object, the ritualized object represents the deity associated with it and becomes an item of worship. To give examples of symbolisms in **Igbo** culture, I shall briefly comment on ten objects.

5.b: Ọfọ Stick (Osisi Ọfọ)
(A ritualized piece of stem or stalk of **Ọfọ** plant) is a symbol of authority and justice, and a medium for petition in prayer. **Ọfọ** stick is traditionally given and accepted in **Igbo** culture as a royal staff of political authority to titular heads, titled chiefs, and elders as well as elected or appointed community leaders obliging them to be fair but firm in their service to the people. During a swearing-in exercise in recent times in **Ihe Shikeaguma**, **Ọfọ** stick is given to non-Christians and the Bible to Christian leaders. **Ọfọ** stick is also

given by the chief priest as a staff of spiritual authority to initiate diviners and priests in **Igbo** traditional religion. Long before the advent of Christianity in Igboland elders installed the **Ọfọ** instrument as a staff of spiritual authority of **Ani** deity over all the other deities and communities in Igboland. Each community usually invoked this staff after the institution of new laws and traditional agreements that were required to be binding on all.

In **Ihe Shikeaguma** before the advent of Christianity, every adult male who had a family or a homestead of his own, had an **Ọfọ** stick installed ceremoniously as his own staff of political and spiritual authority over his household. The family head or any holder of the **Ọfọ** stick was traditionally authorized to invoke this staff as his last line of spiritual defense and authority in all matters affecting his household or domain if he felt that he was not fairly treated. Whenever a staff holder was forced to invoke his staff, the family or community met and whoever was found guilty of offending the staff holder was bound to appease the **Ọfọ** staff ritually as recommended by the elders. If a non-staff holder felt that he was ill-treated, he was free to consult a staff holder who could invoke the **Ọfọ** staff on his behalf. The staff could also be invoked in prayer whenever the holder made any solemn petition to the deities or the ancestors.

5.c: The Kola Nut (Ọjị) is a symbol of **Igbo** hospitality. The kola nut is traditionally presented to a guest as a symbol of cordial reception or acceptance in an **Igbo** family or community. It is also traditionally used as a medium for making a plea or petition during traditional prayers, at socio- cultural ceremonies of marriage, title taking, lease or purchase of land, settlement of disputes, etc. There are two major types of kola nuts in Nigeria. The first type is the traditional **Igbo** kola nut (**Ọjị Igbo**) which is produced mainly in Igboland. It usually has between three lobes and as many as seven lobes. The second type which is produced mainly in Yorubaland but eaten mainly in Northern Nigeria (**Ọjị Hausa**) usually has two lobes. Since this type of kola nut usually has only two lobes, it is not used for prayers in **Igbo** traditional religious rituals and ceremonies.

The overall conceptualization of the kola nut among the Igbo is that it is a life affirming principle. (Onye wetara ọjị wetara ndụ). [32]

Based on this concept the symbolism of the numbers of kola nut lobes gives affirmation to life in **Igbo** culture as follows:

---

[32] E.N. **Onwu,** (2002) **Ahiajoku** Lecture, page 20

* Three lobes of a kola nut symbolize the **Igbo** concept that the three main physical purposes of human existence on earth are; life, wealth, and children.

* Four lobes of a kola nut symbolize the four market days of the **Igbo** native week. The **Igbo** concept of life on earth in the terms of a marketplace (**Ụwa bụ afia**) where we come to sell or buy and return home to spirit land at the end of our stay on earth, reminds the **Igbo** that life on earth is not forever.

* Five lobes of a kola nut symbolize the five fingers of the right hand (**Ikenga**). In **Igbo** culture the right hand (**Ikenga**) symbolizes fortune and industry that give birth to wealth which makes life worthwhile on earth. Also, five lobes symbolize the five realizable aspirations of the **Igbo**: Life, love, peace, wealth and children. Although the **Igbo** believe that life, wealth and children are the three most important physical reasons why man is on earth, they also believe that life must be nourished with love and protected with peace, so that wealth can be created for human life to have a meaningful sojourn on earth.

* Six lobes of a kola nut symbolize the **Igbo** belief in the six forces of creation that

determine the individual life trait of every human being on earth:

1. The force of the right hand (**Ikenga**) facilitates hard work and industry.

2. The force of the tongue (**Uho/ufo**) gives one eloquence

3. The force of the face (**Ihu/Iru**) gives one an imposing personality.

4. The force of the feet (**Ụkwụ n'ije**) leads one into adventure.

5. The force of acquisition (**Ọkụ**) facilitates the preservation of wealth.

6. The force of memory (**Akọ n' uche**) gives one common sense and knowledge. During the **Nri** civilization, AD 800 – 1700, these personality traits were ritualized and transformed into personal and group cults in all the areas of **Nri** influence.

* Seven lobes of a kola nut symbolize approaching good fortune especially for the person who broke the kola nut. In **Igbo** culture this good omen is usually celebrated in anticipation of the good fortune.

The Kola Nut Rite

In **Ihe Shikeaguma**, the kola nut rite has four parts; the presentation of the kola nut, the breaking of the kola nut, the kola nut prayer, and the sharing of the lobes of the kola nut by both the host and the guests.

The Presentation of the Kola Nut: The kola nut is traditionally presented by the eldest male or   a titled adult male among the hosts in a bowl to the eldest male or a titled adult male among the guests in every ceremony. When the eldest male or a titled adult male receives the kola nut, he thanks the hosts and presents the kola nut to his fellow guests starting from the next eldest male. If the guests are from different communities, the holder of the kola nut starts the presentation with the eldest community and passes it round until it comes to the youngest community. If there are many kola nuts, the elder gives out one kola nut each to an adult male from each community represented in the gathering, starting with the eldest community.

The Breaking of the Kola Nut: The guest elder having recognized the communities represented in the gathering with a gift of a kola nut, now returns the kola nut bowl to the host who appoints the youngest adult male from among his own community to break his own kola nut on his behalf; and to produce the bud of the kola nut (which is the life of the kola nut) to the elder who appointed him.

This is done to ensure that the kola nut is alive and worthy for offering. If the bud of the kola nut (**Ile ọjị**) was eaten up by weevils or the kola nut has less than three lobes, it is usually rejected as not good enough for the offering in prayer and another kola nut is produced as a replacement. If the bud is alive and the kola nut has more than two lobes, the bud is given to the elder for the kola nut offering in prayers (**Igọ ọjị**).

The Kola Nut Prayer: When the eldest male or a titled adult member of the host family finally receives the bud of the kola nut, he inquiries about the number of lobes of the kola nut. He announces the symbolism of the number and goes on to say the prayers in the **Igbo** language. He calls on God the creator (**Chukwu okike**) to accept the kola nut offered to him. He also calls on the clan and town deities; other spirit forces such as the sun and the oracle (**Anyanwụ n'agbara**), the ancestral spirits (**Ndi ichie**), and the market days (**Eke, Oye, Afọ** and **Nkwọ**), to also accept the kola nut. He affirms **Igbo** belief in the above spirit forces and prays for the purpose for which the kola nut was presented, and for the realization of the five aspirations of the **Igbo**; life, love, peace, wealth and children. At the end of the prayer, the onlookers give their affirmation to the prayer by saying: "**Ise-e-e**" (May our above mentioned five aspirations be realized).

The Sharing of the Kola Nut: The man who broke the kola nut takes one of its lobes. He shares the remaining lobes to others starting with the eldest man who said the prayer or representative of the eldest community and goes on with the sharing until the kola nut lobes go around. Since the kola nut is a symbolic food, the lobes can be cut into as many pieces as the number of people present. In **Igbo** culture, a woman does not break the kola nut during a kola nut rite, but she can share the kola nut lobes after the kola nut has been broken and the prayer said by a man.

5.d: Alligator Pepper (Oseike or Oseọjị)
The alligator pepper is a symbol of energization. In **Igbo** culture it is traditionally presented with kola nuts by host or guest as a symbol of stimulating intensity in preexisting relationships such as blood relationships, close friendships, or reverence to deities and ancestors. In **Igbo** traditional worship, it is also offered to stimulate amulets, charms, and such deities like **Ngwu** or **Agwụ** to action after a plea, a petition, or an exhortation, to such deities.

5.e: Spear (Alọ)
The spear which is a symbol of valor was carried with the sharp end turned up-wards by **Igbo** warriors as a decoration for bravery and as a defense weapon before and during the arrival of **Eri** (Ancestor of **Nri** clan) to Igboland. In peace time and during

sociopolitical ceremonies, the sharp end was usually covered with a soft piece of wood by the warrior to avoid injury to others, but the spear was always handy. During this time every adult male usually carried a sword or a machete for protection against wild animals and bandits.

5.f: Spear of Peace (Aloeze or Ojji)

The spear of peace was a symbol of diplomatic immunity. During the **Nri** civilization, peace was paramount among its precepts hence it was pacifist and never attempted expansion by force of arms. It was taboo to spill human blood on the land in all the areas of **Nri** influence. For this reason, the spear had four or eight chimes attached to it to alert all and sundry of its presence. It was carried by hand and by every **Nri** agent, priest or diviner with its sharp end to the ground, as part of his diplomatic paraphernalia for easy passage throughout Igboland.

5.g: Tribal Face Marks (Ichi)

Tribal face marks were symbols of tribal identity and allegiance. **Nri** agents and diplomats were decorated with these face marks as diplomatic immunity for free passage in and out of **Igbo** settlements during their business missions.

5.h: Red and Yellow-Wood Body Paint (Ufie and Edo)

The red and yellowwood body paints were symbols of friendship and diplomatic immunity before the advent and during the early years of European influence in Nigeria. During the **Nri** and **Aro** civilizations in Igboland, emissaries and diplomats on friendly, political and trade missions carried either or both of these two body paints in balls or powder for their hosts as diplomatic presents from their community heads. Pawns, men and women, being handed over to creditors usually carried carmine wood body paint in ball or powder for the creditor. This gesture meant that the pawn should not be sold as a slave by the creditor until the debt is paid back and the pawn freed. If the pawn was a female, she could be married by the creditor or any of his relations without any further bride price paid on her. Travelers who had to pass from one community to the other presented carmine- wood body paint from their community head or elder as diplomatic present to the head or elder of each community or settlement, who usually gave them free passage and safe handover to the next community as royal emissaries.

5.i: White Chalk (Nzu)

White chalk is used as a symbol of happiness, spiritual power or retreat depending on how and where used. When a child is born, white chalk powder or paint is rubbed on the face by relatives and friends of the family as a sign of happiness. During festivals and marriage ceremonies, white chalk body paint decorations are made by women especially young teenage girls. Fortune tellers rub white chalk paint around one eye as a symbol of their spiritual power. White chalk is also one of the media for divination in Igboland. In **Igbo** culture, when a white chalk line is drawn by a peace maker between two feuding parties, a note of warning for retreat has been served. It is a declaration of physical or spiritual war against the other party for any of the feuding parties to cross the chalk mark. Traditionally, other marks such as stones or plant beacons do represent the white chalk marks for the separation of disputants during land disputes in Igboland. Important diplomatic and traditional religious guests, especially **Nri** and **Igala** agents and priests, in those days were received with kola nuts and a bar of white chalk.

5.j: Young Palm Frond (Ọmụ)
A young palm frond is a symbol of peace in **Igbo** culture. When a piece of land is disputed, the aggrieved disputant sticks a young palm frond conspicuously on the land to sue for a peaceful settlement, and to warn any intruder to keep his distance from the land until settlement is given by the elders. In any fight or struggle, if one side raises the young palm frond, he is taken to have surrendered or sued for peaceful negotiation. In peace keeping, if the peacekeeper raises the young palm frond, the feuding parties stop fighting and listen to the peacekeeper. In the absence of the palm frond, the right hand is raised in its place by the peacekeeper.

The peacekeeper could be an elder, the community head or any agent of the community assigned to that job. In sociopolitical ceremonies, if participants are told to carry the young palm frond, the message so expressed is that absolute peace is anticipated in the ceremony. On the other hand, the young palm frond (ọmụ) can be hoisted prominently in the center or at the entrance of the arena. In a community ceremony or assembly, if a participant or an observer has a piece of the young palm frond between his lips, the message so expressed is that he is incommunicado and should be left alone.

During the offering of a sacrifice, the young palm frond (ọmụ) is usually waved above the head to invite vultures to come down in peace to accept the sacrifice on behalf of the deities and ancestral spirits. Anybody who harms the vulture that comes down on this invitation incurs the anger of the deities and the ancestors.

5.k: The Vulture (Udene)

During a traditional sacrifice in Igboland, the arrival and eating of the sacrifice by a vulture symbolize acceptance of the sacrifice by the deities and ancestral spirits hence the **Igbo** saying that: "During a traditional sacrifice if a vulture does not come, the implication is that the sacrifice is rejected by the spirits".

I wish to conclude this chapter by looking at language and writing as other means used by the **Igbo** in representing their thought and ideas before the advent of European influence in Igboland. By 3000 BC, **Igbo** language had developed into an advanced stage recognizable as different from other Lower Niger languages. As a result of local differentiations in sociocultural developments, varieties of dialects, mutually intelligible emerged and became a means of sharing ideas and translating the oneness of the **Igbo** as one people.

As a symbolic culture, **Igbo** culture developed some means of putting thought and ideas into some form of graphic or pictorial writing on human skin with plant pigments as **Uli;** on walls with charcoal, chalk and colored soft stones as murals; and on floors with silica pebbles (**aja iyi**), shells (**Eze azụ**), and plant stones (**okwe**) as mosaic. After AD 800, **Nri** civilization introduced **ichi** and **nke** tattoo marks as diplomatic or cult symbols. During the **Aro** civilization AD 1700 – 1850, slaves, trade cattle and initiates into cults were given graphic tattoo marks to identify them. These ideographic signs and symbols had not developed into a pan **Igbo** form of writing before the Atlantic slave trade disrupted the up-and-coming pan **Igbo** civilization in the eighteenth century

Chapter Six

The Influence of Civilizations on Igbo Culture

6.1: UGWUELE CIVILIZATION

We are going to have a look at the influence of the **Ugwuele** civilization on the socially transmitted behavior patterns like arts, beliefs, institutions, and other human work and thought of the **Igbo** and the Lower Niger peoples. From the work of archaeologists, linguists, and historians, one is led to believe that the **Ugwuele** settlement was inhabited by the earliest ancestors of some of the lower Niger and West African peoples for some centuries before they moved out to other settlements. On this settlement at **Ugwuele** and its environs, during the centuries of their habitation and interaction, they must have developed a distinct Stone Age culture or civilization with one language, art, belief, and occupation, before their ancestors moved to their different present-day settlements.

At the **Ugwuele** settlement, they had developed the prototypes of such behavior patterns as arts (in the stone artifacts discovered by archaeologists), language (in the lower Niger languages that have words that are cognates), religion (in the lower Niger traditional religion based on belief in God the creator, and in intermediary spirits); and occupation (in the development of yam culture as the main focus of their farming). Some of the earliest ancestors of the lower Niger peoples left **Ugwuele** with some of the cultural influence of the **Igbo** who stayed behind at **Ugwuele** settlement and its environs and developed these prototypes for the present-day **Igbo** culture. Nwachukwu in his **Ahiajoku** lecture (2003) takes us to **Chikwendu's** archaeological work (1991):

> *Using evidence from the relatively few archaeological investigations that have been so far carried out in Igboland, Chikwendu has shown that all three sub periods of Stone Age culture existed in Igbo prehistory. Early Stone Age culture, also termed Acheulian, has been found at the archaeological site at Ugwuele, in Uturu Okigwe. This culture flourished between 1,000,000 and 500,000 years ago. The discoveries at Ugwuele consisted of heaps upon heaps of stone hand axes. The extent of the site and quantity of stone artifacts found led experts to believe that a hand axe factory existed at Ugwuele. The age and extent of this hand axe factory make Ugwuele Stone Age site a legacy of the entire human race as it is evident that a stone Age civilization flourished there.* [33]

---

[33] **Nwachukwu,** 2003 **Ahiajoku** Lecture Page 8

Onwuejeogwu (1987) takes us to the possibility that the lower Niger people lived together some where before their dispersal and developed one language that now has its cognates in most of the Kwa languages.

> *The lower Niger languages (Kwa languages) extend along the Guinea Coast, from Liberia to Cross River of Nigeria and inland for about 320 kilometers.... It is hypothesized that those languages have a common stock because they have common basic words which are cognates.*[34]

Major Leonard (1991) in his book, "The lower Niger and its peoples", ties the lower Niger people together as a people with an original religious belief when he said:

> *They are in the strict and natural sense of the word a truly and a deeply religious people, of whom it can be said that they eat religiously, drink religiously, bathe religiously, dress religiously, and sin religiously.*[35]

Echeruo (1979) takes us to the development of yam in West Africa as far back as the period before 100 BC:

---

[34] **Onwuejeogwu,** 1987 **Ahiajoku** Lecture Page 9
[35] **Onwu,** 2002 **Ahiajoku** Lecture Page 1

The large-scale introduction of iron in West Africa dates from about 300 AD. At least four hundred years before that (100 BC) several species of yam and oil palm were already firmly established in the forest and woodland regions of West Africa.[36]

Onwuejeogwu (1987) takes us from the **Ugwuele** settlement to the Scarp lands (**Enugwu**) civilization and its Iron Age economy.

The Nsukka-Udi civilization is hereby referred to as the civilization of furnace. In its earliest form, about 4000 years ago, it is contemporaneous with the Afikpo, and both might have evolved from the Ugwuele forms. The late Stone Age evolved in the development and diffusion of this culture which gave rise to a rich civilization characterized by iron industry, agrarian, and commercial economy based on marketing of iron implements, elephant tusks, ivory bracelets and horses from the North.[37]

---

[36] **Echeruo**, 1979 **Ahiajoku** Lecture Page 9
[37] **Onwuejeogwu**, 1987 **Ahiajoku** Lecture Page 45

6.2: NRI (NSHI) CIVILIZATION

The **Nri** civilization which flourished for about nine centuries (AD 800 - AD 1700) was one of the greatest and most stabilizing events in the history of the **Igbo** nation. It was believed that its legitimacy derived from belief in God the creator (**Chukwu Okike**) which the **Igbo** had earlier accepted as God of the **Igbo** centuries before the emergence of the **Nri**. One important contribution of **Nri** myth of their origin towards **Eri**'s religious belief, and the emergence of **Nri** civilization, is its allusion to **Eri**'s possible contact with Egyptian or Jewish culture before his arrival at the **Anambra** River basin. This allusion suggests that **Eri**'s ancestors might have migrated Southwards from North Africa during the drying up of the Saharan lands about 2000 – 1500 BC. The North African influence gave **Eri** the idea of a sacred kingship, slavery, human sacrifice, and a new version of God-worship which was rampant among the Jews of that time but new to earliest **Igbo** culture.

The earliest Jewish history has it on record that: God asked Abraham, a Jew, to sacrifice his son, Isaac, and Abraham consented to the instruction about 1,900 BC. God fed the Jews from the firmament with manna in the desert on their way from Egypt to Palestine about 1,300 BC. There were kings and slaves in Egypt and among the Jews and Arabs about 1,000 BC.

*About 3,000 BC, the Sahara began to dry up, the rivers and pastures began to disappear, then began a steady movement of Saharan people into more favorable lands. Some moved northward and merged with the mixed population of the African Mediterranean. The Saharans who migrated eastward towards the Nile came up against Egyptian resistance, which gradually diminished with the weakening position of the Egyptian kingdoms. The other movement was southward into the heart of the continent. These Saharans mingled with those they found, and a new way of life emerged in various places.*38

In tandem with **Igbo** traditional way of adopting new ideas, the **Igbo** settlers of the **Anambra** River Basin who were farmers and hunters welcomed **Eri** and adopted his new version of God-worship and rulership which were different from those of the earliest **Igbo** culture and civilization before **Eri**'s arrival in Igboland.

Chukwu the creator sent Eri down. Eri came down from the sky. He sailed down the river Anambra and established at Agulueri. Mystical powers he had, which won the people over to him. They had no king and there was no food. Chukwu fed

---

38 **Onwuejeogwu,** 1987 **Ahiajoku** Lecture Page 16

them on firmament. Chukwu said: "Sacrifice your first son". Eri sacrificed his first son and Chukwu gave Eri yam. Chukwu said: "Sacrifice your first daughter". Eri sacrificed his first daughter. And Chukwu gave Eri cocoyam. Eri became king; Great king he was etc.[39]

Later still Nri killed a male and a female slave burying them separately. Again, after Izu atọ, (12 days) an oil palm grew from the grave of the male slave and a breadfruit tree (ụkwa) from that of the female slave. (Afigbo 1981: 41-42).[40]

Nri mythology also has it that the same God that sent **Eri** and directed him to sacrifice his first son and first daughter also called **Nri** to sacrifice two slaves. The same myth also says that the same God gave **Nri** mystical powers, a sacred kingship and made him an intermediary between God and man. The **Nri** with their mystical powers and great wealth established ritualized rule on the residents of the **Anambra** River basin. They perfected the art and business of divination. **Nri** agents established many oracles and new deities in all the areas of their business. They maintained their various spiritual and civil taboos, and their codes of conduct with the manipulation of their various oracles and

[39] **Onwuejeogwu,** 1987 **Ahiajoku** Lecture Page 1
[40] Afigbo, 1981 **Ahiajoku** Lecture Pages 41-42

the art of divination. The **Nri** did not destroy or disregard the deities such as **Chi**, **Ani**, **Ngene**, **Fiajioku**, and the taboos they met in the areas of their influence rather they added more color to their maintenance and established new ones.

The **Nri** established codes of cleansing taboos and abominations, and officiated as priests in cleansing rituals, title taking, initiations, and the establishment of new deities at great cost to those who invited them. They also acted as oracle agents in ascertaining the cause of death and misfortunes of people and how the deities were appeased to forestall future reoccurrences. Money (**anyi** and **okpogho**), yams, animals, etc., were needed for the appeasements, and most of the articles went to **Nri** agents who moved from village to village spreading oracle messages. Where the oracle implicated a person as responsible for another person's death, the oracle recommended that the convict be clubbed to death with **Ọfọ** stick, and his belongings confiscated by the oracle.

The influence of new movements from the drought-stricken areas of West Africa into the lower Niger Area coupled with the coming of new farm crops and new farm tools shifted some of the **Igbo** attention from God's sky above to **Ani**, **Agbala** and the acquisition of wealth below. Upon this foundation, the **Aro** civilization built its Machiavellian economic philosophy.

The importance of the Nri civilization is that it developed a highly ritualized and symbolic culture in Igboland and welded together twelve settlements scattered over two hundred square miles East and West of the Niger into one kingship unit.[41]

The **Nri** civilization exerted more religious and economic influence than political on the settlements that came under its hegemony. This civilization which was on its way out because of **Aro** civilization and European economic interests was sacked by the British colonial Administration that took over the government of Nigeria.

6.3: ARO CIVILIZATION

The **Aro** civilization, AD 1700 – 1850, was an offshoot of the **Nri** civilization which lasted for about nine centuries. The **Nri** civilization laid a solid foundation for a smooth take over by the **Aro** civilization. Even though the ethical philosophy and religious dogma of the **Nri** civilization rejected slave trade, the **Nri** myth of their origin and rise of **Nri** show that the **Nri** practiced domestic slave dealing and human sacrifice in the areas of their influence. Although the **Nri** moral thought rejected slave trade, some of the **Nri** itinerant priests, traders,

---

[41] **Onwuejeogwu,** 1987 **Ahiajoku** Lecture Pages 25-48

and diplomats soon became victims and partakers of the notorious trade.

Arochukwu, a trading town, was founded by **Igbo** traders from **Ohafia, Abriba, Item, Abam, Edda, Aba, Umuahia, Afikpo** and other towns who initially traded on palm produce, elephant tusks and spices as intermediaries between the hinter land and the coastal people who traded directly with the earliest European traders. These European traders exchanged the local goods with such imported goods as guns, gunpowder, iron tools and weapons, hot drinks and fancy goods. The migrant **Arochukwu** traders who traveled to the **Igbo** hinterland to exchange local goods with imported goods came under the influence of the **Nri**; and established trading settlements within the towns under the theocratic rule of the **Nri** and imbibed some of the **Nri** lifestyle.

The **Aro** intermarried with the natives and thus strengthened relations with their neighbors in Igboland and non-**Igbo** tribes such as the **Anang** and the Ibibio who traded with them. Early in the 16th Century, **Arochukwu** had grown into a big commercial town in Igboland. By the middle of the 17th Century when European traders came to the Bight of Biafra in search of their infamous commodity, **Arochuwu** was attractive to them as a slave market for the following reasons:

* **Arochukwu** was well positioned near the banks of a river which was navigable with small boats and canoes to the high seas.
* **Arochukwu** had existing trading relations with the coastal people who traded directly with the white men
* The **Aro** had established trading settlements in the hinterland for the collection of export trading goods.

At the onset of slave trade, the **Aro** civilization was caught between two forces. The first was the spiritual influence of **Nri** civilization. The second was the economic influence of the white trader, who came with a gun in one hand and money (**okpogho/ ikpeghe**) plus trading goods in the other hand. By now the white traders had established slave markets on the Guinea Coast. **Aro** traders who were already becoming decadent were also ill equipped spiritually and physically for any military confrontation with the white men. They eventually decided to do slave business with the Europeans.

"If **Eri** and **Nri**, with their religious dogma practiced slavery and sacrificed their children and slaves to become great, according to **Nri** myth, why would the **Aro** man not sell his own tribe's men to become great too?" they might have reasoned. By the middle of the 18th Century, **Aro** traders monopolized one of the major slave trade routes in West Africa between the hinterland and the coast of the Bight of Biafra. Within one century, towards the end of the 18ᵗʰ Century, **Arochukwu** had become a big slave trading cosmopolitan town inhabited by **Igbo** and non-**Igbo** slaves and slave dealers. As competition in the lucrative slave trade increased among the coastal people; and the procurement of slaves got more difficult, the **Aro** established in **Arochukwu** the notorious **Ibunu Ukpabi** oracle which they imported from the **Ibibio**. **Aro** agents in other **Igbo** towns also imported the **Ekpe**, **Ọkọnkọ**, **Ọbọng**, and **Akang** oracles, in addition to numerous other oracles established by the **Nri** in the hinterland.

The slave agents manipulated these oracles to instigate intergroup and intertown conflicts and wars that produced captives from the hinter land for the slave market. The **Aro**, with the assistance of the white slave traders organized the **Abam-Edda** paramilitary system to aid weaker towns against bigger towns for the purpose of capturing war prisoners for the slave market. The **Abam-Edda** military system was also used to bring down any opposition against slave trade or the **Aro** hegemony.

This military system was funded with the proceeds of the infamous trade and backed with military wares and funds from the white slave traders who were the main beneficiaries of slave trade. Constant intertown wars and slave raiding activities destabilized and depopulated the entire **Igbo** nation and the border ethnic groups such as **Idoma, Tiv, Mbembe, Yako, Isoko, Ijaw, Igala.**

In order to tighten their strangle hold on the **Igbo** nation, the **Aro** slave traders established slave settlements in the **Igbo** hinterland for the purpose of continuous supply of slaves for their evil trade.

> *Aro Ndizuogu, Ndikelionwu, Ndiokolo, (others in Nsukka, Afikpo and Nike area) were funded by Aro slavers. Some lineages in Umuoji, Abatete, and Nkpo are said to be founded by frustrated Aro slavers and hired warriors from Abam, Edda and Ohafia.*[42]

Though the **Aro** did not start slavery in Igboland, they perfected the business of slave dealing with the help of the oracles borrowed from the **Nri** and the Ibibio and intensified it with the financial and military support and protection of the white slave masters. The biggest and strongest **Igbo** men and women that could not be captured during slave raids and instigated community wars were tricked or implicated into slavery with the numerous oracles established by the slavers. It should also be noted that during the **Aro** civilization there were no formal prisons to punish criminals. War captives and criminals sentenced to capital punishments or

---

[42] **Onwuejeogwu,** 1987 **Ahiajoku** Lecture Page 40

banishments became ready commodities for the slave market.

The **Nri** who controlled the economy of the **Igbo** for nine centuries before the onset of the **Aro** civilization opposed the slave trade by the **Aro** because of the destabilizing effect of slave trade with Europeans on **Nri** businesses.

> *The Ọzọ and ritual systems of the Nri that had diffused into Igbo cultural life for five centuries was gradually losing their moral and political significance as the Aro civilization was taking root and overlapping the Nri civilization.*[43]

The infamous and brutal slave trade with Europeans lasted only one and half centuries A.D. 1700-1850, yet it left ugly and indelible marks on the culture and philosophy of the **Igbo** and slowed down the economic growth of the **Igbo** nation. Some elders believe that the part played by some of the **Igbo** during the slave trade provoked the anger of God and the ancestors, consequently attracted the slaughter of thousands of the **Igbo** before the colonization and eventual economic exploitation of their land and people by the British. M. A. **Onwuejeogwu** (1987) highlighted the differences between the **Nri** and **Aro** civilizations, when he said:

---

[43] **Onwuejeogwu,** 1987 **Ahiajoku** Lecture Page 41

*Apart from Nri civilization, the most
exulted civilization in Igbo land by writers
is the **Aro** which flourished in the dark age
of Igbo history between 1700 and 1850. It
is here given the status of a civilization, not
much because of its contribution to Igbo
civilization but for the fact that it portrays
a pragmatic aspect of a Machiavellian
comprador capitalist political economy
sustained on what may be called
Machiavellian diplomacy. It demonstrated
how a black decadent civilization grew out
of opportunities created by another white
decadent civilization.*[44]

6.4: BORDER CIVILIZATION
(A.D. 800 – 1900)

Before A. D. 800, when the **Nri** civilization started,
the **Igbo** living within the **Okigwe, Afikpo, Udi,
Nsukka** triangle had settled down farming at
the fertile low lands of greater **Afikpo, Okigwe,
Awgu, Nkanu, Abakaliki, Nsukka** divisions and
the new settlements at the **Anambra** river basin.
Black smithing at **Achi**, **Udi**, **Nsukka** and **Awka**
flourished and produced the iron farm tools and
hand weapons used within the neighborhood and
the border settlements. There were pottery works
at **Isiagu, Inyi, Ugbo, Ozalla**, etc. Small scale

---

[44] **Onwuejeogwu,** 1987 **Ahiajoku** Lecture Page 55

rearing of livestock took place at the upper fringes of the Scarp lands.

During this time population movements within this theatre which were essentially peripheral were directed to more fertile lands. As more food was produced, the population increased, and this gave rise to the desire for more land which often led to skirmishes and fist scuffles between communities or individuals. The several centuries of **Nri** civilization produced a stabilizing effect on the growing **Igbo** nation. The **Nri** preached peace and love among all the **Igbo** communities by insisting in their observance of **Nri** sacred codes and religious dogma.

The **Nri** civilization which was referred to as the civilization of the sacred and divine by historians, also nurtured and protected the growing economy and technology of the **Igbo**. It also cooperated with border peoples who did business with the **Igbo**. However, the border influence on the **Nri** civilization resulted in non-observance of the very sacred codes and dogma of the **Nri** by some of the **Nri** themselves and some of their agents. This situation of greed and materialistic tendencies prepared some of the **Nri** agents for recruitment into the slave trade, when the European slavers arrived. These agents used their powerful oracles to implicate innocent people into slavery.

By the end of the 19th century, the Igbo theatre had been defined into a culture area bordered by other ethnic groups such as Idoma, Tiv, Mbembe, Yako, Ijaw, Isoko, Urhobo, Edo, Ishan and Igala. Movements of migrant farm labor and smiths while not a new phenomenon in the border intensified with the introduction of money economy, easier means of communication, and the British colonial concept of peace.[45]

Among the ethnic groups mentioned above, the **Igala** was one of the most influential civilizations because it was contemporaneous with the **Nri** and had a ritualized culture and economy. The **Igala** civilization did not have large settlements like the **Nri** or the **Aro** in Igboland but its influence permeated deeper and wider into Igboland because it worked hand in hand with the **Nri** and the **Aro** civilizations.

According to Nri mythology, the second wife of Eri bore Onoja who left for the upper Anambra River near Ogulugu and founded Igalaland.[46]

One can easily see that the **Nri** and the **Igala** worked together as relatives and had one modus operandi in their theocratic influence on the **Igbo** nation. In

---

[45] **Onwuejeogwu,** 1987 **Ahiajoku** Lecture Page 41
[46] **Onwuejeogwu,** 1987 **Ahiajoku** Lecture Page 25

the Northeastern **Igbo** area, the **Igala** were migrant horse agents, diviners, and petty traders dealing in beads and antiquities. In the Western, and the Niger delta areas of Igboland, the **Igala** also operated as diviners, traders, and fisher men.

> *Just as the influence of Benin on the lower Niger basin might be described as more cultural than political, so also the influence of Igala in this part might be described as more economic than political as many writers tend to exaggerate. Trading and fishing posts were established by the Igala. Ebu is a typical Igala settlement acculturated by their neighbors. Traders between Idah and Atani, Illah, Okpanam, Asaba, Oko, Abala, Osomari, Okwe, absorbed Igala migrants through trade, marriage, and migration.*[47]

The Islamic reform movement launched from Sokoto by Arab Muslim leaders in 1804 spread to virtually every part of Northern Nigeria, generating wars that produced thousands of captives for the slave market. By mid-nineteenth century after the abolition of the Atlantic slave trade, external demand for slaves declined but the trade continued within the West African hinterland. The price of slaves in the lower Niger area dropped dramatically yet internal slave raiding activities backed by Arab

---

[47] **Onwuejeogwu,** 1987 **Ahiajoku** Lecture Page 36

slave merchants continued within the middle belt region of Nigeria. Slaves were sent down by road and by river to southern slave markets where they were sold for a pittance.

The **Idoma** and the **Tiv** slave agents brought slaves from the North to the **Igala** who traded directly with **Aro** traders. The **Igala**, trading as **Aro** slave agents brought slaves and horses from Northern Nigeria and the border towns of Northern Igboland, to **Nsukka** slave market where slaves were bought with money or exchanged with imported goods. The horses were bought with the local currency (**okpogho**) or exchanged for slaves by the **Igbo** who used these horses for title taking and burial ceremonies. The same slaves exchanged for horses by the **Igbo** were resold in the same market to **Aro** slave agents by the **Igala**.

It was reported that by A. D. 1880 at the Nsukka slave market ten human slaves exchanged for one horse while at Ubulu slave market, four to six adult slaves exchanged for one horse.[48]

More enterprising farmers and palm oil producers in Igboland took advantage of the situation and amassed cheap labor by buying and maintaining large numbers of domestic slaves. The master-slave relationship under the present economic

---

[48] E.N. **Onwu**, 2002 **Ahiajoku** Lecture Page 12

situation often sparked off many bitter conflicts until 1916 when the British colonial government of Nigeria passed the final law against domestic slavery in the country. The law gave rise to labor shortage problems for the former slave masters and unemployment problems for the freed slaves. Added to these freed slaves were youths who graduated or dropped out from mission schools.

Those youths who could not find employment refused to go back to family farms, but rather joined the group of hungry job seekers of that time who wandered from one administrative center to the other in search of work; "A horde of starving men uprooted from their tribe and from their clan", as described by Frantz Fanon. This period of labor migration and harsh colonial taxation gave rise to food shortages and political instability that sparked off sporadic **Igbo** insurgencies against British rule towards the beginning of the twentieth century.

The Ibibio who traded and intermarried with the Southeastern **Igbo** contributed a lot to the sustenance of the slave trade by their supply of slaves and slave labor, in addition to the introduction of the notorious **Ibunu Ukpabi** oracle to **Arochukwu**. The riverine people on their own part had long standing trade and marriage relations with the **Igbo** before the onset of the slave trade. The Southern **Igbo** took advantage of the sparse population and rich fertility of the rivers area, and moved into the area originally for farming, fishing and trading purposes, and thus established many **Igbo** settlements such as **Diobu, Umuokoroshe, Umuola, Ikwere and Etche**. This area supplied the food that sustained the slave trade and the **Aro** civilization.

6.5: EXTERNAL CIVILIZATION (A. D. 1700 – 2000)

I have shown in the previous chapters of this book that before A. D. 1700, the **Igbo** nation had emerged as a distinct people with one language; and was occupying a geographical area covering parts of the lower Niger, **Imo**, and upper Cross-river basins, and having both political and economic influence in the area now known as South Eastern and South Southern Nigeria. By this time, the **Igbo** had become a force to reckon with in the emerging European trade, in the fast-growing export trade of the African West Coast. Off the coast of the Bight of Biafra, the internal export trade routes were monopolized by the **Igbo** who acted as intermediaries in the European trade with the hinterland. Within the **Igbo** heartland, farming, livestock rearing, processing of palm produce, black smiting, pottery, weaving, and petty trading thrived and sustained the growing economy and the export trade of the **Igbo** with Europeans on the West African Coast.

The **Nri** civilization was on its way out yielding place to the emerging **Aro** civilization; but had however created a stable and ritualized economy which propelled the **Igbo** into a leadership role in the emerging economic and political prosperity which but for the transatlantic slave trade, might have developed the entire lower Niger area. About the same time A. D. 1700, the trade in palm produce took a satanic turn to the infamous transatlantic trade in human beings who worked in tobacco and sugar plantations established by Europeans in America.

To ensure a steady flow of slaves for the evil trade, **Aro** traders assisted by Europeans established and maintained secret cults, oracles, various deities, and paramilitary squads which they manipulated to sustain the slave trade. The **Aro** civilization which was sustained by the slave trade had a blatant disregard for human dignity which resulted in the devaluation and desecration of human life in several ways. **Igbo** people were traded by fellow decadent **Igbo** for money and other material things like guns, and fancy goods from European traders. Tens of thousands of able-bodied men and women were carried away in European instigated inter-town wars or were tricked into slavery by oracle priests and diviners. Eventually the **Aro** civilization through its own moral weakness and co-operation with Europeans depleted the **Igbo** wealth of able-bodied men and women and thus destroyed the peoples' respect for its leadership that watched helplessly as the **Igbo** were herded away into slavery.

According to Uche, the estimates of Igbo population between A. D. 1700 and A.D. 1800, was steady at 300,000 plus, due to the effect of the notorious trans-Atlantic slave trade...., but went up to above 3,000,000 by A. D 1900, as a result of the abolition of the trans-Atlantic slave trade.[49]

Let us examine the slave statistics of Captain Adams, (1823), who made many slave voyages to West African coast between 1786 and 1880. He recorded that 20,000 slaves were sold yearly at Bonny; of these, 16000 were Igbo. According to his estimation, for twenty-year period, 320,000 Igbo were sold at Bonny and 50,000 at old and new Calabar. There is therefore an extraction rate of six per cent per annum and most of these slaves came from the North East of Igboland, the area skilled in iron industry which would have been the backbone for further industrial development in Igboland [50]

---

[49] M.A. **Onwuejeogwu**, 1987 **Ahiajoku** Lecture, pages 42 and 43
[50] M.A. **Onwuejeogwu**, 1987 **Ahiajoku** Lecture, page 43

It is to be noted that the **Nri** civilization that held
sway over the external and internal politics of over
half of **Igbo** culture area before the onset of
Atlantic slave trade was pacifist and had no army
or any military regimentation. Consequently, it
never attempted stopping the slave trade militarily
or building an empire by force. It was
abomination to spill human blood by violence on
the surface of the earth (**Ani**); which the **Nri** saw
as a supernatural force. For about ten centuries,
AD-800-1800, a civilization and hegemony based
on religious ascendancy with a ritualized concept
of peace, harmony and truth was nurtured. The
Igbo practiced ancestral democracy in segmentary
governments and had only poorly organized
village-type defense arrangements for over ten
centuries, AD-800-1850, until the European
backed slave raids and inter community wars that
raged in Igboland during the period, AD-1700-1850.
These slave raids and inter settlement wars
disorganized the relative peace that prevailed in
Igbo communities during the **Nri** civilization, and
put some arms and ammunition into the hands of
Igbo youths which they used against British
colonial agents and officials during the early days
of colonial activities.

By the middle of the nineteenth century the effect of
the slave trade came down fully on the **Igbo** nation,
to the extent that the usual exuberant morale of the
Igbo fell so low that the **Igbo** nation was neither

politically nor militarily disposed to effectively face the military onslaught of the British. There was no organized pan **Igbo** resistance of British imperialism, but each community or settlement reacted according to its immediate involvement and strategic readiness. An example of the many group reactions to British imperialism was the "**Ekumeku** movement" (the silent ones), the violent winds that blew in the Western **Igbo** area at that time.

> *The first Ekumeku was organized and directed against the Royal Niger Company in 1889; the second was organized and directed against British colonialism between 1900 and 1910.*[51]

When the British colonialists arrived Eastern Nigeria, which is the heart land of **Igbo** culture area, they got treaties of protection negotiated and signed with some **Igbo** community leaders and took to swift military expeditions to silence the small units of unprepared and poorly armed **Igbo** resistance. In **Ihe Shikeaguma** for instance, the elders recollected that a British contingent made up of, a British commander, hired coastal people, freed slaves, and conscripted natives arrived **Ihe Shikeaguma** about 1910. Earlier, by 1908, the British soldiers attacked and took **Ufuma**. By 1909, they were at **Inyi**. While the British soldiers were

---

[51] M.A. **Onwuejeogwu,** 1987 **Ahiajoku** Lecture, page 54

still at **Inyi**, elders of **Ihe Shikeaguma** under the leadership of **Ude Agunevo** sent a reconnaissance group (**Ẹgẹbẹ**) through **Achi** on one **Eke Egbo** market day, to get information from **Inyi** about approaching British soldiers under a white man called **Mgbagọyigọ** (McGregor).

The reconnaissance men came back the following day to warn against any military resistance by **Ihe Shikeaguma** based on the devastations they saw and the stories they heard. They advised that women and children should be evacuated since it was likely that **Ihe Shikeaguma** would be attacked because of the popularity of its hunters. This advice gave rise to the great evacuation (**Ọsọ Bekee**) of 1909 – 1910. By 1910, the British soldiers came through **Achi** and arrived at **Ọhụete** farm on the eastern bank of Oji River in **Amagu Ihe Shikeaguma** in May of that year when the farm was cleared and tilled for planting. The soldiers camped in the clearing and sent words to those who did the clearing to come to their camp. **Ude Agunevo** and some elders went to see the white men. Through their interpreter, a British soldier asked **Ude Agu** why they cleared the land. He told the white man that they heard of the coming of the British soldiers and cleared the land for their camping.

The white man thanked them and asked the owners of the land to mark out the boundaries of their village with young palm fronds (**ọmụ**). The leaders of **Amagụ** village marked out the boundaries of their village the following morning in readiness for some promised presents. **Nwugo Agụ of Ụmụsike** who saw **Amagụ** people marking out the boundaries of their village with palm fronds, included his family with palm fronds as part of **Amagụ** village. On the same day the white men sent words to all hunters of **Ihe Shikeaguma** whom they said they heard were great hunters to bring their cap-guns for exchange with more efficient British rifles. The hunters happily took their guns to **Ọhụete** army camp for the exchange.

All the guns were collected and burnt in their presence. The soldiers summoned all the gun owners, to come with their leaders and elders the following day to **Eke** market square for the exchange of the burnt guns with new guns. While the men were in the market square the following morning for the gun exchange, British soldiers surrounded and attacked most of the villages of **Ihe Shikeaguma** excepting **Amagụ** and part of **Ụmụsike** villages. They set fire on houses and fired at any man seen in the villages. There was a stampede in the market square and many people lost their lives. In a matter of hours, the town was destroyed and deserted. Those people left alive scampered into the bushes and nearby towns. A group of warriors from **Agbogugu** who heard of the attack of **Ihe** and were on their way to assist

Ihe were ambushed after they crossed the **Iyiakwa** River. From **Ihe Shikeaguma** the British soldiers continued their rampaging exercise in other communities with an unstoppable fury. Many communities fought back but were mowed down.

Later, a British colonial officer returned to **Ihe Shikeaguma** when the British colonial office wanted to establish the British type of Native Administration in Igboland. As a compensation for the "friendly" role he played during the arrival of the British soldiers at **Ọhụete** farm in **Amagu Ihe**, the British Administrative Officer asked **Ude Agunevo** to nominate one of his sons to be the chief of **Ihe Shikeaguma**. He nominated his sister's son, **Agunevo Ọtụsa**, who became the first warrant chief of **Ihe Shikeaguma**.

Both **Onwuejeogwu** and **Isichei** recorded the history of European resistance in Igboland.

> *Between 1700 and 1900 the devastating effect of the slave trade on **Igbo** culture and civilization was total and final. The ancestors of Igbo were beaten hands-down by European canons and guns between 1880 and 1920; the longest history of European resistance in Africa South of the Sahara, apart from that of the Zulu* [52]

---

[52] M.A. **Onwuejeogwu,** 1987 **Ahiajoku** Lecture, page 69

It took the British over twenty years of constant military action to subdue the Igbo who flung themselves against the British with only cap guns, Dane guns, and machetes. The Igbo were slaughtered in their thousands by the British rifles and machine guns with unlimited supplies of ammunition[53]

By 1914 the **Igbo** theatre of civilization was integrated into what we today call Nigeria. By this exercise the **Igbo** nation lost its political independence to the British colonialists; who approached the enforcement of their political domination and economic exploitation from three positions: military, administrative, and religious.

6.5a: Military Position: Already the British military force had silenced the divided and poorly organized armed resistance of the **Igbo** who had lost their most able bodied young men to European instigated inter town wars, slave raids, and slave trade before the British constant military action to subdue the **Igbo**. The surviving **Igbo** leaders were either killed or imprisoned by the British and their guns and gunpowder, earlier on exchanged for palm produce or slaves were seized and destroyed.

---

[53] **Elizabeth Isichei,** A history of the **Igbo** people

The British military force made up of British commanders, coastal people, conscripted natives and freed slaves kept watch over and contained **Igbo** insurgents.

6.5b: Administrative Position

The British colonial administrators, who did not understand or refused to use the **Igbo** traditional democratic system of governance, rather forced their native administration system on the **Igbo**. They recognized or appointed freed slaves or former slave trade collaborators as chiefs and government agents. These British government agents protected only the interest of the colonial masters who appointed them and treated their fellow **Igbo** with disdain and utter hatred. On the home sector the **Aro** civilization which had dealt with the **Igbo** mercilessly had become powerless. The **Igbo** economy was devastated. **Igbo** deities that could not protect the **Igbo** were thought by the **Igbo** to be dead. Even God of creation and of tender heart (**Chukwu Okike obi ọma**) of the **Igbo** seemed to have remained inactive. There was no hiding place for the remaining **Igbo** population. Remaining pockets of **Igbo** resistance continued in one form or the other. The surviving **Igbo** traders became indignant with the white men and disappeared into the bush.

6.5c: Religious Position

The Europeans who had known the Igbo before

the slave trade and who knew how religious and enterprising the Igbo could be, realized that only spiritual medicine could reduce the anger of the Igbo and enliven their productive spirit and continued faith in God. Also, the British experience of Igbo insurgency during the period 1880–1920, probably influenced the British decision to encourage the activities of Christian missionaries in Igboland to soften anti-British feelings. Then Christianity arrived at the scene.

The European missionaries condemned slavery and human sacrifice. They loved and protected the slave, the lowly and orphaned children in the community. They gave them hope for here on Earth and for hereafter in Heaven. These earliest Christian missionaries taught the same **Igbo** concept of human life as God's property (**Chi nwe ndụ**) which no one could toy with. This teaching and the humanitarian considerations given to the demoralized **Igbo** attracted their acceptance of the teaching of the white Christian missionaries. The missionaries taught the futility of idol worship some of which took human sacrifice and proved the lifelessness of these idols by destroying their shrines and building churches in their places. They built schools and hospitals and fed the poor and the homeless. They brought with them European goods and exchanged them with local goods and services thereby preparing grounds for the normalization of trade with the people of the African West Coast.

Thus, the missionaries won back for the British the confidence of the **Igbo** and laid a new foundation on which the present day educational, political and economic development were built. We should nevertheless be aware of how African religions in general and **Igbo** traditional religion in particular suffered neglect, misinterpretations, and distortions in the hands of some missionaries and colonial government agents who treated Africans as sub-humans, without history, and without religion.

Most of the earliest **Igbo** converts and associates of the Christian missionaries were freed slaves and the down trodden who gladly took European and Jewish names, and saw their membership of the then new Christian churches as an opportunity to fight the **Igbo** tradition that brought the stigma of slavery and lowly status on them. They gave only the negative interpretations of the **Igbo** tradition to the white missionaries and encouraged the destruction of **Igbo** cultural artifacts such as musical instruments, and shrines as instruments of Idol worship. Some of these earliest Christian converts encouraged the replacement of the entire **Igbo** culture with Jewish and European cultures especially in relation to the belief and worship of God. Even after most of the white Christian missionaries left Nigeria and handed over the churches to **Igbo** missionaries, some of these **Igbo** church leaders surprisingly became even more hostile to **Igbo** culture and tradition instead of enculturating the **Igbo** way of worship like other free nations have done. In some cases where **Igbo** traditional religious worshippers were tolerant and accommodating on inter religious issues some fanatical **Igbo** Christians were aggressive. Fortunately, majority of **Igbo** Christian church leaders today are very understanding and Christlike in their approach to the teaching and conversion of non-Christians, and have invested lots of treasure, talent and time in Igboland for the propagation of the faith and for the education and welfare of our people.

In less than two centuries we have produced world renowned princes. Achebe in literature, Chris Okigbo in poetry, Animalu in mathematics, theologian, Francis Cardinal Arinze of the Roman (Catholic) Curia, and many others.[54]

---

[54] **M. A. Nwachukwu,** 2003 **Ahiajoku** Lecture, page 26

Chapter Seven

Evaluation of **IGBO** Culture

7.1: THE ORIENTED VALUES OF THE IGBO

In recognizing our sense of worthwhileness or values let us give a thought to the comment of Innocent **Chuka Okonkwo** (2002):

> *People acquire, maintain and enrich their sense of worthwhileness only if they at least vaguely recognize the source of what personal dignity they have, their family, their friends and neighbors, their associates or fellows, their group ties or their nation* [55]

The earliest **Igbo** were forest dwellers in the lower Niger, **Imo** and Cross River basins. They lived a hazardous life of wandering, gathering of wild edible roots, fruits and leaves. Originally this situation left them in a tough world where they were exposed to wild animals, hunger and disease coupled with strife for existence among various competing earliest tribal groups of the lower Niger basin. These groups had contacts with the **Igbo** or passed through **Igbo** settlements to their present-day

---

[55] **Chuka Okonkwo**, 2002, **Ahiajoku** lecture, citation

habitations within and outside the lower Niger area. These contacts with tribal or linguistic groups, and their passage of **Igbo** settlements is implied by M.A. **Onwuejeogwu** (1987) in his linguistic evidence of **Igbo** origin.

> *Geographically, Benin, Yoruba, Igala, Idoma, Urhobo, and Isoko are all neighbors of Igbo and their languages also belong to the lower Niger group of languages having many basic words which are cognates.*[56]

For the basic words of a group of languages to be cognates is suggestive that those languages separated from one mother-language which was developed and spoken over a period by the ancestors of a people living together in one settlement before their dispersal to various places.

The **Igbo** hazardous lifestyle of struggle demanded that he be courageous, fearless, determined and hard working to survive. This lifestyle led him to the concept that man does not rest (**nwoke ezuike**). The earliest **Igbo** had a strong belief that as long as he obeyed the traditional laws (**Nsọ Ani**) God of creation and of tender heart (**Chukwu okike obi ọma**) would always protect him in his hazardous life (**Chi nedu**). This achievement orientation of the **Igbo** has been found in their industry, courage

---

[56] M.A. **Onwuejeogwu**, 1987, **Ahiajoku** Lecture, page 10

and determination evidenced in the **Igbo** itinerancy in search of adequate means of livelihood in all nooks and crannies of the world in all human endeavors. Professional begging was unknown in early **Igbo** tradition and stealing was a terrible crime in a traditional **Igbo** society. Stealing was punishable with death, banishment, amputations, isolation or fine, depending on what was stolen.

The traditional **Igbo** had a deep sense of community, with individual existence tied to life in the community and individual effort for overall community good. The life-in-community concept of the **Igbo** is reflected in their belief in the extended family units of father's and mother's relations (**ikwunna** and **ikwunne**). The **Igbo** concept of consultation (**igba izu**) for consensus and agreement made the idea of living together for the **Igbo** a necessity.

This concept of consultation for consensus is the basis for **Igbo** republicanism which makes room for individual input and derives from the traditional **Igbo** belief in individual effort or input for the overall community good. It is also responsible for the **Igbo** living only in Igboland in crowded village settlements, from prehistoric times, unlike the Hausa or Yoruba who can be found in other parts of Africa as natives of those places.

Permanent residence outside Igboland for any **Igboman** was out of the question since it was an established way of life that the **Igbo** must return to his community at the end of his work or mission from any part of the world he visited whether he was successful or not. Today, while the **Igbo** believes in, works and prays for the wellbeing, wealth and unity of his community, he knows very well that he is not going to be judged, recognized or rewarded by what his father or relations had achieved, but by what he personally is able to achieve by himself for the benefit of his community.

The concept of every **Igboman** living and working for his wellbeing is proof that the **Igbo** knows that he would definitely return to his community at the end of his business for assessment, whether dead or alive. The **Igbo** loves and protects every community where he finds himself in the course of his business and respects the authority placed over him while in school or at work, but the **Igbo** does not worship human beings. He has great respect for elders and leaders but traditionally he does not tolerate oppression and authoritarianism. Even **Igbo** slaves in Haiti during the slave trade as reported by **Isichei**, 1976:44 and Herskovit 1931:20-21, were said to be:

Excellent for work in the fields yet difficult to handle they kept a strong sense of their Igbo identity and gave help, care and instructions to new arrivals from Igboland.

In the midst of other ethnic groups or people the **Igbo** sees himself as a superior person from a superior race and strives to prove it, especially in competitive ventures like sports, business and lately Western education. Today the **Igbo** believes in Western education (**Onye amaghi, ibe Ezi ya**) as a tool for economic and political growth.

Perhaps the most outstanding quality of the Igbo is his innate receptivity to new ideas, and adaptability to change, which under the stimulus of Christianity and Western education, readily triggered in him an obsessive desire for self-improvement and modernity through education.[57]

Onwu (2002) agrees with **Nwabueze** on the achievement orientation of the **Igbo** but observes:

Admittedly, this Igbo achievement and performance orientation as an important aspect of Igbo life is one area in which the Igbo have been badly misunderstood and misrepresented.[58]

---

[57] Ben **Nwabueze**, 1985, **Ahiajoku** Lecture, page 6
[58] E. N. **Onwu**, 2002, **Ahiajoku** Lecture, page 30

We must also admit to ourselves that our usual **Igbo** approach in competitive ventures: "I go before others", while healthy internationally, excites fear and hatred in other Nigerians and this approach exposed us to exploitation by others in the past. Like the goldfish we have not been able to hide ourselves from exploitation due to our orientations. During the slave trade, European slave masters preferred **Igbo** slaves to slaves from other ethnic groups because **Igbo** slaves were more productive and exhibited much more intelligence than others.

During the early days of the British administration in Nigeria, British colonial Government agents and other European traders and contractors noticed that the **Igbo** were outstandingly hardworking and honest and were prepared to work anywhere in Nigeria.

Consequently, many **Igbo** youths were prematurely taken out of mission schools and employed as laborers, clerks and artisans in their companies and colonial government establishments all over Nigeria; not because the British loved the **Igbo** more but because the **Igbo** were the materials they needed at the time. This British observation and consequent action triggered the **Igbo** movement to every nook and cranny of Nigeria and beyond. Another neutral observer, a European for that matter, J. Jordan, 1971:115, reported Bishop Shanahan, also another European who lived and worked with the

Igbo, and was buried at **Onitsha**, as saying that the average **Igbo** was not materialistic:

> *The average native was admirably suited by environment and training for an explanation of life in terms of the spirit, rather than of the flesh. He was not materialistic. Indeed, nothing was farther from his mind than a materialistic philosophy of existence. It made no appeal to him.*[59]

The achievement orientation of the **Igbo** was defended by Ben **Nwabueze** (1985) where he said:

> *In their enterprising spirit and aggressive individualism, the Igbo may appear to be exploitative, grasping and greedy, but these are attributes, which characterize all aggressively enterprising people everywhere. These attributes are not therefore proper grounds on which resentment can justifiably be nursed against the Igbo by other Nigerians.*[60]

It is hoped that as the present-day **Igbo** youths get to know what **Igbo** attributes really are, their orientations shall be guided by a little more caution and tact in their relations with other people, to avoid

---

[59] J. Jordan, 1971: 115, Bishop Shanahan
[60] Ben **Nwabueze**, 1985 **Ahiajoku** Lecture, page 8

unnecessary misunderstanding or exploitation as a people. In his call to the **Igbo** to deeply reflect on why they are resented and discriminated against, Ben. **Nwabueze** (1985) observed:

> *However, his success in education and trade has inclined the Igbo toward a noisy exhibitionism, over assertiveness, over confidence, and too-know air, an over-weening pride, and a patronizing and condescending attitude towards the less successful communities among whom he settled. The latter are despised and mocked to their face for not being as successful. For all this, I think the Igbo are justifiably resented.*[61]

7.2: REFURBISHING IGBO CULTURAL HERITAGE

Our cultural heritage which started from prehistoric times was passed down to us by our ancestors; and it is all about our life and times, as related to our home, birth, food, language, relationships, worship, death, burial and afterlife. These ancestors experienced nature first-hand and established our present-day culture that has survived thousands of years of oral preservation, apart from our cultural artifacts. With our scientific, technological and religious advancements, we still cannot fully understand or assess the intellectual and spiritual

---

[61] Ben **Nwabueze**, 1985 **Ahiajoku** Lecture, page 8

attainments of our ancestors, notwithstanding the fact that these attainments were not documented. These high intellectual and spiritual attainments of our ancestors produced some of those age-old ethnic issues that we should not just throw away as nonsensical, because truth does not die. It lives on and on.

> *The Igbo cannot give up his ethnic identity because therein lies the eternal order of existence.*[62]

> *Scholars and a few other people know how indebted humanity is to the Arabs for their numerals, to the Egyptians for geometry and irrigation, to the Greeks for athletics and politics, and to the Romans for their law, only to mention but a few from the European classical times. Even today, each country and each culture try consciously or unconsciously to articulate some worthy strands of its culture.*[63]

Some of our cultural achievements such as the **Igbo** ancestral democratic system of governance, the **Igbo** community service system, and the extended family system (**Igbo** brand of social security system), were older or at least contemporaneous with some of the above achievements yet little study is being made

---

[62] A.O. **Animalu**, 1990, **Ahiajoku** Lecture, page 3
[63] **Kemjika Anoka**, 1979, **Ahiajoku**, Lecture, citation

about them even by our own people. It is our duty to refurbish these strands of our culture, project and market them for consideration and recognition, first by our own people, our neighbors, and then, the modern world.

"An unexamined life is not worth living", says the ancient Greek philosopher, Socrates. We have all the potential we need to carry out this examination and refurbishment so that our cultural achievements are reinfused through our own effort into the present-day life of our people and the modern world. The **Igbo** are among the best gifted humans created by God on earth, with a rich endowment of spiritual, intellectual, and physical attributes.

These attributes have been abundantly proven in such achievements as the **Ugwuele** and **Igboukwu** artifacts of old, and the present day world acclaimed **Igbo** clerics, professors, sportsmen and women, artists, and the ubiquitous **Igbo** business gurus who thrive in all sorts of businesses everywhere on earth, including those areas where difficult business conditions exist. With all these successes credited to the **Igbo**, it is time for us to find our roots, increase our awareness of our cultural heritage, and give all the recognition and support we can to culture awareness projects of our people in order to refurbish and enliven our cultural heritage and industry.

Igboland in Southern Nigeria of West Africa is one of the choicest places to live in because there is availability of fertile land. There is a great variety of easily grown food and economic crops. There is a good and warm climate, and an abundance of human and mineral resources. There is an absence of constant natural disasters like volcanoes, earthquakes, hurricanes, tsunamis, tornadoes, cold-waves etc.

If nations who have an abundance of the above natural disasters and little natural resources have survived as culture-conscious and progressive nations of the world today, there is no reason why we, the **Igbo**, who are greatly endowed with abundant natural gifts should allow our own rich cultural heritage to rot away while we spend time and money studying and copying other people's cultures including those aspects that are injurious to our very existence as individuals and as a people. We should increase our awareness of our cultural heritage and give moral and financial support to community development projects in Igboland, in line with M. A. **Onwuejeogwu's** observation (after the Nigerian Civil War):

> *Igbo have learnt one lesson that they can, like their ancestors, transform Igboland into a big theatre of modern civilization.... But this can only be achieved when the Igbo elites might have discovered their*

roots and how these roots are related to the roots of their ethnic groups in Nigeria. Understanding their roots will enable them regain confidence in themselves, develop the spirit of self-reliance, inventiveness and creativity lost by the intervention of the slave trade and colonialism.[64]

In refurbishing our cultural heritage, our "charity" should begin at home, by our own day to day life at home; by the way we speak, dress, work and worship God. That is a debt we owe to our parents, our ancestors, and the Igbo nation.

As Igbo parents we should be bearers and teachers of Igbo culture. We should be proud of our cultural orientations and socio-economic achievements because there in lies our pride and our heritage as a people.

---

[64] M.A. **Onwuejeogwu,** 1987, **Ahiajoku** Lecture, page 71

Bibliography

AHIAJOKU LECTURE
SERIES AND MORE

I intentionally made most of my references to Igbo authors and elders because these elders received cultural transmissions from their parents and elders, in addition to their professional training; they are Igbo culture bearers and creators.

Afigbo A. E.	The Age of Innocence: The Igbo and their neighbors in Pre-colonial time. 1981 **Ahiajoku** Lecture, Government Printer, **Owerri**.
Animalu A. O.E.	**Ucheakonam**: (A way of life in the modern scientific age) 1990 **Ahiajoku** Lecture, Government Printer, **Owerri**.
Echeruo M. J.C.	A Matter of Identity: 1979 **Ahiajoku** Lecture. **Imo** Newspaper Ltd. **Owerri**
Emenanjo E. N.	**Igbo or Igboid: Asụsụn'agbụrụ ndi Igbo**. Language in **Igbo** civilization, 2001 **Ahiajoku** lect.

Eteng I. A.	Onye ajụrụ ajụ anaghi ajụ onweya: **Ndigbo** in post-civil war crisis of disunity: 2004 **Ahiajoku** Lecture, Government Printer **Owerri**.
Nwabueze B.O.	The **Igbos** in the context of modern government and politics in Nigeria, a call for self-examination and self- correction: 1985 **Ahiajoku** Lecture, Government Printer **Owerri**.
Nwachuku MA.	Beyond **Tecnuzu**, Reflections on Igbo perception and practice of technology: 2003 **Ahiajoku** Lecture, Government printer **Owerri**.
Obiechina E.	**Ncheta ka**: The story, memory and the continuity of Igbo culture. 1994 **Ahiajoku** Lecture, Government Printer **Owerri**.
Okigbo B. N.	Plants and food in Igbo culture: 1980 **Ahiajoku** Lecture, Government Printer **Owerri**.
Onwu E. N.	Uzọ ndụ n'okwu: Towards an understanding of Igbo traditional religious life and philosophy. 2002 **Ahiajoku** Lecture, Government Printer **Owerri**.
Onwuejeogwu M. A.	Evolutionary trends in the history of the development of the **Igbo** civilization in the culture theatre of **Igbo** land in Southern Nigeria: Government Printer **Owerri**.
Onwumechili C. A.	**Igbo Enwe Eze**? The **Igbo** Have no Kings?: 2000 **Ahiajoku** lecture, Government Printer **Owerri**.

Uchendu E.	**Ezi n'Ụnọ**: The extended family in **Igbo** civilization. 1995 Ahiajoku Lecture, Government Printer **Owerri**.
Ohadike D. C	**Aniọma**: A social history of the Western **Igbo** People. Ohio University Press, Athens U.S.A.
Onuigbo S. N (Rev. Fr.)	The history of **Ntuegbe** Nese Afro-orbis Publication ltd **Nsukka**.

www.ingramcontent.com/pod-product-compliance
Lightning Source LLC
Chambersburg PA
CBHW060000100426
42740CB00010B/1354